THE
RISE
OF THE
ENTERPRISE
SOCIETY

VOLUME 8
1973·1991

THE
RISE
OF THE
ENTERPRISE
SOCIETY

INTRODUCTION BY
ASA BRIGGS

HAMLYN

Project editor Peter Furtado

Project art editor Ayala Kingsley

Text editors Robert Peberdy, Mike March, Sue Martin

Cartographic manager Olive Pearson

Cartographic editor Zoë Goodwin

Designers Frankie Wood, Janet McCallum, Wolfgang Mezger, Gill Mouqué, Niki Overy, Linda Reed, Nicholas Rous, Tony de Saulles, Dave Sumner, Rita Wütrych

Picture research manager Alison Renney

Picture research Jan Croot, Diane Hamilton, Rebecca Hirsh, Angela Murphy, Diana Phillips, Linda Proud, Christine Vincent, Charlotte Ward-Perkins

Editorial assistants Elaine Welsh, Monica Byles

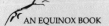

AN EQUINOX BOOK

© Andromeda Oxford Ltd 1994

Devised and produced by
Andromeda Oxford Ltd
11–15 The Vineyard
Abingdon Oxfordshire OX14 3PX
England

This edition published by
Hamlyn, part of Reed
Consumer Books Ltd,
Michelin House,
81 Fulham Road,
London SW3 6RB

ISBN 0-600-57996-4

Printed in Germany by
Mohndruck Graphische Betriebe
GmbH. Gutersloh.

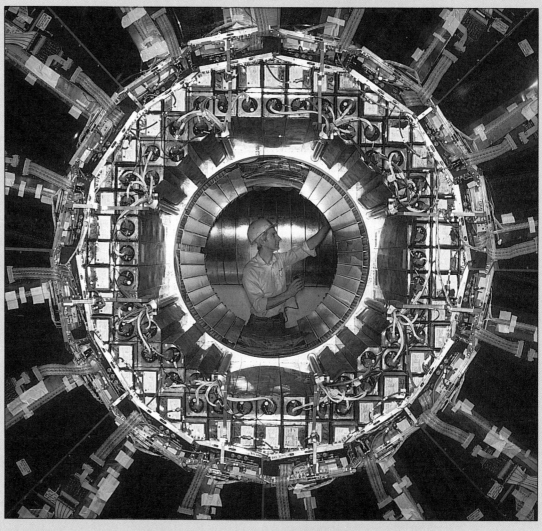

ADVISORY EDITORS

Alan Borg
Imperial War Museum,
London

Asa Briggs
Worcester College, Oxford

Carlo Cipolla
University of California,
Berkeley, USA

Sir Napier Crookenden
Formerly Lieutenant of Her
Majesty's Tower of London

Andrew J. Goodpaster
US Army (retired)

Wolfgang Krieger
Ebenhausen, Germany

David Landes
Harvard University, USA

William McNeill
University of Chicago, USA

Peter Pulzer
All Souls College, Oxford

**Hartmut Pogge von
Strandmann**
University College, Oxford

Philip Waller
Merton College, Oxford

Geoffrey Warner
Open University

M.L.H.L. Weaver
Linacre College, Oxford

Charles Webster
All Souls College, Oxford

EDITORS

John Campbell
Freelance writer, London

John Harriss
London School of Economics

Richard Maltby
University of Exeter

C. S. Nicholls
St Antony's College, Oxford

Sidney Pollard
Formerly of University of
Bielefeld, Germany

J. M. Winter
Pembroke College,
Cambridge

CONTRIBUTORS

Gerold Ambrosius
University of Bremen,
Germany

Duncan Anderson
Royal Military Academy,
Sandhurst

Ian Beckett
Royal Military Academy,
Sandhurst

Geoffrey Best
Formerly of University of
Sussex

Robert Bideleux
University of Swansea

Simon Boughey
Corpus Christi College,
Cambridge

Gail Braybon
Freelance writer

Sir Julian Bullard
All Souls College, Oxford

Kathleen Burk
Imperial College, London

Angus Calder
Open University

Peter Carey
Trinity College, Oxford

Jane Carmichael
Imperial War Museum,
London

Malcolm Cooper
Freelance writer

P. L. Cottrell
University of Leicester

Robert Dare
University of Adelaide,
Australia

Martin Dean
Formerly of University of
Cambridge

Anne Deighton
University of Reading

John Erickson
University of Edinburgh

Keith Faulks
Freelance writer

David Fletcher
The Tank Museum, Wareham

CONTENTS

James Foreman-Peck
University of Hull
Brian Foss
Freelance writer
Michael Geyer
University of Chicago, USA
Robert Gildea
Merton College, Oxford
Anthony Glees
Brunel University
Roger Griffin
Oxford Polytechnic
Alfred Grosser
Paris
Jennifer Hargreaves
Roehampton Institute,
London
Nathaniel Harris
Freelance writer
Nigel Harris
University College, London
Gundi Harriss
Birkbeck College, London

David Horn
University of Liverpool
Julian Jackson
University of Swansea
Keith Jeffery
University of Ulster
Matthew Jones
St Antony's College, Oxford
Paul Kennedy
Yale University, USA
Ghislaine Lawrence
Science Museum, London
Peter Lowe
University of Manchester
Keith Lyons
London School of Economics
Dermott MacCann
Brunel University
Peter Martland
Corpus Christi College,
Cambridge
Roger Morgan
London School of Economics

Lucy Newton
Leicester University
A. J. Nicholls
St Antony's College, Oxford
David Penn
Imperial War Museum,
London
Brian Holden Reid
King's College, London
Catherine Reilly
Freelance writer
Denis Ridgeway
Formerly of Royal Navy
Scientific Service
Gowher Rizvi
University of Warwick
Keith Sainsbury
University of Reading
Harry Shukman
St Antony's College, Oxford
Penny Sparke
Royal College of Art, London

Jill Stephenson
University of Edinburgh
Stanley Trapido
Lincoln College, Oxford
T.H.E. Travers
University of Calgary,
Canada
S.B. Whitmore
Formerly British Army of the
Rhine, Germany
Paul Wilkinson
University of Aberdeen
Elizabeth Wilson
North London Polytechnic
Roger Zetter
Oxford Polytechnic
Ronald Tamplin
University of Exeter
Ruth Pearson
University of East Anglia
Peter Lambert
University of East Anglia

INTRODUCTION

It is increasingly difficult to write history the nearer that we approach the present, particularly when there is a speeding up of news as occurred throughout the 1970s and 1980s, largely as a result of the development of communication by satellite and the spread of television sets. Inevitably neither people nor events can be seen in perspective until their consequences can be assessed.

The role of the journalist, which increased in importance between 1973 and 1990, is necessarily different from that of the historian, just as news is different from history. There were times, too, however, as in 1989, a vintage year for journalists, when news itself moved so fast – and carried with it so many surprises – that it was difficult for the public even to keep up with the news. Television carried it directly into the home: history unfolded before people's eyes. Tomorrow was already here. Yet dramatic events, like the pulling down of the Berlin Wall in 1989 and the subsequent reunification of Germany in 1990, have long-term consequences that cannot be foreseen. They will certainly affect the shape of the 21st century – a question which has fascinated people for decades. From the 1960s onwards, futurologists have been looking forward toward 2000, the end of a millennium as well as of a century, or in imaginative mood to 2001. In an age of space travel, science has sometimes caught up with science fiction; and during that age biological sciences have advanced more rapidly than the physical sciences, bringing with them new problems, some of them moral problems relating to life and death, like abortion and euthanasia, as well as new opportunities of raising health standards and further prolonging the expectations of life. During the 1980s Americans began to speak of the "greying of America". Some people approached the impending millennium with despair at the overriding questions facing the world community: inexorably rising population and growing gaps between rich and poor spread a gloom that technological advances could not dispel.

Speeding up of news, like futurology, has been associated with increasing globalization and with recognition at different levels that for good or ill – and for all the enormous differences in standards of health and wealth in different parts of the world – the planet is one. Thus, in 1989 itself, a year of great events, *State of the World 1989, A World Watch Institute Report on Progress Towards a Sustainable Society* concentrated not on political or military events – it had only one chapter called "enhancing global security" – but on themes like "halting land degradation", "re-examining the world food prospect", and "protecting the ozone layer". The survey described the world as a "world at risk" – with the threat of "global warming" – and as a "world without borders" since environmental and ecological problems were transmitted from one country to another and were ultimately shared by all. What happened to the tropical rain forests could be as devastating in its planetary effect as what happened in crowded, noisy, polluted cities, one of the worst of them a Latin American capital, Mexico City.

Human beings were always at the center of the story, however, as they were at the core of disasters, like the wreckage of oil tankers during the 1970s or in the wreckage of the nuclear reactor at Chernobyl in the Ukraine in 1986. It was their decisions, including their errors and, above all, their ways of life, which ultimately forced decisions to be taken, that made history. The explosion and fire at the nuclear reactor plant at Chernobyl was one of the most dramatic events of the period. The crisis was brought on by technicians conducting unauthorized experiments with the aging reactor. More than seven tonnes of radioactive material were hurled into the atmosphere, contaminating land, food and water and scattering disaster far beyond the borders of the Soviet Union as far as the Welsh hills. In the immediate vicinity of the reactor more than 100,000 people were evacuated from their homes and 2,500 square kilometers of land became uninhabitable.

One chapter in the *State of the World* dealt not with a single human disaster but with a new and continuing biological danger for human beings everywhere. In 1981, physicians in California and in New York had identified a frightening new complaint: the immune systems of a number of male homosexual patients had been destroyed, leaving them prey to infections, cancers and, it soon became apparent, early death. Similar symptoms were noted by physicians in Africa and in Haiti, and within a year the complaint had been given a name known, however, largely by initials, AIDS, acquired immune deficiency syndrome.

The following year, the "cause" of AIDS was identified also – a human immunodeficiency virus, HIV. It soon became apparent that the spread of the disease was not confined to homosexuals. Drug use could carry it: so, too, could medical blood transfusions. It could affect the heterosexual community and it could be passed on to babies. By the end of the decade the disease had spread throughout central Africa, and in the Far East, despite strenuous efforts at health education and an expensive search for an elusive vaccine. World action was needed to tackle the AIDS problem, and, like pandemics before it, it raised profound questions and exposed weaknesses in the existing social and administrative order.

The end of Communism
AIDS provided an ominous example of what could happen in a world "without borders". Yet borders continued to matter in politics and in some cases to matter more than they ever had done. Thus in 1991 and 1992 there was fierce fighting concerned with borders in the former Yugoslavia as the old country broke up into pieces.

The country where the most dramatic events of 1989 and 1990 took place, the Soviet Union, broke up also in 1991. A vast area of the world once held together by the power of the Communist party organized from Moscow, it could not survive as one when the party lost its grip. The story of change had begun in 1985 when Mikhail Gorbachev became general secretary of the party, ending a period of stagnation and, behind the scenes, of increasing economic strain. By unleashing changes which realigned the Soviet Union in international politics and which were to break up his country into different component parts, Gorbachev altered the whole balance of power in the world. The chain of consequences could certainly not be foreseen in the mid 1980s as he extolled the importance of openness, *glasnost*, and of reform, *perestroika*. The Soviet

▶ Life in the Calcutta slums in the 1980s.

Union as such ceased to exist in 1991, when not only did formerly independent countries like the Baltic states – Latvia, Lithuania and Estonia – secure their independence, but so also did parts of the Union, like the Ukraine and Kazakhstan, which had never been independent before.

Gorbachev always faced hostile critics inside and outside the party and an abortive attempt was made in 1991 to reverse his policies by a hard-line coup. Its failure was followed by his loss of power to one of his sharpest critics, Boris Yeltsin, who after ensuring the failure of the coup, acquired preponderant power for himself in Russia at the center of the old Soviet Union. However, neither under Gorbachev nor under Yeltsin were the economic problems of the country tackled effectively. The transition to a market economy was rough and disordered even though it was hailed – and to a degree supported – in Washington, London and Brussels.

Marxism as an international force seemed to crumble with Gorbachev. Indeed, it had already crumbled in Poland, Czechoslovakia, Hungary and East Germany before it crumbled in the Soviet Union itself. The centenary of the death of Karl Marx had been celebrated in 1983 as much in Western Europe as in the East. Yet under the pressure of economic forces, without losing its appeal to a significant number of intellectuals, by 1989 it no longer provided the basis for a working socialist citizenry. Before the Berlin Wall, which separated East and West, was pulled down in 1989, large numbers of East Germans had already crossed their own frontiers to find freedom outside. Indeed, it was their determination to move and, above all, the fact that they could and did move, that toppled the regime of Erich Honecker who had been head of state in East Germany since 1976.

One country which remained Communist in 1989, Albania,

Marxism declined (except in China), the power of Islam increased. With the heart of a militant Islamic movement now in Iran, where under Ayatollah Khomeini gained power after the fall of the Shah in 1979, there was a new center of authority. It was strong enough to reach into Britain, where the novelist Salman Rushdie was placed under threat of death for publishing his allegedly blasphemous novel *The Satanic Verses*.

Iran was also at war with neighboring Iraq from 1980 to 1988, a war during which chemical weapons were used. It was Iraq, however, rather than Iran, which was at the focus of world news in 1991 with an invasion of Kuwait, planned and carried through by the dictatorial supremo of the ruling Ba'ath party, Saddam Hussein. United Nations action, led by the United States, freed Kuwait after a brief war in early 1991. Huge military power was employed, but it did not totally destroy Hussein's own power base. The United Nations intervention marked a new chapter in the history of international cooperation – and it would not have been possible had not Gorbachev and the American president George Bush been drawn close enough together to bring to an end the long years of great power vetoes in New York. The end of Cold War rivalries now meant that Hussein could be isolated.

Bush had succeeded Reagan as Republican president of the United States in 1989. For a time he had been American ambassador to the United Nations from 1971 to 1973 and in 1980 he had lost the Republican presidential nomination to Reagan. The years from 1980 to 1988 had been dominated by two figures who seemed to characterize the decade – Ronald Reagan himself and Margaret Thatcher, who became prime minister of Britain in 1979 and went on to win three successive general elections. Committed to conservative policies on the two sides of the Atlantic, they developed a special relationship with each other.

It was Mrs Thatcher, however, who gave her name to the new political *ism* of the period. Thatcherism was an ideology which encompassed a monetary economic strategy and a set of individual moral imperatives as well as a political party program. It offered strong government combined with a reliance on market forces single-minded enough to challenge the political consensus that had existed since 1945. Thatcherism influenced other countries besides Britain in a period of economic transition when government expenditures were curbed. It also influenced the program of Britain's Labour party. Yet Mrs Thatcher herself fell from power as Conservative leader and Prime Minister in a welter of recriminations in 1990. When she fell, there was mass unemployment in Britain on a scale that would have been inconceivable even in 1973 when, under her Tory predecessor Edward Heath, Britain was suffering from a combination of unemployment and inflation.

The changes in Eastern Europe raised many questions about the directions to be taken in the West, especially in the European Community where the end of the Cold War mentality brought a debate between those who would widen the Community, and those who would deepen its integration. Throughout her years of power Mrs Thatcher was suspicious of many of the new moves towards greater European political union being pressed in Brussels. Yet she supported the moves towards greater economic integration and the advent of a single European market in 1992. There had been many Europeans who had been looking forward as eagerly to 1992 as they were to 2000 or 2001, but in a world of change there was as much uncertainty in the old West as there was in the new East as the new century grew closer and closer.

went through revolutionary disturbances itself in 1992 which destroyed what had for long seemed an impregnable regime backed by force in support of ideology. There were similar changes also in Third World countries, like Ethiopia, where Marxism had become an official religion.

A world in flux

For all the excitement of these changes, the world did not become a significantly more secure place in the early 1990s. In some respects, indeed, the destruction of Marxist regimes restored to life old regional, national and religious rivalries and enmities that had been forced underground since 1945 or even 1917. Thus, Sarajevo, capital of Bosnia and Herzegovina, which had been the Balkan town in the news before the beginning of World War I, hit the headlines again in 1992 when it was besieged by the Serbs. And in Asia, too, as the power of

THE EXPLOSIVE WORLD

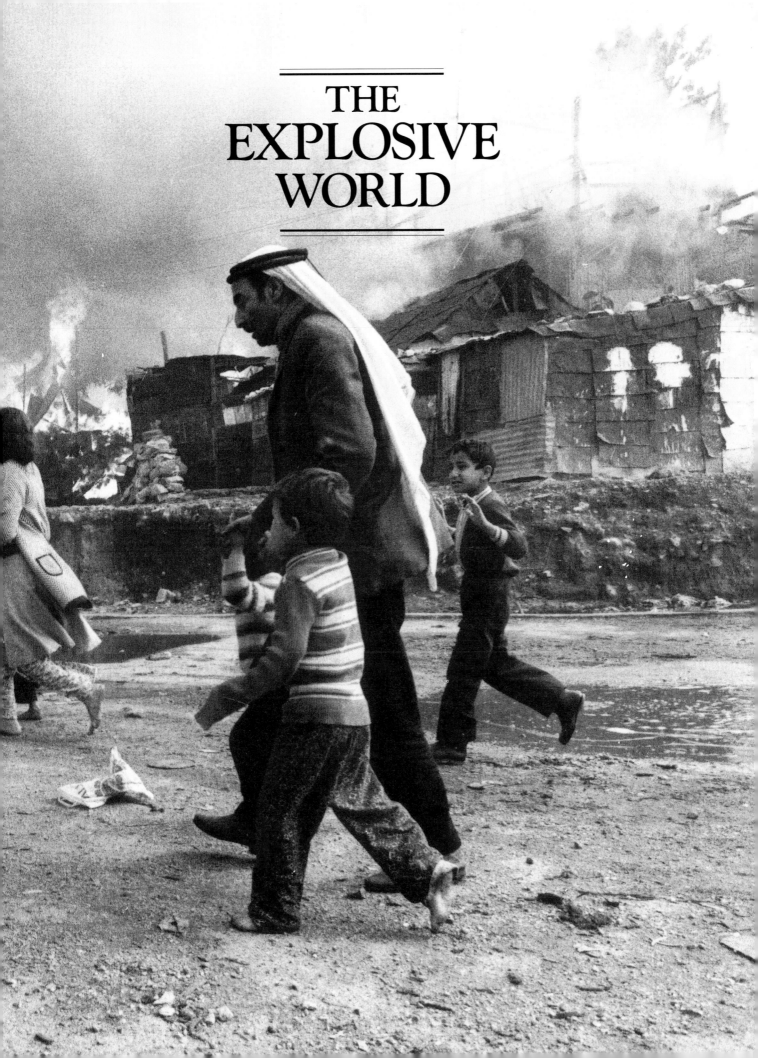

Time Chart

	1974	1975	1976	1977	1978	1979	1980	1981
Europe/Mediterranean	• 4 Mar: 1st UK minority cabinet since 1929 • 2 Apr: Valéry Giscard D'Estaing elected Pres. (Fr) • 6 May: Willi Brandt succeeded by Helmut Schmidt (W Ger) • 29 May: UK resumed direct rule of Ulster • 15 Jul: Coup in Cyprus; Turkish invasion, 20 Jul. UN cease-fire, 22 Jul	• 24 Apr: Siege of W German embassy, Stockholm, by terrorists demanding release of members of Baader–Meinhof group • 20 Nov: Death of dictator Franco (Sp); succeeded by King Juan Carlos (22 Nov)	• 6 Jan: Resignation of Prime Minister Aldo Moro and cabinet after claims of CIA funding of noncommunists • 16 Mar: Resignation of UK prime minister Harold Wilson (since 4 Mar 1974): succeeded by James Callaghan • 23 Jul: In Portugal, Mario Soares was 1st constitutional prime minister since coup (25 Apr 1974)	• 23–24 Jan: Spanish constitutional rights suspended for 30 days after political violence and strikes in Barcelona and Madrid • 15 Jun: Adolf Suarez elected in 1st free elections in Spain for 41 years • 16 Jun: Brezhnev named USSR president as well as party chief – the 1st time in Soviet history	• 16 Mar: Kidnap of former Prime Minister Aldo Moro by Red Brigade – discovered dead, 9 May (Ita) • 6 Aug: Death of Pope Paul VI. 28 Sept, death of John Paul I. 16 Oct, 1st non-Italian Pope elected since 1523: John Paul II of Poland	• 3 May: 1st UK woman prime minister, Margaret Thatcher, elected with large majority • 27 Aug: UK Earl Mountbatten killed in IRA bomb explosion • Dec: USSR invaded Afghanistan in support of Marxist regime following coup	• 4 May: Death of Tito (Yug): succeeded by collective rotating presidency • 30 Aug: After labor unrest, workers at Gdansk Lenin Shipyard allowed to form independent trade unions: unprecedented in Soviet bloc	• Greece became a member of the EEC • 2 Mar: Social Democrat Party formed (UK) • 11–12 Apr: Nationwide racial riots, also in July (UK) • 10 May: François Mitterrand elected President • 13 Dec: Martial law declared (Pol) and Solidarity banned. Labor unrest continue
The Middle East	• 10 Apr: Resignation of Golda Meir; Itzhak Rabin replaced her • 18 May: India became the 6th nation with a nuclear bomb • 31 May: Agreement signed by Israel and Syria for armistice on Golan Heights • 28 Oct: 20 Arab nations called for an independent Palestine state and recognized PLO leader Arafat	• 21 Feb: UN Human Rights Commission censured Israel for actions in occupied Arab territories • 13 Apr: Fighting started between Moslems and Christians (Leb) • 5 Jun: Suez Canal reopened after 8 years except to Israeli traffic • 26 Jun: State of emergency declared in India	• 3 Jul: Entebbe hijack ended, Uganda, when plane held by pro-Palestinian terrorists was stormed by Israeli commandos	• 24 Mar: Morarji Desai replaced Indira Gandhi as prime minister (Ind) • 21 Jun: Menachem Begin elected prime minister (Isr) • 5 Jul: General Zia ousted Prime Minister Bhutto (Pak) • 5 Dec: President Sadat (Egy) broke diplomatic ties with Syria, Iraq, Libya, Algeria and S Yemen	• 17 Sep: Camp David Accords between Sadat (Egy) and Begin (Isr) to fix schedule for peace negotiations: denounced by 20 Arab League nations at Baghdad summit (5 Nov) • 19 Dec: Indira Gandhi expelled from Indian Parliament and imprisoned on charges of conspiracy, electoral misconduct and abuses during emergency rule	• 16 Jan: Exile of Shah. 11 Feb, Islamic law imposed on Iran by Ayatollah Khomeini • 26 Mar: Peace treaty signed by Sadat (Egy) and Begin (Isr). Egypt censured by Arab League: diplomatic ties and economic boycott imposed • 4 Nov: Iranian militants captured US embassy, Teheran. Most of 90 hostages freed 20 Jan 1981	• 6 Jan: Indira Gandhi reelected as prime minister of India • 22 Sep: Start of Iran–Iraq war (cease-fire and start of UN-backed peace talks, Aug 1988)	• 5 Sep: Coptic Pope deposed and religious and other "dissidents" arrested through fear of religious factionalism (Egy) • 6 Oct: President Sadat assassinated by extremist Moslem soldiers: succeeded by Hosni Mubarak (Egy) • 18 Oct: 1st socialist government elected under Andreas Papandreou (Gre)
Africa	• 2 Sep: Emperor Haile Selassie deposed in bloodless coup by military leaders. 20 Dec, Ethiopia declared a socialist state	• 25 Jun: Mozambique gained independence from Portugal under Marxist President Samora Machel	• 16 Jun: Soweto racial riots started against legislation to force Afrikaans use in some teaching (S Afr) • 4–5 Aug: Sudan broke relations with Libya and USSR after failed coup	• 4 Nov: UN voted embargo on military wares to S Africa in protest against racist policies	• 3 Mar: Pact for power to Rhodesian blacks by 31 Dec • 22 Aug: Jomo Kenyatta succeeded by Daniel Arap Moi • 28 Sep: PW Botha elected (S Afr)	• 11 Apr: Idi Amin deposed by Ugandan exile force and Tanzanian soldiers • 21 Dec: Peace pacts signed in London to end conflict, Rhodesia	• 17 Apr: Rhodesia became independent Zimbabwe: end of 90 years of white rule. Robert Mugabe was 1st black prime minister	• Nov: Forays by S African troops into Angola to counter SWAPO guerrillas fighting for Namibian independence
The Americas	• 1 Jul: Death of Perón: widow Isabel succeeded him as 1st woman head of state in the Western Hemisphere • 9 Aug: Resignation of Nixon following Watergate scandal. Gerald R Ford sworn in as next president, gave Nixon unconditional pardon (8 Sep)		24 Mar: Overthrow of Isabel Martinez de Perón (Arg) by General Jorge Rafael Videla • 2 Nov: Jimmy Carter elected next US president	• 28 Apr: 1st formal negotiations between US and Cuba when fishing rights pact approved. Diplomats posted in each country (3 Jun) within foreign embassies without full restoration of relations • 1–2 May: Arrest of Clamshell Alliance protestors in 1st mass civil disobedience against nuclear plant construction (US)	• 22 Aug: National Palace and 1,500 hostages seized by Sandinista guerilas. President Somoza refused to step down after strikes, and cutting of US military aid (Nic)	• 17 Jul: Sandinista rebels captured Nicaraguan capital: junta took power after resignation and flight of President Somoza • 1 Oct: Panama took control of territory of American Canal Zone • 21 Nov: US evacuated all non-essential personnel from embassies in 10 Islamic nations	• Jan: US trade embargo imposed after USSR invasion of Afghanistan • 24 Mar: Assassination of RC Archbishop Oscar Romero (Sal) • 4 Nov: Ronald Reagan elected as US President • 13 Dec: José Napoleon Duarte was 1st civilian president in 49 years (Sal)	• 30 Mar: Failed assassination of President Reagan • 6 Aug: Reagan decided on production of neutron weapons – 100 new MX missiles called for (2 Oct) • 20 Sep: British Honduras became independent Belize with contingent of UK troops to guard against attack from Guatemala who claimed it
Asia and Pacific	• 9 Apr: India, Pakistan and Bangladesh restored diplomatic relations after agreement on dispute concerning Pakistani prisoners of war	• 16 Apr: Khmer Rouge took Cambodia • 30 Apr: S Vietnamese surrender to the communists • 23 Aug: Communist takeover of Laos completed	• 8 Jan: Death of Zhou Enlai. 9 Sept, death of Mao Zedong. Hua Gofeng succeeded Mao as chairman of Communist party • 2 Jul: N and S Vietnam reunited as one nation	• 22 Jul: Gang of Four expelled from Communist Party and Deng Xiaoping "rehabilitated". 11th congress marked by creation of 26-member Politburo, new party constitution and arrest of Mao's widow	• 1 May: Ethnic Chinese "boat people" began to flee Vietnam • 3 Jul: China cut all aid to Vietnam. 13 July, cut aid to Albania • 3 Nov: Pact signed by US and Vietnam	• 1 Jan: Diplomatic relations established between China and US. US broke relations with Taiwan • 26 Oct: President Park assassinated by director of Korean CIA after 18 years in power	• 23 Jun: Invasion of Thailand by Vietnam via Cambodia • 7 Sep: Resignations as part of pro-modernization campaign against lifelong incumbency of official posts (Chn)	• 25 Jan: Sentences passed in trial of Gang of Four (Chn) • 29 Jun: Hua Gofeng replaced as head of Communist Party (Chn) by Hu Yaobang. Mao discredited for mistakes in leadership
World	• 4 Sep: US and E Germany established diplomatic relations (US was the last major Western power to recognize E Germany since its emergence from international isolation in 1971)	• 1 Aug: Nonbinding security and cooperation pact signed in Helsinki by 33 European nations, Canada and US to freeze postwar borders, extend détente, renounce force and aid to terrorists and respect human rights	• 24 Feb – 5 Mar, 25th Soviet Communist Party Congress: Increased independence of Western Communist Parties • 28 May: US and USSR signed 5-year treaty limiting size of underground nuclear test explosions and allowing US to inspect Soviet tests on-site	• 7 Sep: 2 Panama Canal treaties signed by US and Panama: canal to be under full control of Panama from 1999 and to be permanently neutral • 21 Sep: USA, USSR and 13 nations signed nuclear non-proliferation pact to limit spread of nuclear weapons		• 18 Jun: US Senate refused SALT II treaty with USSR after Afghan invasion • 17 Jul: 1st meeting of European Parliament • 12 Dec: NATO agreed to install 572 medium-range missiles in Europe by 1983		• Mass European demonstrations for nuclear disarmament started in UK

1982	1983	1984	1985	1986	1987	1988	1989
14 Dec: Garret Fitzgerald replaced Charles Haughey (elected 9 Mar, Ire) / 1 Oct: Election of Helmut Kohl (W Ger) / 18 Oct: Solidarity trade union banned (Pol). 21 Dec: martial law lifted / 28 Oct: Election of Felipe Gonzalez (Sp) / 10–12 Nov: Brezhnev succeeded by Yuri Andropov (USSR)	• 5 May: France expelled 47 Soviet diplomats and nationals on charges of espionage: unprecedented in French–Soviet relations / • 9 Jun: In UK, Conservative party under Margaret Thatcher reelected / • 16 Jun: Yuri Andropov elected president of the Soviet Presidium	• 9 Feb: Death of Andropov, succeeded by Konstantin Chernenko as general secretary of the Communist Party (Feb) and president of the Supreme Soviet (Apr) / • 22 Apr: UK cut diplomatic ties with Libya / • 12 Oct: IRA bomb attack on Uk Conservative Party at Annual Conference, Brighton	• 10 Mar: Death of Chernenko; succeeded by Andrei Gromyko as Soviet president (2 Jul) and Mikhail Gorbachev as general secretary of the Communist Party / • 28 May: UK was found guilty of sex discrimination in immigration policy by European Parliament / • 27 Nov: Anglo–Irish accord signed: Eire to be consulted in running of Ulster (UK)	• Kurt Waldheim elected President (Aut) / • 16 Feb: Dr Mario Soares became 1st civilian president in 60 years (Por) / • 28 Feb: Assassination of Prime Minister Olof Palme; succeeded by Ingvar Carlson (Swe) / • 24 Oct: UK broke off diplomatic relations with Syria	• 10 Mar: Charles Haughey became prime minister of Eire / • 17 Aug: Death of Rudolf Hess in Spandau Prison, Berlin (W Ger)	• Jan: Joint army brigade (Fr, W Ger) / • 8 May: Francois Mitterrand reelected president (Fr) / • Jun: Poul Schlueter reelected (Den) / • 30 Sep: Opponents to Soviet reforms voted out of office. Gorbachev appointed Soviet president (1 Oct) / • 20 Oct: Abolition of criminal suspect's right of silence (UK)	• 1st democratic Soviet elections / • 4 Jun: 1st partly democratic elections in Poland; Solidarity prime minister appointed (Aug) / • 24 Jun: German–Soviet treaty / • Jul: Southern Irish elections failed to find acceptable government / • 10 Nov: Berlin Wall opened
24 Mar: Military coup and martial law (Bang) / 6 Jun: Attack on Israeli ambassador by Palestinian terrorists countered with invasion of southern Lebanon. Israel agreed to PLO evacuation plan under multinational peace-keeping force / 28–30 Aug: Start of war between Druse Moslem militia and the Lebanese Army	• 11 Feb: Resignation of Israeli Defense Minister Ariel Sharon after inquiry into massacre of Palestinian refugees in West Beirut (16–18 Sep 1982) / • 12 Sep: Resignation of Prime Minister Menachem Begin; succeeded by Yitzhak Shamir (Isr) / • 15 Nov: Turkish Republic of Northern Cyprus declared	• 21 Feb: With deterioration of situation in the Lebanon, international peacekeeping forces withdrawn / • 31 Oct: Indira Gandhi assassinated by 2 Sikh bodyguards; succeeded by her son, Rajiv Gandhi (Ind)			• Peace accord signed with India to end bloodshed in Sri Lanka between separatist Tamil guerrillas and mainly Sinhalese government	• mid-Apr: (Pak) Afghan peace accord for Soviet pullout by Feb 1989 / • Aug: Cease-fire agreed in Iran–Iraq war / • 17 Aug: Death of General Zia (Pak); succeeded by 1st woman leader of Moslem country, Benazir Bhutto (1 Dec) / • 14 Dec: Yasir Arafat (PLO) renounced terrorism, recognized Israel	• 4 Jun: Death of Ayatollah Khomeini after 10 years' power; succeeded by Hojatoleslam Ali Akbar Rafsanjani (29 Jul) as prime minister with extended powers under new constitution
17 Feb: Opposition leader Joshua Nkomo dismissed from regime of Mugabe (Zim). 16 Aug: he retook his seat in government after exile in Botswana and UK / 7 June: Capital of Chad fell to rebel forces		• 20 May: Most serious black terrorist bomb attack against regime outside air force HQ, Pretoria (S Afr) / • 3–4 Aug: US involvement in Chad crisis publicly angered French government	• 15 Apr: End to ban on mixed marriages announced: 1st ceremony took place 15 Jun (S Afr) / • 27 Jul: President Milton Obote ousted in bloodless coup, Kampala (Uga)	• 19 May: S African forces carried out raids on Zambia, Zimbabwe and Botswana / • 12 Jun: State of emergency declared with widespread unrest on 10th anniversary of Soweto uprising (S Afr)		• 8 Aug: Agreement between S Africa, Cuba and Angola over disengagement of troops from Angola / • Oct: President Kenneth Kaunda reelected for 6th term in office (Zambia)	• 1 Jan: Namibia granted independence from S Africa / • 11 Jan: Start of Cuban troop withdrawal from Angola
28 Mar: 1st free elections held in 50 years (Sal) / 2–3 Apr: Start of Falkland Conflict with Argentine invasion of UK territory / 17 Apr: British North America Act of 1867 terminated (UK, Can) / 8 Jun: Reagan became 1st US President to address joint session of parliament	• 25 Oct: US troops landed on Grenada to "protect US citizens" after Marxist coup. Cuban and Soviet presence discovered	• 6 Nov: Ronald Reagan reelected as US President	• 30 Apr: Reagan planned total trade embargo on Sandinista regime in Nicaragua after request for aid for Contra rebels blocked by House of Representatives / • 1 Aug: US House of Representatives voted to impose sanctions on S Africa			• Mar: US-backed coup to oust General Noriega failed (Pan) / • May: Belize and Guatemala agreed a permanent commission to formulate treaty to end territorial dispute / • 6 Oct: Gen. Augusto Pinochet refused to step down after election defeat (Chi) / • 8 Nov: George Bush elected US president	• 2 Feb: Carlos Andres Perez reelected (Ven) / • May: 1st free elections in Argentina
12–13 Sep: Hua Guofeng lost his position as successor to Mao Zedong. Deng Xiaoping was elected chairman of new Central Advisory Commission to the Communist Party (to 2 Nov 1987)	• 5 Mar: Election of Labour Party under Robert Hawke (Aus) / • 9 Oct: Death of Korean government officials in bomb explosion during ceremony in Burma: N Korea was blamed			• 2 Mar: Australia Bill signed by the Queen severing constitutional ties with UK / • 26 Feb: Corazon Aquino chose her cabinet after flight of ex-President Ferdinand Marcos (Phil)	• 14 May: Failed coup in Fiji against Indian political dominance: state of emergency declared. 1 Oct: Col. Rabuka declared himself head of state	• Feb: Cease-fire for Laos and Thailand / • Feb: 1st democratically-elected president (S Kor) / • 18 Sep: Military coup after civil unrest when 1st civilian elected (Bur)	• 7 Jan: Accession of Emperor Akihito (Jap) / • 4 Jun: Student revolt quashed, Beijing (Chn) / • 25 Jul: Liberal Democrats received first major electoral reverses for 30 years (Jap)
10 Dec: The Law of the Sea Convention signed after 10 years by 119 nations (refusal to sign by UK, US and other industrialized nations): in favor of profit-sharing and cooperation / 1 Jan: Javier Perez de Cuellar (Per) became Secretary-General of UN	• 14 Mar: OPEC group agreed to cut oil prices in view of world glut / • 28–30 May: Economic summit (US, UK, Can, Fr, W Ger, Ita, Jap) / • 22–23 Nov: Breakdown of US–USSR arms reductions talks as NATO and USSR announced increase in nuclear forces	• 30 Mar: US and several S American nations agreed to package of loans totaling $5 billion to aid Argentina with international debts / • Aug: Equipment and experts sent by several countries to clear the Red Sea of mines placed by the Islamic Jihad	• 2 Jan: Official withdrawal of US from UNESCO	• 1 Jan: Perez de Cuellar (Per) appointed for 2nd term as UN Secretary-General		• 14 Apr: Afghan accords, Geneva (Afg, Pak, USSR, US) / • mid-Jun, Economic pact: EEC and Gulf Cooperation Council / • Nov: Space technology cooperation agreement (Chn, Aus) / • 7 Nov: UK and Iran restored diplomatic ties	• 12 Jan, Chemical weapons conference, Paris (Fr): 149 nations signed total ban on use of gas, toxins and bacteriological weapons / • Salman Rushdie affair: UK/Iran relations broken after Moslem death threats to UK author. International controversy ensued

Datafile

The years after 1973 saw the arms race between the superpowers reach its most frenetic level since the 1950s and then begin to slacken as the long-obstructed channels of negotiation gradually opened to allow for real progress with arms reduction agreements. The intensification of competition in the late 1970s and early 1980s was caused by the arrival of new generations of nuclear and conventional weapons, while diplomatic positions became more rigid as the US reasserted itself after the trauma of Vietnam and the USSR intervened militarily in Afghanistan. The trend began to reverse as superpower allies in Europe began to question alliance arrangements which could turn their homelands into nuclear battlegrounds, as popular opposition to nuclear weapons began to grow, and as the staggering cost of modern military development began to do real damage to the flagging economies of the USA and USSR. In an era of economic retrenchment, the governments of both the US and USSR began to adopt less rigid stances toward each other.

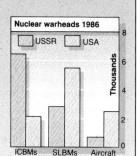

Strategic warheads

◀ By 1990 superpower arms budgets were being cut back in the face of economic difficulties in the Soviet Union, and arms limitation agreements. Iraq, however, which was rearming after its long war with Iran, was spending heavily on armaments from both East and West. These weapons would be used in the Gulf War of 1991.

▲ ▼ The number of US and Soviet nuclear warheads, both land (ICBM, intercontinental ballistic missiles) and submarine (SLBM, sea-launched ballistic missiles) based, rose steeply in the 1970s, the US attaining a dramatic lead in the first half of the decade and the USSR making a huge effort to catch up thereafter.

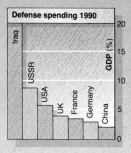

Defense spending 1990

◀ While the massive nuclear arsenals of the US and USSR were relatively equal in aggregate, they depended on a different mix of bases and launch systems. Preparing for war in Europe, the USSR's strategic missile forces were overwhelmingly land-based. The US depended far less heavily on fixed sites.

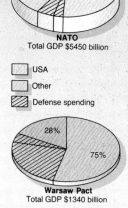

Arms budget 1982

NATO
Total GDP $5450 billion

☐ USA
☐ Other
▨ Defense spending

Warsaw Pact
Total GDP $1340 billion

☐ USSR
☐ Other
▨ Defense spending

◀ The USSR and its Warsaw Pact allies spent a far higher proportion of their GDP on defense than the US and its NATO allies. Both superpowers carried the greater proportional share of the total spending within their alliances, particularly in the Eastern bloc where the smaller countries were economically far weaker.

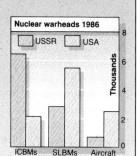

Nuclear warheads 1986

☐ USSR ☐ USA

ICBMs   SLBMs   Aircraft

▼ Membership figures for the Campaign for Nuclear Disarmament (CND) in Britain typify changing public opinion to nuclear weapons. CND expanded rapidly between 1979 and 1984, driven by controversy on the basing of US Cruise missiles on British soil. With progress in arms reduction negotiations, membership fell.

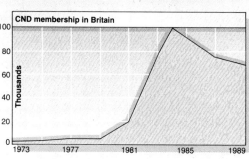

CND membership in Britain

From the late 1960s superpower relations had been complicated by the Soviet premier Brezhnev's "doctrine" that any attempt by an Eastern bloc country to abandon socialism would be resisted by all the other members of the "socialist commonwealth". At the same time, however, the hardline from Moscow seemed to be tempered by promises of détente. In March 1976 Brezhnev publicly endorsed "the principles of peaceful coexistence to reduce and eliminate the danger of world war" and spoke of "negotiation and not confrontation" as "the natural state of things".

The case for détente

Leading Western politicians believed that by accepting Soviet hegemony in Eastern and Central Europe (about which it could do very little), they could secure Soviet agreement on the urgent issue of arms limitation. Moreover, they reasoned that the greater contacts that would ensue from détente might even incite some of the satellite countries to press for greater independence from Moscow. By accepting that the Soviet Union would not abandon its military presence in Central Europe, which it regarded as the key to its security, the United States and its NATO allies hoped to defuse potential flashpoints of superpower confrontation such as the Cuban missile crisis of 1962.

Between 1970 and 1976 the superpowers held four summit meetings, of which three took place on American soil, and in 1972 Richard Nixon became the first US president to visit Moscow. Nixon's resignation on 9 August 1974, after a scandal over the bugging of the Watergate building, the Democratic party headquarters, both weakened the Republican party and cast doubt on all of Nixon's actions, including his foreign policy, in which he had been so ably assisted by his secretary of state Henry Kissinger. However, Nixon's successor, Gerald Ford, remained undeterred in pursuing détente, fortified by Kissinger and by the belief that the development of better relations with the People's Republic of China would concentrate the mind of the Soviets enough to ensure further negotiations with them on arms limitation and a general reduction in East–West tension.

This approach led to a meeting between Ford and Brezhnev in Vladivostok on 23 November 1974 and the signing of the SALT (Strategic Arms Limitation Talks) II treaty. They also agreed to hold a general conference on security and cooperation in Europe (CSCE) in Helsinki in 1975. SALT II placed a ceiling on numbers of missile launchers and bombers and was designed to extend and complement SALT I (which had for five years frozen the numbers of ballistic missiles). However, this second treaty was never

SUPERPOWER RELATIONS

ratified, largely because of American disquiet over the Soviet invasion of Afghanistan at the end of 1979. The signing, in August 1975, of the Helsinki agreement, which was the culmination of the CSCE process, was attended by representatives from 33 European countries as well as the United States and Canada. Widely interpreted as legitimizing the Soviet hold on Central and Eastern Europe, the agreement actually did no more than guarantee the integrity of all European borders. Moreover, the regimes within those borders were committed to promote better East–West relations and uphold the primacy of "human rights". (Ultimately, the Soviet Union's failure to comply on human rights' issues was the ostensible – and certainly most emotive – reason why Helsinki did not succeed, though the most compelling reasons were certainly military.)

Further hope for better East–West relations in 1975 came with the ending of US support for the government of South Vietnam. Thus, when a Soviet *Soyuz* spacecraft docked in space with an *Apollo* from the United States, the union appeared to symbolize a new era in US–Soviet relations and fulfil Nixon's 1972 promise of the superpowers locked into "interdependence for survival". However, American optimism was short-lived, as intelligence reports suggested that the Soviets had begun to rearm.

▶ A US mobile Cruise missile launcher in the early 1980s. The introduction of Cruise threatened to upset the strategic balance. A mobile land-based nuclear weapon system did not fit into the idea of mutually assured deterrence, built around fixed missile sites.

▼ The dialogue of détente. US president Carter and the Soviet leader Brezhnev at arms limitation talks in 1979. Mutual suspicion and strategic intransigence ensured that the rate of change was slow.

With the election of Jimmy Carter as the 39th President of the United States in the autumn of 1976, a shift in US foreign policy took place. Whereas the Nixon–Ford–Kissinger line had been clearcut, Carter's was far less so. A former governor of Georgia, with little experience of foreign affairs, Carter relied on his secretary of state, Cyrus Vance, and his national security advisor, Zbigniew Brzezinski, for guidance on foreign policy. Vance, however, was a "dove" who supported détente, whereas Brzezinski, an expatriate Pole, was a "hawk" who distrusted the Russians. Meanwhile many experienced US politicians had begun to feel that Ford had conceded too much in the name of détente.

By the early 1970s the United States had stopped increasing the number of nuclear missiles, concentrating instead on developing multiple-warhead missiles (MIRVs) and Cruise missiles (an updated version of Hitler's V1 rockets). Meanwhile the Soviets had built a new bomber, launched the Kiev-class aircraft carrier and greatly expanded the Red Navy as well as developing SS20 and SS21 missiles. The SS20 was a powerful medium-range missile, highly mobile and impossible to monitor, and, like the short-range SS21, was deployed in Europe. By early 1983 the Soviets had 650 SS21s, compared with NATOs 100 equivalent weapons.

NATO rearmament

By the end of 1978 Carter was under pressure, both from inside the United States and in Europe, to act more firmly against the Soviets. On 1 July 1979 General Haig (who later became President Reagan's secretary of state) resigned as NATO supreme commander because of his differences with Carter. At about the same time, the West German chancellor, Helmut Schmidt, and the British prime minister, James Callaghan, both urged Carter to begin the much-needed process of rearming NATO even at the risk of arousing Soviet hostility. They proposed a "twin track" approach, combining rearmament with talks on disarmament. This policy was formally ratified in Brussels on 12 December 1979. It stipulated that NATO would deploy 572 Cruise and Pershing missiles (intermediate-range nuclear forces, or INF) in Europe if negotiations failed to bring about reductions in armaments on the Soviet side.

In 1980 President Carter increased the US military budget by five per cent for the following year, introduced a grain embargo against the Soviet Union (alienating farmers of the American Midwest, whose anger cost him dear in the presidential elections) and urged the US Olympic team to boycott the 1980 Moscow games as a protest against the Soviet invasion of Afghanistan.

To many in the West it seemed that the Soviets had cynically used the decade of détente to massively reequip and rearm. Soviet armed forces in Europe now outnumbered those of NATO: 2.75 to 1 in artillery and 2.5 to 1 in tanks and tactical aircraft. The basis of détente had ultimately been the MAD (mutual assured destruction) doctrine: a strategic balance in nuclear weaponry whose intention was to deter an attack by either side since neither could hope to win an ensuing war. A strategic advantage, particularly, as in this case, in the European theater, was perceived as greatly increasing the vulnerability of Western Europe. NATO's answer was to threaten to deploy Cruise and Pershing missiles, and eventually to do so.

President Jimmy Carter's reputation for vacillation and his botched attempts to secure the release of American hostages seized from the US embassy in Iran highlighted American impotence under his stewardship and cost him the presidency in the 1980 elections. Indeed, his new, harsher policy towards the Soviet Union effectively endorsed the "new right" cause being advanced so eloquently by his Republican rival Ronald Reagan, who claimed that compromise had weakened the United States and disturbed the international equilibrium.

Reagan's election as 40th president of the United States on 4 November 1980 sounded the

► ▼ The Reagan presidency witnessed a perceptible shift in US policy towards the rival superpower. Early in his first term, Reagan reasserted the traditional anti-Soviet stance, describing the USSR as an "evil empire", but his attitude softened as dialog developed, and by the late 1980s he and Gorbachev exchanged visits.

▼ The British prime minister, Margaret Thatcher – nicknamed the "Iron Lady" by Moscow – emerged as a committed advocate of deterrence through strength – in terms of both nuclear and conventional military force. In the early 1980s, both NATO and the Warsaw Pact maintained huge forces in Central Europe.

Sino-Soviet Relations

A heavy Soviet military buildup in East Asia and along disputed border regions increased Chinese fears for their security in the mid 1970s, while the Soviet Union felt growing unease with China's developing strategic nuclear capability in the early 1980s. Tensions were heightened by Soviet support for Vietnam (a traditional Chinese enemy) when it invaded Cambodia in December 1978 and overthrew the Pol Pot regime (backed by China). China responded by launching a brief offensive against Vietnam in February 1979. Relations further worsened after the Soviet occupation of Afghanistan in December 1979.

By the late 1980s relations showed signs of improvement, with China and the new Soviet leadership keen to reduce the economic costs of confrontation and boost mutual trade. After Moscow's withdrawal from Afghanistan and reduction of its forces on the Chinese border, the first Sino-Soviet summit since the Khrushchev era was held in Beijing in 1989. The summit led to the demarcation of the eastern section of the Sino-Soviet border, and the process of reapprochement between Beijing and Moscow continued despite the collapse of the Soviet Union in 1991.

◀ Chinese missile forces for deployment in the north.

death knell of détente, which he declared had been a "one way street that the Soviet Union had exploited to pursue its own aims". Reagan came to the White House firmly resolved to present an uncompromising face to the Soviet Union and to execute NATO's rearmament. In November 1983 the Soviets walked out of the INF talks at Geneva as a protest against the "twin-track decision" to deploy Cruise and Pershing missiles in Europe and refused to restart arms limitation talks unless the missiles were withdrawn.

Earlier in 1983 Reagan had proposed the "zero option": the total dismantling of all intermediate missiles in Europe. Yuri Andropov, who succeeded Brezhnev as president in November 1982, dismissed this as "unrealistic", but in October 1983 made a counter offer for a mutual 25 percent reduction in intercontinental missiles and in return for no deployment of Cruise or Pershing, to reduce Soviet medium-range missiles to the number possessed by Britain and France. At that time, Reagan and his chief advisers, secretary of state Schulz and the hawkish Caspar Weinberger, showed no enthusiasm either for a summit to discuss these issues or for any compromise that might give the Russians the advantage. Instead they persisted in their attacks on the Soviet Union as the "evil empire", as Reagan called it. The shooting down, on 1 September 1983, of a South Korean Airline jumbo jet that had strayed over the Kamchatka peninsula, home of some of Russia's most sophisticated strategic technology, hardened American attitudes still further.

Perhaps the biggest sticking point following the rearmament of NATO was Reagan's "Star Wars" proposal, the Strategic Defense Initiative (SDI). Its purpose was to construct a laser shield around the American continent making it imper-

vious to attack from Soviet missiles. SDI alarmed the Soviets by undermining the principle of MAD, which depended upon both superpowers being equally vulnerable to attack by long-range strategic missiles. To the countries of Europe, it represented an isolationist, "fortress America" policy that potentially spelled danger for the European continent.

The appointment of Mikhail Gorbachev as head of the Soviet Communist party on 10 March 1985 began a new era in US–Soviet relations. On 19 and 20 November 1985 Reagan and Gorbachev met in Geneva, where the Americans proposed an interim agreement on INF missiles to limit their number, with the long-term intention of eliminating them totally. The leaders also agreed in principle to halve the number of offensive weapons.

In this new, optimistic political climate, Reagan and Gorbachev spoke to each other's nations on television in January 1986. Gorbachev in his address proposed to the American people a 15-year timetable for ridding the earth of all nuclear weapons. He also showed that he was not inflexible on human rights issues and the following month he freed the dissident Jew Anatoliy Shcharansky, exchanging him for a Soviet agent.

Following a visit by the French president Mitterrand to the Soviet Union in July 1986, Gorbachev proposed the immediate withdrawal of six Red Army regiments in Europe.

The US administration remained wary, however, and NATO's first response was to announce support for an American proposal to resume the manufacture of chemical weapons. Not surprisingly, the second Reagan–Gorbachev summit in Reykjavik, Iceland, in October was a disappointing failure. The Soviet leader felt himself snubbed while Reagan refused to be pressured into abandoning his prized Star Wars scheme.

Yet the Soviets did not stop trying: they agreed with 33 other European countries, the United States and Canada to a new system of prior

► "This way to the last peace – with dead certainty": German anti-nuclear demonstrators make their attitude to the missile buildup very clear. The intensification of the arms race and the deployment of short and medium-range nuclear missiles (like the US Pershing and Cruise, and the Soviet SS20) on European soil, brought the peace movement back to life in the early 1980s. Persistent mass protest at developments which could place European targets at direct, early risk in any superpower confrontation exposed the NATO and Warsaw Pact alliances to unprecedented strain. While other factors contributed to withdrawal of missiles in the late 1980s, popular protest also played a key role.

Women for Life on Earth

◄▼ The women's peace camp protests at Greenham Common, in Britain, presented the stark contrast between the values of life – represented here by images of dancing on a missile site during a mass-protest, or by family photographs attached to the fence of the airbase – and values of war implicit in the existence of Cruise.

In September 1981, a group of women set up a "peace camp" outside the US air base at Greenham Common in Berkshire, UK, as a protest against the NATO decision to site 96 ground-launched Cruise missiles there in December 1983. It was feared that these "theater" nuclear weapons made possible the concept of a "limited" nuclear war. It seemed to many women that the government, without parliamentary support or public debate, had taken a decision which endangered them and also, in their name, threatened the lives of Russian women and children.

For some of them the only way to deal with the fear, powerlessness and anger they felt, was to take action. Many came to Greenham to stay until the missiles were removed: they protested by demonstrating, by blockading construction work, by trespassing, by talking to anyone who would listen. They lived in primitive conditions outside the gates of the base, where harassment and arrest were daily events.

Greenham Common women's peace camp became a focus for the peace movement. On 12 December 1982, 30,000 women from all over Britain, as well as groups from Sweden, Holland and West Germany, gathered at the base and encircled the 15km perimeter fence in a massive demonstration of collective and personal commitment. Many returned time and again over the next years so that a constant presence and vigil was maintained. Similar peace camps were set up at other missile sites in Europe and America: some were, like Greenham, women-only protests. All looked to Greenham as a model of a form of political activity in which ways of living and being – decentralized, non-hierarchical, supportive – were offered in opposition to the allegedly masculine, militaristic world view represented by the missile bases.

notification of any military activities, as one of a series of measures to promote confidence and security in Europe. They also reaffirmed their commitment to quit Afghanistan and undertook not to resume atmospheric nuclear testing unless the Americans did so first (which they did).

In February 1987 Gorbachev further proposed that US and Soviet INF missiles be removed from Europe over a five-year period and conceded that SDI need not be part of this package. This was a most warming introduction to the major Soviet-American arms talks that opened in Geneva in May and carried on throughout the summer. By August the West Germans had agreed to put their own Pershing rockets into any INF agreement thus removing one obstacle to a deal; and another fell when the Soviet Union accepted the principle of open inspection. When Gorbachev and Reagan met again, in December 1987, in the United States, they agreed to eliminate all land-based INF weapons and to meet again in Moscow early in 1988 in order to finalize the details of the agreement.

In May the INF treaty was ratified by both American chambers and by the Supreme Soviet, so that when Reagan visited the Kremlin, he and Gorbachev became signatories in an historic first step toward the denuclearization of at least part of US and Soviet weaponry. Not only did the dismantling of INF weapons begin at once throughout Europe but television viewers in both the Eastern and Western blocs were treated to the rare sight of inspections by the forces of the other side to verify that the nuclear warheads were truly being destroyed.

The prospects for further and more extensive arms reductions looked even more promising with the collapse of Communist rule in Eastern Europe and the USSR (1989–91). President Bush and Boris Yeltsin, the new president of Russia, signed the START II treaty in 1993, which agreed substantial reductions in the US and Russian nuclear arsenals.

▼ Withdrawal of Cruise – a US missile launcher is loaded into an aircraft for transportation home from a European airbase. Mobile nuclear missile systems produced mass popular opposition, and threatened to upset the delicate balance of deterrence. Their withdrawal gave momentum to further arms reductions.

Datafile

The 1970s and 1980s saw an increase in conflicts around the world in which either the participants consciously challenged the authority of the superpowers in their regions, or from which the Soviet Union and the United States chose to remain aloof. New political movements such as Islamic fundamentalism challenged the old certainties of global geopolitics, and it became increasingly difficult to group the nations into the categories of East, West and nonaligned.

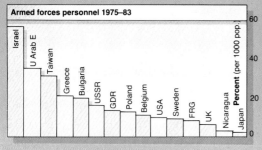

Armed forces personnel 1975–83

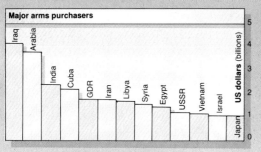

Major arms purchasers

▶ The large industrial powers are major consumers of oil, and while some rely on domestic production, others, notably Japan and the countries of Western Europe, need to import billions of barrels. When the oil producers of the Middle East cut production in 1973 the Western industrial world was forced into a severe energy crisis.

◀ The Western nations generally made less heavy military demands on their people than those of the Eastern bloc. Israel arms a large proportion of its relatively small population in defense against its far more populous Arab enemies; Japan is restricted by treaty to maintaining only a small force for purely defensive purposes.

◀ The major importers of arms are concentrated heavily in the Middle East and the remainder of the Arab world where oil provides ready cash, while political instability offers a pretext for remaining heavily armed. There are few nations that do not receive a significant proportion of their military equipment from abroad.

Oil consumption 1978

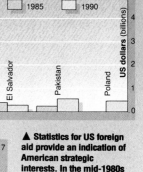

US foreign aid

▶ The international arms trade was dominated by the two superpowers, and the industrial countries of Western Europe. Governments may frequently use the negotiations for the sale of arms to further their diplomatic interests and to reinforce alliances. The need to supply technical backup commits the exporter and purchaser to close cooperation. It is sometimes suggested that arms manufacturing nations may welcome limited wars on distant continents to see their products tested on the battlefield.

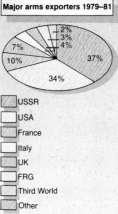

Major arms exporters 1979–81

2%
3%
4%
7%
10%
37%
34%

USSR
USA
France
Italy
UK
FRG
Third World
Other

▼ The stark division of the world into rich and poor is illustrated by figures for refugees and contributions to refugee assistance. Across much of Africa, South Asia and Central America, poverty and overpopulation produce misery which can easily turn into a demographic disaster. In Afghanistan and Palestine, the refugee problems are the direct result of war and foreign occupation; elsewhere disturbances of this nature help trigger off shortages of food, housing and the other necessities of life which drive millions away from their homes.

Refugees 1991

▲ Statistics for US foreign aid provide an indication of American strategic interests. In the mid-1980s Israel still received huge support from the United States, almost twice the amount sent to any other country; but by the end of the decade this support had fallen away in the face of Israeli intransigence over the Palestinian question. Pro-Western Egypt was a staunch Middle Eastern ally of the United States through the period while money sent to Pakistan and El Salvador reflected global security issues.

◀ Afghanistan still provided by far the largest number of refugees in 1991, even though three years had elapsed since the withdrawal of Soviet troops from the country. There as elsewhere, civil disturbance and economic dislocation now provided the main impetus for the movement of large numbers of people. In the 1990s, with ever-increasing numbers on the move, and particularly within Europe after the collapse of Communism, Western governments applied a stringent definition of refugee status.

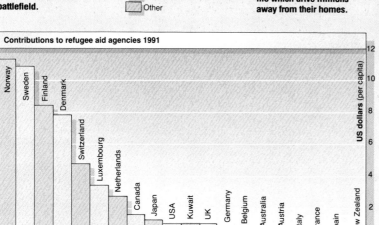

Contributions to refugee aid agencies 1991

BEYOND THE SUPERPOWERS

The nonaligned countries of the Third World found it difficult to develop independently of superpower interests. The United States, having withdrawn its combatants from Southeast Asia, became increasingly involved in supporting pro-US groups in Central America, while stopping short of military intervention. At the same time the Americans punished those who, like Nicaragua and Libya, opposed US surrogates or challenged US supremacy. The Soviet Union became embroiled in a war in Afghanistan and, like the United States in Vietnam, was later ignominiously forced to withdraw.

In Vietnam and Afghanistan nationalism was an important weapon in the fight for independence and freedom from superpower interference. Likewise, the Islamic revolution in Iran won support because of its emphasis on religious nationalism and its rejection of both the US and Soviet systems. Equally, among ethnic minorities (or, in the case of South Africa, the black majority) nationalism represented a potent force for opposition and hope for change. The Palestinians on Israel's West Bank, the Sikhs of the Indian Punjab, the Iraqi Kurds and the Tamils of Sri Lanka all rebelled against the racial and cultural oppression of the countries within whose boundaries they resided and demanded the right to self-determination.

Southeast Asia after US withdrawal

Events in Southeast Asia were overshadowed by the collapse of the South Vietnamese government and the terrible massacres in Cambodia. Following the armistice agreement of 1973 and the withdrawal of US forces. South Vietnam fell to the invading North Vietnamese in April 1975. President Nguyen van Thieu resigned and fled to the United States. Saigon, the South Vietnamese capital, was renamed Ho Chi Minh City, after the late North Vietnamese leader. Meanwhile relations between the Communist regime of Vietnam, led by Ton Duc Thang (who enjoyed the full support of the Soviet Union) and the Chinese government deteriorated after disagreement over Cambodia.

In April 1975 the pro-US Cambodian leader Lon Nol was forced to flee in the face of the advancing Communist Khmer Rouge army. The erratic Prince Sihanouk, whom Lon Nol had deposed with US help, tried to take control of the country, but was removed by the Khmer Rouge

▼ Looting in Phnom Penh, 1975 – public order collapses as the US-backed regime crumbles before the advancing Khmer Rouge. The failure of the American war effort in Southeast Asia left former client regimes at the mercy of their Communist enemies. In Cambodia, where the Khmer Rouge had emerged as one of the most extreme Communist groups, the shift in power produced cataclysmic results.

The civil war in Lebanon in the 1970s and 1980s summed up the apparent hopelessness of Middle Eastern politics

◀ **Life among the ruins – a Beirut woman collects water against a background of demolished building in the mid-1980s.** Lebanon suffered the most severe consequences of destabilization in the Middle East. Israeli invasion, the Palestinian refugee problem, the emergence of rival forces of Islamic extremism and the interference by all the surrounding powers combined to reduce the small country to a battleground. A host of rival power groups fought out a confused and bloody civil war. Intervention by Israel and Syria, and interference by other powers ensured that no lasting settlement could emerge. The inhabitants continued to live under the threat of bombs and bullets.

▶ **Ayatollah Khomeini, the Iranian Muslim avenging angel, tramples the devil of US capitalism underfoot.** The Islamic revolution in Iran gave expression to the rising tide of religious fundamentalism – its identification of US interference as the villain of the piece transformed local rivalries into an explosive clash of values.

▼ **Bound and blindfolded, the staff of the US embassy in Tehran are paraded before a hostile mob soon after their capture by revolutionary Islamic students in November 1979.** The hostages were held to ransom with the connivance of the new Iranian regime for 14 months. The plight provided a focus for the confrontation between the superpower that had once dominated the Middle East, and the new forces that had swept that domination aside. The dangers and difficulties of military intervention were highlighted by the failure of a rescue mission in 1980.

leader Pol Pot, who took over the government on 4 April 1976. Inspired by Chinese Communism, he emptied the towns and turned the whole country into a vast agricultural penal colony. Many hundreds of thousands died there or were killed in a regime of immense cruelty and savagery. Fighting between Vietnam and Cambodia (renamed Kampuchea) that began in 1975 culminated in a Vietnamese invasion in 1978. Pol Pot, who managed to escape, was sentenced to death in his absence for crimes against humanity but continued to lead the Khmer Rouge from Thailand. Almost one million people fled the upheavals in Vietnam and Cambodia. The new republic of Kampuchea (today, Cambodia; the name was changed back in 1989) became an increasingly troublesome source of contention between the Soviets and the Chinese, who resented Soviet support for the Vietnam-backed regime. In the post-Cold War era, however, it seemed that the Cambodia problem might at last be resolved through the intervention of the United Nations. In 1992 a peace agreement was signed between the Vietnamese-backed government and the Khmer Rouge, ending the civil war. It remained to be seen whether the UN could bring about a lasting solution.

Israel-Egypt peace agreement
Another traditional trouble-spot, the Middle East, remained a lasting source of conflict despite some optimism in the late 1970s. In May 1977, three and a half years after the Arab–Israeli Yom Kippur war, Menachem Begin, leader of the right-wing Likud party, became prime minister of Israel. Begin, himself a former terrorist and a hardline Israeli nationalist, was not, however, averse to seeking peace with his old enemy, Egypt.

In fact, as early as 1973, the Egyptian premier Anwar Sadat had proposed troop reductions with Israel and in November 1977 he amazed the world by traveling to Jerusalem to address the Knesset (Israeli parliament). Carter, the US president, invited both Sadat and Begin to Camp David, his presidential residence, where, in September 1978, the three leaders signed a historic "framework for peace in the Middle East".

Egypt for the first time guaranteed Israel's right to exist while the Israelis agreed to return the Sinai desert to Egypt (completed on 25 April 1982). Both Begin and Sadat received the Nobel Peace Prize for the work. However, the more extreme voices in the Arab world branded Sadat a traitor to the Arab cause. President Carter tried to encourage other moderate Arab states such as Jordan and Saudi Arabia to join in the peace process, but met with no success. Egypt remained isolated and was expelled from the Arab League. On 6 October 1981 Sadat paid the ultimate price for breaking ranks when he was assassinated at a military review.

War in the Lebanon
At the root of the conflict in the Middle East was the Palestinian problem, which had attended the creation of the state of Israel in 1948 and had grown steadily worse since then. Many Palestinians lived precariously in refugee camps in the state of Lebanon, Israel's northern neighbor. From 1975 a Lebanese civil war raged between the Maronite Christians (a minority who wielded the power in Lebanese public life) and the Muslim Sunnis, Shiites and Druse. The presence of the Palestinians, who had made Beirut their operational base for guerrilla attacks on Israel and attracted Israeli reprisal raids, heightened the conflict.

In 1976 Syria, allegedly in the name of all Arab states, sent in its armed forces, prompting some, like Walid Jumblat, the left-wing Druse leader, to

Iran–Iraq War

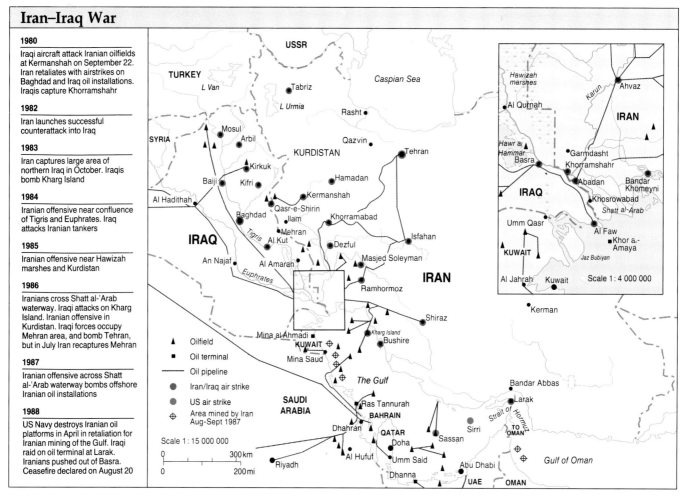

1980
Iraqi aircraft attack Iranian oilfields at Kermanshah on September 22. Iran retaliates with airstrikes on Baghdad and Iraq oil installations. Iraqis capture Khorramshahr

1982
Iran launches successful counterattack into Iraq

1983
Iran captures large area of northern Iraq in October. Iraqis bomb Kharg Island

1984
Iranian offensive near confluence of Tigris and Euphrates. Iraq attacks Iranian tankers

1985
Iranian offensive near Hawizah marshes and Kurdistan

1986
Iranians cross Shatt al-'Arab waterway. Iraqi attacks on Kharg Island. Iranian offensive in Kurdistan. Iraqi forces occupy Mehran area, and bomb Tehran, but in July Iran recaptures Mehran

1987
Iranian offensive across Shatt al-'Arab waterway bombs offshore Iranian oil installations

1988
US Navy destroys Iranian oil platforms in April in retaliation for Iranian mining of the Gulf. Iraqi raid on oil terminal at Larak. Iranians pushed out of Basra. Ceasefire declared on August 20

▲ Oilfield
■ Oil terminal
— Oil pipeline
● Iran/Iraq air strike
● US air strike
⊕ Area mined by Iran Aug-Sept 1987

Scale 1 : 15 000 000
0 ——— 300 km
0 ——— 200 mi

take up arms against them. In March 1978 Begin for the first time invaded the southern Lebanon to try to destroy the Palestinian bases but withdrew under UN pressure. Three years later, having rejected a Saudi peace plan, Begin annexed the Golan Heights on the Syrian border and, on 6 June 1982, invaded the Lebanon a second time. Israeli forces penetrated as far as West Beirut, but most of the Palestinian forces escaped, including Yasir Arafat, the leader of the Palestine Liberation Organization (PLO). Two days later a massacre of Palestinians by Christian forces took place in the Shattilla camp virtually in full view of the Israeli army.

The situation in Lebanon continued to grow worse. On 14 September the Christian Falangist leader, and president elect, Beshir Gemayel was assassinated. He was succeeded by his brother Amin. The next year 260 US Marines, part of a UN peace-keeping force, were killed trying to keep the warring factions apart from each other.

Israel was increasingly paying the price of its involvement, both in money and in reputation. The war cost more than one million US dollars a day, leading, in 1984, to 300 percent inflation. Israel also attracted growing hostility against actions that were seen as adventurist and expansionist. Begin had openly called for the annexation of the biblical lands of Judea and Samaria and continued to build Jewish settlements on the West Bank of the Jordan.

Israel began its withdrawal from Lebanon in

1985, but the deep scars remained. By then, Begin had retired through ill health and his successor, and leader of the Likud party, Yitzhak Shamir, had been forced in a coalition with the Labour party under Shimon Peres, who was keen to extricate Israel from the Lebanon.

Israel under pressure

The Israelis found it increasingly difficult to contain Palestinian nationalism within the occupied West Bank and Gaza Strip and retain the sympathy of the West.

In February 1988, television pictures showed

▲ The Gulf War began with a massive Iraqi offensive aimed at achieving territorial expansion while Iran was convulsed by revolution. Initially wavering, the Iranian forces managed to push back the Iraqis and a struggle of attrition set in along the original frontier.

▼ The success of the Tehran regime in mobilizing religious enthusiasm transformed the war into a religious crusade involving masses of fanatical revolutionary volunteers.

▲ The horrors of static warfare in the 1980s – bodies rot in foxholes and buildings burn as a soldier surveys the chaos of the war zone around Basra. The combat zone in front of the strategic Iraqi city of Basra soon resembled the Western Front of 1914–18, with tens of thousands of troops being fed into a confused and devastated battlefield where a decisive breakthrough remained impossible. Iran committed itself to the overthrow of the "heretic" government in Baghdad: Iraq, for all its anti-Khomeini rhetoric, was intent only on survival. In the end, mutual exhaustion would pave the way for a ceasefire in 1988.

Israeli soldiers forcing four Palestinians to lie down on a road while a bulldozer buried them with sand. The soldiers were also seen beating them and breaking someone's arm. The Israeli authorities promised to curb such excesses, but they remained as a solemn reminder of the bitterness of the conflict.

Consequently, the Western states decided to promote the fortunes of Yasir Arafat, the PLO leader. In September 1987 Arafat met left-wing Israeli parliamentarians in Geneva and in April 1988 he traveled to Moscow to meet Gorbachev (who told him to recognize Israel's right to exist). Further meetings in 1988 and 1989 with Western politicians and a declaration by the PLO that it no longer sought to destroy the state of Israel, encouraged both Britain and the United States to put pressure on the Israeli government to negotiate a settlement with the Palestinians.

The Iranian revolution
Elsewhere in the Middle East, US diplomatic endeavors received a savage rebuttal. Mohammed Reza Pahlavi, who had been Shah of Iran ever since 1941, was fully supported by the United States and the West. They saw in him a liberalizing and modernizing force in the Arab world, strongly pro-Western and anti-Soviet and a reliable supplier of oil. Even after the oil price hike in 1973, of which the Shah was one of the instigators, he was still regarded as an important ally. By 1978, however, opposition to his rule had

begun to destabilize his hold on power. The Shah's chief rival was the Muslim fundamentalist Ayatollah Khomeini, who had been exiled to Paris in 1946. There he recorded his denunciations of the Shah's "secularizing policies", which were smuggled into Iran on cassettes and widely broadcast. Despite forceful repression by the army and Savak, the notorious secret police, the Shah's situation rapidly became untenable.

On 16 January 1979 he handed over power to a regency council and left the country. On 1 February 1979 Khomeini returned to Tehran to a massive welcome to launch his Islamic revolution. Four days later, a provisional Islamic government was established with revolutionary tribunals, who condemned many thousands to death. On 31 March 1979 a referendum on whether Iran should become an Islamic republic returned a 99 percent vote in favor.

In November 1979 an international crisis inspired by Khomeini occurred when revolutionary students broke into the US embassy in Tehran and seized officials as hostages in a bid to force the United States to return the Shah to stand trial. Some blacks and women were released shortly afterward but 52 continued to be held. An attempted rescue mission by US marines in April 1980 failed miserably when their helicopter crashed in the Iranian desert. The crisis emphasized Carter's weakness and the hostages were not released until a settlement was negotiated the following year.

The "War of the Cities"

From 23 September 1980 Iran and neighboring Iraq were at war following a border dispute. Khomeini dismissed his president Bani-Sadr, who opposed the war, and replaced him first with Mohammed Rajai, who was later assassinated, and then by Ali Khamenei, a radical Islamic fundamentalist and supporter of the war.

It was a mark of the new caution governing superpower relationships that neither the United States nor the Soviet Union became deeply embroiled in the conflict though both stood to lose by it. The war threatened Western oil supplies, while to the Soviet Union it represented an in-

ternecine feud between two anti-American Muslim states. In fact, Iraq, despite violations of human rights in its treatment of its Kurdish minority, received arms from pro-Western Saudi Arabia and Egypt as well as France.

The Iran–Iraq war – often called the War of the Cities – rapidly led to an escalation of tension in the area. In May 1987 both Soviet and American ships came under fire in the Gulf, prompting the UN Security Council to call for a ceasefire, but the call was not heeded. The Iranians' claim that the Iraqis had used nerve gas and cynanide bombs added to the war a new and ugly dimension. By May 1988, when Iran seemed to have lost the war, Iraqi planes bombed the oil terminal of Hormuz and destroyed five tankers. On 18 July the Ayatollah Khomeini declared that he accepted the cease fire, but the central issue of rights in the Shatt al-Arab waterway was only resolved in 1990, when Iraq invaded Kuwait and made concessions to Iran to secure its borders.

The presence of US warships in the Gulf to protect commercial interests led to an incident that brought Iran and the United States close to war. In August 1988 the USS *Vincennes*, a warship, shot down an Iranian airliner, killing everyone on board. The *Vincennes* had misread its radar and believed itself to be under attack. At the end of the year, an American civilian airliner was blown up over Lockerbie, Scotland, in what was thought to be a reprisal action.

Even after its war, Iran continued to show an

▲ A civil war in Angola – Marxist UNITA forces parade beneath a poster of their leader. In Angola, as in many other new African nations, the withdrawal of the colonial power (Portugal) in 1975 transformed a war of independence into a civil war. The presence of well-armed guerrilla groups, some like the MPLA with Soviet and Cuban support, was seized on by powers such as South Africa to destabilize uncongenial new regimes.

◄ President (soon to be self-proclaimed Emperor) Bokassa of the Central African Republic (right) outshines his host President Amin on a state visit to Uganda in 1976. At their worst, the post-colonial conflicts in Africa allowed military strongmen like Amin (President of Uganda from 1971 to 1979) and Bokassa to use armed force and tribal rivalries to instal themselves as dictators. The comic-opera bombast of their rule could not compensate for widespread brutality, inefficiency and corruption. Although they were soon overthrown, the damage they caused made the tasks of their successors all the more difficult.

uncompromising face to the world. In 1989 Khomeini put a price on the head of a British writer for publishing a blasphemous novel. The British government ordered full police protection for the author, Salman Rushdie, a former Muslim, and Britain's European partners also condemned such behaviour by a head of state. Khomeini's death in 1989 led to a power vacuum which no individual could fill adequately. Consequently a struggle ensued between "hardliners", such as the Ayatollah Khamenei who became Iran's new spiritual leader and who was repeatedly to confirm the fatwa on Rushdie, and "moderates", such as Hashemi Ali Akbar Rafsanjani, who considered that Iran needed better relations with the West, to boost its sagging economy. By 1990 the moderates seemed to have won out, for in October 1990 the national elections were a victory for Rafsanjani's supporters and Iran began to enjoy improved diplomatic relations with the West.

War and famine in Africa

During the 1970s superpower relations, already uneasy over arms buildups, were further exacerbated by political and military conflict in Africa. Soviet support for the Angola liberation front led by Agosthino Neto enabled him and his Cuban troops to defeat both the pro-American FNLA and the UNITA forces led by Jonas Savimbi and backed by South Africa, who continued to fight a guerrilla war against the Marxist government. South Africa also supported antigovernment mercenaries in Mozambique.

Cuban troops also gave military support to General Mengistu's Marxist regime in Ethiopia

during the war against neighboring Somalia (formerly Moscow's ally), which supported secessionist rebels in Ethiopia's Ogaden province, and Cubans assisted in the fight against Eritrean rebels on the Red Sea coastline. From 1977, the Soviets had poured arms into Ethiopia even though the country faced terrible famine, which was worsened by government attempts to collectivize agriculture. In 1985, Ethiopia received aid in the form of money raised by the Irish rock-star Bob Geldof, in a concert staged in London and televised worldwide. The Ethiopian government, too, took measures, and by 1986 some 500,000 people had been resettled.

As in Angola, Mozambique and other African states, so in Rhodesia independence brought with it civil war. In 1965 Rhodesia had illegally declared its independence from Britain and maintained white-minority rule. However, by the late 1970s, under economic pressure and amid growing international condemnation and intensification of the civil war, the white minority government led by Ian Smith agreed to British proposals to end its rebel status. On 1 June 1979 Rhodesia became the Republic of Zimbabwe. In elections held the following February Robert Mugabe became prime minister and quickly established himself as one of Africa's most dynamic leaders. After independence differences emerged between Mugabe's ruling ZANU-PF (Zimbabwe African National Unity – Patriotic Front) party and that of his former guerrilla ally, Joshua Nkomo, whose ZAPU (Zimbabwe African People's Union) party drew its strength from Matabeleland. In particular, ZAPU opposed Mugabe's plans for a one-party state. However, in 1986 talks began with a view to merging the two parties.

Crisis in South Africa

In South Africa, the only African state that was still ruled by whites, the situation deteriorated rapidly. In September 1978 Pieter Willem Botha succeeded Johannes Vorster as prime minister and also became the minister for national security. Announcing that South Africa was "multiethnic", he attempted to buy off the Asian and "colored" communities, who together represented 14 percent of the population, by offering them limited political consultative rights. The real power, however, still resided with the whites (19 percent of the population), while the two-thirds blacks majority remained disenfranchised. At the same time, Botha took apartheid – the policy of so-called "separate development" – a stage further by establishing *Bantustans* or "tribal homelands", which virtually made blacks aliens in their own country. In 1985, however, he repealed some apartheid laws, including the ban on marriage or cohabitation between blacks and whites.

From 1983, South Africa experienced a severe recession, made worse by foreign investors losing confidence in the South African economy. In succeeding years, political tensions heightened and in 1986 a state of emergency was declared and reporting restrictions were imposed on the Western media. Thousands of people were imprisoned without trial and many hundreds are

▲ Imprisoned by the South African authorities in 1963 for terrorism, the African National Congress leader Nelson Mandela proved as potent a threat to white minority rule behind bars as he did an inspirational leader of black resistance during his active political career. His isolation in prison had the effect of providing the black nationalist with a form of symbolic leadership, and the attention he attracted all over the world made it difficult for the South African government to execute or release him.

◄ One of the 23 victims of the Soweto riots of June 1976, when young blacks protesting about conditions in the black townships around Johannesburg were gunned down by police. Kept at boiling point by economic hardship, overcrowding and police interference, black opposition in the squalid townships of South Africa periodically erupted into widescale rioting. The beleaguered white regime never hesitated to use force to reimpose order, with the result that each outbreak has produced a new group of martyrs – killed by police bullets or beaten into prison – to keep the campaign against apartheid alive.

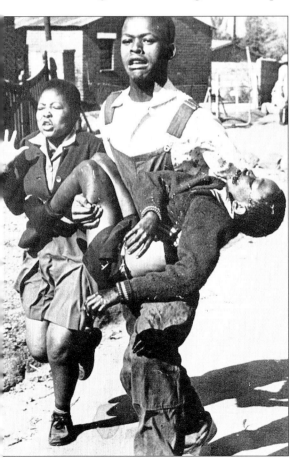

believed to have been tortured and killed at the hands of the South African security forces. Botha now faced opposition not only from the blacks but increasingly from white neo-Nazi extremists. Outside the country, too, pressure was mounting to force South Africa to bring about changes. However, an attempt by the Commonwealth in 1986 to introduce economic sanctions against South Africa was blocked by the British prime minister, Margaret Thatcher. She argued that such measures would harm the black population, cause chaos in the "front line" states whose economies depended on South Africa, and encourage a siege mentality in South Africa itself. Britain had many business ties with South Africa, and indeed its economic importance for the West as a whole was considerable. South Africa supplied 97 percent of the West's platinum, 70 percent of its gold and manganese and 20 percent of its uranium.

To assuage world opinion after the introduction of emergency powers, Botha announced the abolition of the hated pass laws, which restricted the movement of blacks about the country, and promised new constitutional rights for both blacks and coloreds. In 1987 he even agreed to reform the group areas act, which was seen as the mainstay of apartheid. However, despite appeals from the European Community states and others, he refused to release the jailed African National Congress (ANC) leader Nelson Mandela. The United States extended its sanctions, begun in

1985, and banned airline flights to South Africa from American carriers. Several American, British and Canadian firms also closed down their South African operations.

Botha faced an invidious choice. Too much liberalization internally would promote a right-wing backlash and his National party (NP), which ruled the country since 1968, might be driven from power. Too little reform, on the other hand, would lose South Africa whatever little sympathy that remained in the West for it. In 1987 Botha suffered a stroke and with much reluctance gave way to F. W. de Klerk. Although he too promised reforms, his election and that of the NP, was marked by new levels of violence and police savagery in putting down protests against the limited franchise. However, he did permit an anti-apartheid march in Cape Town, which attracted tens of thousands of supporters.

South African aggression abroad

Despite P. W. Botha's pledge of South African neutrality in foreign affairs, in 1983 South Africa invaded Angola. Politicians in Pretoria refused to accept the independence of Southwest Africa (Namibia), and attempted to destroy the SWAPO (South West African Peoples' Organization) guerilla bases on Angolan territory. South Africa refused to bow to UN pressure to withdraw from Southwest Africa while Cuban troops remained in Angola. However, in 1984 an armistice was signed by the two states, leading to the weaken

Olympics and declining to attend official functions held in Moscow.

In fact, the Muslim insurgents, or Mujaheddin, received increasing support from Pakistan and, indirectly, the United States. Encouraged in their struggle by the outrage felt in the Western world at the Soviet invasion and the pressure on the Soviet Union to withdraw, they agreed to a ceasefire in January 1987 to give themselves time to regroup. In the autumn, Dr Najibullah succeeded Karmal as president and plans were made for the Soviets to withdraw. Karmal was arrested and taken to Moscow. Najibullah offered a program of national reconciliation, which the Mujaheddin, sensing that victory was close, rejected.

The withdrawal of Soviet troops continued in a worsening situation for both them and their Afghanistan comrades. The war had claimed the lives of thousands of Soviet troops, despite superior Soviet firepower, and the Mujaheddin pressed ever closer to the capital, Kabul. By August 1988 half the Soviet troops had withdrawn across the Friendship Bridge separating the two states, the rest following in December. However, Kabul did not fall, as was expected, and stiff resistance by government forces, coupled with dissent and faction-fighting among the rebels, led to stalemate.

Political turmoil in Southern Asia

In 1977 a military coup in Pakistan led by General Zia Ul-Haq ousted Zulfikar Ali Bhutto, the prime minister and leader of the Pakistan People's Party. Bhutto was hanged in 1979. Zia imposed harsh measures, banning political parties and waging a campaign of Islamification. However, he failed to eradicate corruption or the burgeoning opium poppy trade. Severe drought and poor harvests in 1983, and an inflation rate of 20 percent, as well as growing friction with India over the status of the border province of Kashmir, all added to his problems.

To improve relations with India, he visited the Indian prime minister Rajiv Gandhi in January 1986. However, he could not stifle political opposition at home from Bhutto's Oxford-educated

▼ Continuity and change in India – Rajiv Gandhi lighting the funeral pyre of his assassinated mother Indira in 1984. The death of Indira Gandhi at the hands of her Sikh bodyguard brought her politically inexperienced son Rajiv to power in an explosive but politically hopeful situation.

▼ The assassination of Pakistan's military leader general Zia ul-Haq left the way clear for the return of Benazir Bhutto, daughter of Zulfikar, former president and Zia's political opponent who was executed during the early years of his reign. Bhutto swept to power in the subsequent election, the first elected female leader of a strongly Islamic state.

ing of SWAPO, though it was recognized by the UN as the sole representative of the Namibian people. In 1989 Namibia became an independent state. South Africa also concluded a deal with Mozambique, another former Portuguese colony, promising to withdraw support from rebel mercenaries in exchange for Mozambique's denial of bases to the ANC.

The Soviet invasion of Afghanistan

If East and West were united in their condemnation of South Africa, they were deeply divided over events in Afghanistan. Since 1973 Afghanistan had been ruled by a left-wing regime, but a coup in April 1978 by Mur Taraki brought the country fully into the Soviet orbit. The Muslim population revolted, allegedly killing a thousand or so Soviet military "advisors". In September 1979 Taraki was overthrown by Hafizullah Amin who, according to the Soviets, asked for their help to "defend the revolution".

However, on 26 December Amin, his family and closest advisers were murdered and replaced by Babrak Karmal (whose assumed name means "workers' friend"), who had spent a period in exile in the Soviet Union. Aided by Soviet troops, he tried to crush Muslim resistance to the Soviet-backed regime. Outside Afghanistan, 35 Muslim states joined together in January 1980 to call for Soviet troops to withdraw. The West confined itself to a public condemnation of the Soviet action, including a boycott of the 1980 Moscow

daughter Benazir. Zia imprisoned her and then had her placed under house arrest in August 1986, but riots forced him to release her the following month. The tenth anniversary of his rule was marked by civil unrest and a bomb in Karachi that killed over 70 people. To make matters worse, in October, the Americans halted their aid program to Pakistan because they feared it had become a nuclear power.

In May 1988, under growing pressure, he announced new elections. Zia was assassinated shortly afterward, together with the US ambassador to Pakistan, while flying to review troops. Benazir Bhutto swept to power in the elections as her nation's first woman leader.

India too, experienced political crises beginning in the 1970s. In 1974 India carried out a successful nuclear test to become the sixth country to possess a nuclear bomb. However, the United States was concerned at the prospect of nuclear weapons falling into the hands of unstable states even if, like India and Israel, they were democracies. (The thought of Pakistan acquiring and sharing the secrets of its "Islamic bomb" with

Iran after 1979 filled them with horror.) In fact, American fears about India's instability were soon justified. In 1975, Indira Gandhi, India's prime minister, proclaimed a state of emergency to prevent opposition to her reforms, which included compulsory sterilization as a means of birth control. She suffered a humiliating defeat at the polls in 1977 but was re-elected and took office as prime minister once again in 1980. Five years later, however, she was assassinated by Sikh extremists who had penetrated her bodyguard and sought to avenge the storming of their shrine, the Golden Temple at Amritsar, which Gandhi had ordered to root out Sikh nationalist guerrillas. She was succeeded by her son, Rajiv.

Other South Asian states also experienced violent political upheaval. In December 1985 in the Philippines the chief of staff of the armed forces and several others were acquitted of the murder of Benigno Aquino, a respected democrat who had been shot on his return from exile to stand against President Ferdinand Marcos in the presidential elections. He was replaced as a candidate by his redoubtable wife, Corazon Aquino, who received massive popular support. When in the February elections Marcos claimed victory no one believed him. Indeed, television pictures had shown the intimidation and violence that attended his campaign and there were strong suspicions that the ballot had been rigged.

Both Aquino and Marcos were sworn in as presidents, but fighting around the presidential palace forced Marcos and his wife Imelda to seek safe conduct in a US helicopter to Hawaii. Investigations revealed that Marcos had embezzled millions of dollars and invested them in property and art. Aquino's murderers were tried and convicted. The new administration, however, though no longer corrupt, did not satisfy the Communists, who continued with guerrilla activities in their struggle to bring about a redistribution of resources in a country divided by extreme wealth and extreme poverty. When Marcos died in 1989 Mrs Aquino refused to allow his body to be returned home.

▶ In Argentina during the Falklands war the British prime minister became the focus of a propaganda campaign against the enemy; this magazine claims to expose Mrs Thatcher as "The Lady of Death – her husband hates her; her daughter is a drug addict; her grandfather was a thief…".

▼ US anti-Communist policy in Central America committed it to supporting rightwing militarist dictatorships, despite their corruption, inefficiency and disregard for human rights. In Nicaragua, the US threw its support behind the Somoza dynasty, but was ultimately unable to save it from the populist guerrilla forces of the Communist Sandinista movement (seen here). Following the Sandinista triumph. US support was transferred to a motley collection of resistance groups, collectively known as the Contras.

Human Rights

▲ Argentineans with photographs of dead children.

Classical liberalism asserted the universal rights of the individual for life, liberty and the pursuit of happiness, a position developed since 1945 actively to protect all people against oppression, even from the agents of their own state. The United Nations charter pledged all members to achieve "respect for, and observance of, human rights and freedoms without distinction as to race, sex, language or religion", a position endorsed in 1948. Concern for human rights was also expressed in a European Convention in 1950, and by the Organization of African Unity in 1981.

The public advocacy of human rights as part of national foreign policy by leading world statesman – particularly US president Jimmy Carter – and the growth in voluntary agencies aiming to protect human rights against the power of the state, brought the subject to wider public awareness in the 1970s. Protests against torture or judicial murder could lead to international action against the perpetrating government.

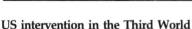

▲ The Argentinean invasion of the remote Falkland Islands transformed an unwanted relic of the British imperial past into a symbol of national pride for which the Thatcher government and the majority of the British public were prepared to fight. The early sinking by the British of the elderly troopship *Belgrano*, with heavy loss of Argentine life (above) was condemned as an irresponsible act which destroyed any chance of a peaceful solution. Yet war was probably inevitable from the moment of invasion. While the Argentinean air force caused serious losses, superior British training and logistics allowed a relatively swift reconquest.

US intervention in the Third World

Because of his fervent anti-Communism President Marcos had received the support of the United States until he became a political embarrassment. Elsewhere in the Third World too the American criterion for support was based on US interests rather than allegiance to democracy. In the Central American state of Nicaragua, where the pro-American dictator Somoza was overthrown by the Sandinista guerrillas in 1979, and El Salvador, where on 10 October 1982 rebels mounted a major offensive against the government, the CIA armed and trained anti-Communist forces. In 1983, US troops even invaded the West Indian island of Grenada, a member of the Commonwealth, to remove a Marxist regime. President Reagan's policy toward Central America, which he called "America's backyard", attracted criticism both in the United States and in Europe, if only because it made it harder to condemn Soviet actions in Afghanistan and risked escalating the Central American crisis into a new Vietnam.

The US bombing of Libya in 1986, following acts of terrorism by Palestinian guerrillas in Europe, was equally controversial. In December 1985, 17 people were murdered at Rome and Vienna airports, and in 1986 a bomb planted in a Berlin nightclub killed a US serviceman and injured many others. Further explosions caused havoc in Paris, and a bomb thrown at Israelis praying at the Wailing Wall in Jerusalem killed one person and injured 69 others. In Britain, a Palestinian terrorist, Nezar Hindawi, received a jail sentence of 46 years for having concealed a bomb in the suitcase of his pregnant girlfriend, who was booked on a flight to Israel.

The United States claimed that the Libyan leader Colonel Qadhafi was behind these attacks. It was well known that he supported terrorism with money derived from oil and that he also supplied arms and training to guerrilla groups (including the IRA). Britain, however, blamed the Syrian government, which had been strongly implicated in the Hindawi affair.

Matters came to a head when the US airforce bombed Libyan radar installations in retaliation for an alleged earlier Libyan transgression against the US Mediterranean fleet. Then, in April, US F111 aircraft attacked Libya itself, killing many civilians including Qadhafi's adopted baby daughter. The British prime minister Thatcher acquiesced in the bombing by permitting the F111s to fly from bases in Britain. The French and Spanish, by contrast, refused permission to overfly their airspace.

War in the South Atlantic

Ever the faithful ally of the United States, Britain itself was thrust to the front of the world stage when, in 1982, a crisis developed in the South Atlantic. For many years Argentina had tried to negotiate for the Malvinas (Falkland Islands), which Britain had taken as a colony 150 years earlier. On 3 April 1982, after a scaling down of the British military presence in the South Atlantic, Argentina invaded the Islands.

The move took Britain wholly by surprise and forced the resignation of the foreign secretary, Lord Carrington. The British prime minister Thatcher demanded an immediate Argentine withdrawal, at the same time preparing to send a massive task force to the South Atlantic. After some wavering, the Americans, whose anticolonial stance made them naturally sympathetic to the Argentinean case, supported Britain, allowing Britain to use Ascension Island as a base. The European Community, including Italy who had close ties with Argentina, also gave Britain diplomatic support. After some very hard fighting in which 700 Argentineans and 255 Britons lost their lives, Britain retook the Falkland Islands in June 1982. Argentina's failure led to the fall of its military junta, and its replacement by a democratic government, while in Britain the war restored Mrs Thatcher's popularity.

INTERNATIONAL TERRORISM

Terrorism is the systematic use of coercive intimidation to create a climate of fear among a wider target group. Perpetrators of terrorism include regimes and agencies of states as well as nationalist, ideological and religious extremist movements. Terrorism may be used to compel the target to comply with the perpretrators' demands, to "neutralize" particular sectors of the population, to publicize a cause, to demoralize and disorient perceived enemies, or to provoke a rival group of governmental authority into over-reaction. Terrorism since the 1960s has been experienced in its "pure" form mainly in Western European and other industrialized states. In most Third World countries it has been intertwined with far more extensive and lethal conflicts as an accompaniment to civil and even international wars, as for example in Vietnam, the Lebanon, and Central America. A valuable distinction can be made between domestic terrorism, confined within a single state, and international terrorism, involving the citizens of more than one country.

Following World War II, major terrorist campaigns were waged in the course of anticolonial insurgencies in many countries, including Palestine, Cyprus, Algeria and Aden. Terrorism proved a very effective weapon of attrition in undermining the will of the colonial powers to sustain their colonial presence. Strategic political objectives were gained, mainly because of the enormous domestic support enjoyed by the insurgents and by the growing desire of the colonial authorities to withdraw from their heavy overseas commitments.

Far from ending terrorism, the process of decolonization paradoxically fueled international terrorism in the late 1960s and early 1970s, as numerous militant ethnic movements chose to challenge the new international order to gain self-determination. The best-known and most influential of these groups were the Palestinian PLO militants, who opted for terrorism as a weapon of last resort following the disastrous defeat of Arab conventional arms in the June 1967 war with Israel. Other factors conducive to the burgeoning of international terrorism in the late 1960s and early 1970s were the strategic nuclear balance between the superpowers which made low-cost, low-risk, potentially high-yield clandestine methods more attractive to both terrorist movements and their state sponsors; the shift of emphasis among revolutionary leaders in the Third World away from heavy reliance on rural guerrilla and toward greater use of urban terrorism; the emergence of the new-left student generation in the industrial countries such as West Germany, which created small residues of militants dedicated to the use of terrorism against Western capitalism in general and the United States in particular; modern technologies such as international jet travel, television satellite communications, and plastic explosives, which have greatly increased both the capability of the terrorist to cause terror and publicize the cause, and the vulnerability of society.

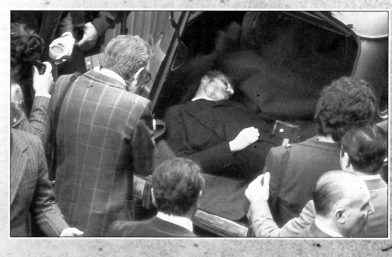

▼ The bomb exploding in the hold of a Pan-Am jumbo jet over Scotland in December 1988 led to an international search for culprits, yet no-one accepted responsibility.

▲ Aldo Moro, leader of the Italian Christian Democrat party, was kidnapped in 1978 by Red Brigade terrorists and killed after the government refused to negotiate.

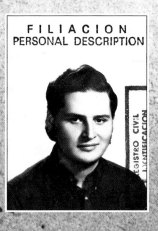

FILIACION
PERSONAL DESCRIPTION

◄ In the 1970s fears arose about the activities of "freelance" international terrorists. One of the most notorious was the Venezuelan Ilich Ramirez Sanchos, known as Carlos Martinez, who was implicated in actions involving Palestinian terrorist groups in Paris and London in the mid-1970s.

► The Provisional Wing of the Irish Republican Army (IRA) undertook paramilitary activity in their fight for a united Ireland in the 1970s and 1980s. As well as conducting a clandestine program of terror against civilian and military targets in Northern Ireland and mainland Britain, they openly patrolled areas of Northern Ireland and created "No-go" areas for British troops.

▼ Airlines – expensive, vulnerable and prestige targets – have often been terrorist targets. This Boeing 707 was blown up in Amman in 1970, after the PLO had negotiated the release of a number of hostages.

► Terrorist tactics may be used by state organizations, as well as those seeking power. In 1985 the Greenpeace environmentalist ship Rainbow Warrior was sunk by French secret agents while conducting a campaign against French nuclear testing in the Pacific.

◄ In 1986 the United States, enraged by Libyan support for terrorism, tried to take revenge by bombing Tripoli. Some 16 adults and four children were killed. After this incident, both countries have been accused of fostering state terrorism.

Datafile

The appointment of Mikhail Gorbachev as leader of the Soviet Union in 1985 eventually brought to an end the bipolar system of international politics, which had endured since World War II. One consequence of this was that the United Nations became a more effective organization, as was demonstrated in the Gulf War of 1990–91, when a US-led coalition, under UN authority, evicted Iraqi forces from Kuwait. After the war, US President George Bush declared the existence of a "New World Order", in which nations would cooperate to maintain peace. However, it was not to last. At the end of 1991 the Soviet Union collapsed, leaving the USA as the world's only superpower.

Desert Storm costs

5% 7% 9% 23% 13% 22% 21%

☐ Saudi Arabia
☐ Kuwait
☐ USA
☐ Japan
☐ Germany
☐ UK
☐ UAE

▼ **Serious cracks in Soviet-dominated Eastern Europe began to appear in the form of the Solidarity movement in Poland during the 1980s. Up to this point the USSR had shown its willingness to resort to force to maintain its empire; for example in Hungary and Czechoslovakia in 1956 and 1968. However, it became clear to dissidents that under Gorbachev violence would not be used so readily. In 1989 Eastern Europe became gripped by popular revolution and a domino effect occurred, spreading to the USSR.**

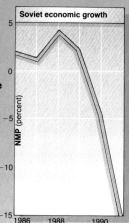

Soviet economic growth

NMP (percent)

1986   1988   1990

▲ **The chart shows the financial contributions made to the Allied effort to remove Iraqi forces from Kuwait. Japan's and Germany's payments reflect their growing status as economic and political powers.**

◄ **This graph clearly shows the poor economic performance of the USSR as Gorbachev's tentative market reforms were introduced to replace the failed state-led economy. The failure of reform encouraged a coup attempt by hardliners in 1991.**

Chronology: The fall of Communism in Eastern Europe and the USSR

1989

11 January
Hungary: Communist-dominated parliament allows formation of independent political parties

February–April
Poland: talks between Communists and other parties provide for multi-party elections

June
Poland: multi-party elections in which Communists win only reserved seats

August
GDR: start of exodus of East Germans to the West via Hungary

24 August
Poland: Solidarity candidate, Tadeusz Mazowiecki elected prime minister

10 November
GDR: the Berlin Wall is opened

10 November
Todor Zhivkov, president of Bulgaria, resigns

17 November
Czechoslovakia: student rally turns into anti-Communist protest; protesters are attacked by the police

29 November
Czechoslovakia: parliament abolishes leading role of Communist party

December
Yugoslavia: assemblies of Slovenia and Croatia agree to multi-party elections

1 December
GDR: parliament voters to abolish leading role of Communist party

11 December
Bulgaria: Communist government proposes free elections

16 December
Romania: clashes between police and dissidents in Timisoara, NW Romania

21 December
Romania: demonstrators force President Nicolae Ceausescu and wife Elena to flee

22 December
Romania: National Salvation Front, based on Communist party, takes power

1990

25 March, 8 April
Hungary: first multi-party elections

April
Yugoslavia: first multi-party elections in Slovenia and Croatia

3 October
Reunification of East and West Germany

11 December
Albania: pro-democracy demonstrations; opposition parties legalized

1991

12 June
Albania: opposition parties join government

18–22 August
Soviet Union: attempted Communist coup against rule of Mikhail Gorbachev

23 August
Soviet Union: President Boris Yeltsin of Russia suspends Communist party in Russia

11 December
Soviet Union: Republics establish the Commonwealth of Independent States

25 December
Soviet Union: Mikhail Gorbachev resigns as president of defunct Soviet Union

---

In November 1982 the 75–year-old Soviet president Leonid Brezhnev died and was succeeded by Yuriy Andropov, a former head of the KGB. However, Andropov himself died in February 1984 and was replaced by Konstantin Chernenko, Chernenko's leadership only lasted a year before he too died, in March 1985.

The rapid demise of a string of Soviet leaders seemed to symbolize a decaying regime. The problems facing the USSR in the 1980s were immense. Marx's utopian dream of a workers' paradise, where the state had become redundant, finally "withering away" to allow the emergence of true democracy, based on equality and collective ownership of the means of production, seemed to have turned into a bureaucratic and undemocratic nightmare. Since the Bolshevik revolution of 1917 the Soviet state had become increasingly centralized. The ruling Communist party had become a highly corrupt and inefficient institution, more concerned with the preservation of its own privileges than with the well-being of the society it ruled. The Brezhnev era in particular (1964–82) was characterized by economic stagnation and mismanagement. The vast natural resources of the Soviet Union remained largely untapped and the consequences for the people were longer food queues and increasing desperation. As the people starved, the Soviet government poured massive resources into building up their military machine, as much to maintain their highly unstable East European empire as to counter the NATO forces of the West. In short, by the mid-1980s the USSR was on the brink of disintegration, having lost any claims it had to legitimate rule. It was the vision of one man that finally led to the collapse of Communist rule, although his initial aim was not to end Communism but to reform the system from above – before it could be destroyed from below.

The appointment of Mikhail Gorbachev

Gorbachev was named successor to Chernenko as general secretary of the Soviet Communist party in 1985 and became president in 1988. He had two main aims: to heal the wounds between East and West, and to modernize the ailing Soviet system. He charmed Western leaders such as the British prime minister Mrs Thatcher, who declared that the West could "do business" with him, and scored considerable diplomatic victories, taking the lead on arms reductions. At home he took a two-pronged approach to reform. On the political and social front, he declared a new "openness" (*glasnost*) to encourage the circulation of new ideas. To remedy the severe problems of the planned command economy, he introduced *perestroika* ("reconstruction"). Gorbachev targeted bureaucratic inefficiency, corrup-

THE NEW WORLD ORDER

tion, and shortages of food and other basics of life. Whilst not wishing to give up centralized Communist control, he attempted to make the party more accountable, through, for example, the setting up of an elected Soviet parliament which was to meet annually, elect the state president for a five-year term, select his deputy and nominate a watchdog body of 15 deputies.

Gorbachev's move towards democratic structures and economic reforms sent shock waves through Eastern Europe, the governments of which became even more unsustainable. The effects of Gorbachev's actions did not end there however.

The impact of Gorbachev's reforms

By implementing *glasnost* and *perestroika*, Gorbachev hoped to secure the survival of the Soviet Communist party and the Soviet Union, through a modernized economy and a greater tolerance of alternative views to orthodox Communist thinking. Once the road to reform had been taken, however, it proved impossible to stop this from accelerating into wholesale revolutionary change.

During the Gorbachev era public opinion, for the first time in the Soviet Union, began to matter. With the advent of *glasnost* hitherto taboo subjects were debated. Censorship was greatly reduced, and non-Communists were allowed to air their views. Religion and intellectuals were tolerated and, in some cases, encouraged. A significant turning point in the growth of openness was the explosion of a nuclear reactor at Chernobyl in 1986. Following 19 days of silence, the problem was publicly admitted. After this event

▶ The appointment of Mikhail Gorbachev, shown here with Italian opera star Luciano Pavarotti, marked a clear break in style compared to his aged and dour predecessors. Gorbachev conducted a "charm offensive," using his relative youth to his advantage in his dealings with Western leaders. His efforts earned him the nickname "Gorby," and in his visits to Western countries he aroused much popular interest.

▼ The Soviet premier visits Chernobyl. Gorbachev's diplomatic success abroad was in contrast to his lack of success at home. The explosion at the Chernobyl nuclear power station in 1986 symbolized the failure of an archaic system.

Gorbachev appeared to gain in authority and confidence and declared a new intention to instigate much more open government and to "call things by their name." In an important symbolic action he removed the ban on the writings of the exiled long-time dissident writer Alexander Solzhenitsyn. Historians began to question the excesses of the Stalin era and present the attempted reforms of Khrushchev in a favorable light.

On the economic front reform met with much inertia. People had become used to the state providing for their needs. Whilst many desired better living standards, they were afraid of the uncertainties of a market system. Within the highest echelons of the Communist party, there appeared a cleavage between conservative hardliners, who wished for a return to the old ways, and radicals led by Boris Yeltsin, who desired extensive modernization, based on the Western model.

As time passed Gorbachev increasingly found himself in the middle of this struggle, trying to placate both sides. This position soon became untenable. Yeltsin, who became president of Russia in June 1990, was soon to emerge as a powerful rival to Gorbachev and in July 1990 he left the Communist party, thus disassociating himself from Gorbachev and from any actions he might take to hold the Soviet Union together. Indeed, in September 1990 Gorbachev was forced to accept emergency powers to allow him to rule by decree. In another damaging split the foreign minister Edward Shevardnadze resigned on 20 December 1990 and declared that "dictatorship is coming".

Modernization and reaction in China

During the 1980s China's leaders, too, were intent on improving their country's poor economic performance. Unlike Gorbachev, however, China's Communist leaders were not prepared to tolerate any real challenge to the authority of the party. Certain elements of market economics were introduced, such as allowing peasant farmers to sell their surplus for profit, but progress on the economic front began to falter by the mid 1980s. Economic growth, however, had fueled, rather than quietened, public discontent with the political system. Disagreements grew at the very core of the party, as talk of reform increased; so too did the size of the armed police force. In January 1987 a modernizer, Zhao Ziyang, became general secretary, but to show that the hardliners still had much influence, Li Peng was made prime minister.

In summer 1989 there were massive student demonstrations in Beijing. Protesters demanded democratic reforms. The visit of Gorbachev to Beijing earlier that year had helped intensify demands for change, but under the orders of Li Peng the army brutally crushed the student demonstrations on Beijing's Tiananmen Square, leaving several hundred dead.

Two years later, the Chinese leadership still faced the dilemma of working out how to reform the economy while attempting to avoid the natural implications of such upheaval. The Chinese government's dealings with Britain over Hong Kong in the early 1990s showed the Chinese still to be wary of democracy: they repeatedly opposed any moves toward democracy in the colony, over which they would assume control in 1997 when the British lease expired.

Revolution in Eastern Europe

The link between the reforms of Gorbachev in the Soviet Union and the revolutions in Eastern Europe during 1989 was a direct one. His reforms unleashed latent aspirations for self-determination, which had hitherto been suppressed by Soviet-backed coercion.

In Poland the movement for reform had begun before the arrival of Gorbachev. In 1980 the Polish Communists were frightened into limited reform by a series of strikes, triggered by imminent rises in food prices. Most significantly, an independent trade union, Solidarity, led by Lech Walesa, was legalized. In December 1981 this organization had become a strong outlet for protest against communism. The government reacted by

► East meets West – a man conducts a conversation with a soldier through the ruins of the Berlin Wall. The collapse of the Wall allowed for the reunification of Germany in 1990. However, the speed of this change brought with it new problems, including the rise of neo-Nazi activity. Reconstruction in the east proved very costly, and unemployment rose to very high levels.

▼ Student demonstrations in Tiananmen Square, Beijing, May 1989. Under the influence of Gorbachev's reforms in the Soviet Union, Chinese students attempted to force their Communist government into introducing democratic reforms. Although some intellectuals supported the students, the workers stood largely on the sidelines. Outside Beijing the efforts of the students went unreported, and China's peasant majority remained ignorant of the struggle.

banning the union and declaring martial law. With the intervention of the Polish-born Pope John Paul II, a compromise was arrived at, and in 1983 martial law was lifted. By January 1988, however, further economic problems led to further strikes. Under immense popular pressure, the government was forced to hold elections which Solidarity was allowed to contest. The result was a humiliating defeat for the Communists and Tadeusz Mazowiecki, representing Solidarity, became prime minister in May 1989.

Hungary also witnessed great change in May 1989. The funeral and reburial of Imre Nagy, the reformist leader of Hungary at the time of the Soviet invasion of 1956, led to a vast demonstration against the government. The regime, under the influence of Gorbachev, had already started limited reform, but this only had the effect of raising expectations. By 1990 the Communist party was changing its name in a vain attempt to win free elections, which they had been forced to hold. A center-right coalition was formed, which removed restrictions on its frontiers with Austria, thus allowing East Germans on holiday in Hungary to flee to the West.

Erich Honecker, the Communist leader in East Germany, hoped to crush revolution in that country as it became clear that his rule was crumbling. East Germany had, however, relied upon the Soviet Union more than any other of the satellites for its legitimacy. After Gorbachev made it clear that he would not support violent repression of the revolution, Honecker was lost. In November 1989 the Berlin Wall was pulled down and in elections in 1990 the Communists were reduced to 16 percent of the vote.

Bulgaria and Romania could not escape the monumental changes that Gorbachev had sparked. In Bulgaria the final death knell for communism was rung when Todor Zhivkov, the Communist leader, attempted to suppress popular calls for *glasnost* by violent means. Zhivkov failed to hold onto power, elections were eventually held, and the Communist leader was later tried for crimes against the state.

Romania saw the most violent reaction. Since 1967 Nicolae Ceauşescu had ruled Romania as a megalomaniacal emperor. He refused to give up his self-styled crown without a bloody fight. In December 1989 a combination of a popular uprising and revolt by the army overthrew Ceauşescu. Thousands were killed in battles between Ceauşescu's private army and the people, before he was finally captured and, along with his wife, put to death.

In Czechoslovakia mass popular demonstrations swept away communism without bloodshed. Václav Havel, a popular author and long-time political prisoner, became president. The leader of the aborted reforms of the Prague Spring of 1968, Alexander Dubček, was given the post of chairman of the parliament.

The year of 1989 was one of the most important of the 20th century, and was a triumph of human courage and fortitude. The revolutions proved that states cannot have stability without legitimacy. Gorbachev was the catalyst that finally, and, amazingly quickly, rendered Communism

unviable. The new governments of Eastern Europe, however, were faced not only with the challenge of overcoming years of economic mismanagement: the maintenance of democracy was likely to be dependent upon outside aid, and possibly the inclusion of the newly democratic states in the European Community. Meanwhile the main political structures of the West – NATO and the European Community – were faced with an identity crisis, no longer faced with a superpower enemy but rather with a plethora of poor, unstable states in Eastern Europe.

Reform in South Africa

With the appointment of F.W. de Klerk as state president of South Africa in September 1989, the hope for a new constitution was increased. De Klerk pledged to transform South Africa. In particular he showed a highly conciliatory attitude to the banned African National Congress (ANC), eventually legalizing it along with other outlawed groups. In an important practical and symbolic action the ANC leader Nelson Mandela was released from prison in February 1990, as were other important black leaders.

De Klerk also attempted to curb the power of the military by asserting cabinet authority over the powerful state security council. The state of emergency, declared in 1986, was also lifted.

▼ The body of Romanian dictator Nicolae Ceauşescu. He was executed, after a hasty trial, for crimes against the people. His rule had been marked by personal indulgence while ordinary people suffered as a result of his brutal policies.

◀ Nelson Mandela returns home after 26 years in prison. As the African National Congress's most famous and influential leader it was essential to F. W. de Klerk's reform program that Mandela was released. Reform in South Africa still remained precarious, with violence threatening from all sides.

▼ ▶ An allied plan attacks Iraq's military communications (right). The ousting of Iraq from Kuwait in 1991 was achieved through the vastly superior technology of the UN forces. The campaign was largely based on pinpoint air assaults, thus placating US fears of a rerun of Vietnam. Iraq's only answer was to burn Kuwait's oilfields (below), which caused massive environmental damage.

However, this did not put a stop to violence. The conflict between Mandela's ANC and the Zulu *In-khata* movement led by Chief Gatsha Buthulezi intensified. Buthulezi, as chief minister of the KwaZulu Bantustan ("tribal homeland"), was highly reluctant to agree to the ANC policy of abolishing the bantustans as this system greatly increased his own power. Violence between the two groups was intensified by the suspicion of an involvement in the conflict by sections of the military, intent on discrediting the ANC.

It remained to be seen whether de Klerk could enact concrete reforms that all groups could accept, and which would bring lasting peace to South Africa. It seemed, however, that he had the support of the majority of whites, who voted overwhelmingly for him in a referendum about his reform program in March 1992.

Instability in sub-Saharan Africa
In sub-Saharan Africa economic stagnation remained a huge problem. In 1989 the World Bank found that food production and per capita income had actually decreased. This helped fuel political instability, although the general trend was away from socialist, one-party systems and towards at-tempts of multi-party democracy. Countries such as Mozambique, Angola and Zambia sought economic aid from the IMF. In exchange the IMF operated a policy of "structural adjustment" which aimed at implementing market reforms and pluralism in these countries. This policy had limited success. In Angola, for example, the results of multi-party elections in 1992 were disputed by UNITA, the losing party.

Latin and Central America
In these two regions of the world a checkered pattern of development emerged in the late 1980s and early 1990s. In some countries, such as Argentina and Chile, there occurred the development of embryonic democracies. In 1992 there was a breakthrough in one of the bloodiest civil wars of the century, in El Salvador, where a truce was declared, and the holding of general elections agreed. In Peru, however, the US-backed government was involved in conflict with the Maoist-inspired guerrilla group. "The Shining Path", and was forced into declaring martial law.

In Central America the US government, under President Ronald Reagan, again showed its willingness to give aid to antisocialist movements. In the case of Nicaragua, the Americans backed the coalition of anti-democratic forces known as the contras, against the left-wing Sandinista government, which had replaced the violent dictatorial regime of Anastasio Somoza in 1979. Eventually the US government got what it had wanted – not through the efforts of the contras but via the ballot box: in 1990 a coalition led by Mrs Violeta de Chamorro defeated the Sandinistas who had lost popularity, largely because their rule had brought with it damaging US economic sanctions.

With the advent of the Gorbachev era, the US perhaps felt less need to confront leftwing movements in these regions of the world. Another consequence of the demise of Communism in Europe was the end of aid from Communist countries to the regime of Fidel Castro in Cuba. Without this aid, Cuba was forced into heavy rationing, particularly of oil.

The United Nations in the Gorbachev Era

With the end of the Cold War in 1989–90 the potential for the UN to assert its authority was greatly increased. The ideological nature of the Cold War conflict undermined international cooperation in seeking solutions to regional conflicts, since either side could, and often did, veto the other's plans. After Gorbachev began reforming the Soviet Union UN involvement in world affairs grew in significance. With the end of East–West conflict, many more avenues for UN involvement were opened, for example, in Angola and Mozambique.

In the Cold War era an operation such as that mounted against Iraq in 1990–91 would have been impossible, and such operations greatly increased expectations that the UN might reduce, or even eradicate, aggression in the states system. It was arguable whether this expectation would prove to be optimistic, since any UN operation was dependent upon individual states being willing to commit troops. Rich and powerful states still had as their main priority their own best interests and in some conflicts, for example Yugoslavia in the early 1990s, the political and military complexity of the situation rendered effective intervention problematic.

A more active UN also raised the question of interference in state sovereignty. Should the UN, for example, intervene when a country violated the civil rights of its own people? The widespread infringement of such rights in many countries made such action highly contentious.

It was possible, however, that as the UN increased its involvement in world affairs, more concrete rules of procedure would be established through experience, and individual states would come to see that it was in their own longterm interest to support the UN in order to prevent renegade states from acting with violence to further their interests.

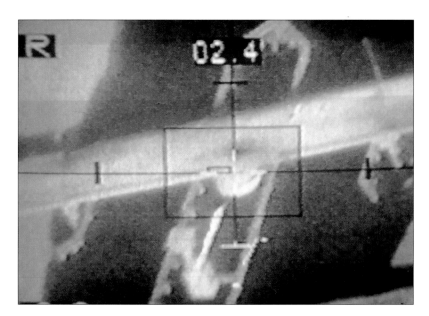

The Middle East: Iraq's invasion of Kuwait

In the Middle East the continuing problem of the Arab–Israel conflict was briefly overshadowed by a second Gulf War, again precipitated by Saddam Hussein's Iraq. On 2 August 1990 Iraq attempted to annexe its small but rich neighbor, Kuwait. It was clear that Hussein did not anticipate a strong reaction from the international community, but in fact he quickly faced an unprecedented display of unity by a broad coalition of countries, operating through the authority of the United Nations.

Having gained the appropriate resolutions from the UN, the US-led coalition swiftly removed Iraq from Kuwait, once it was clear that economic sanctions might not destroy Hussein's resolve. Hussein attempted to split the Arab states from the coalition by attacks on Israel using scud missiles, but this proved futile. Within a week of the allied military invasion, Kuwait was liberated with huge Iraqi losses, of up to 100,000.

The resurgence of nationalism in the USSR

One of the most powerful forces unleashed by Gorbachev's reforms was nationalism. As the fifteen republics that made up the Soviet Union grew impatient with the continuation of economic problems and the inability of the Communists to solve them, the force of independence movements grew.

The Soviet government's response was a destructive mixture of conciliation and state violence. Whilst it attempted to negotiate a new reconstructed union, through a pact signed on 1 April 1991 (promising more power to the republics), it ruthlessly attempted to crush independence movements in the Baltic states through military intervention, especially in Lithuania. This, however, did not deter the republics from their struggle for self-determination. In a series of referendums, the people of several states, including Estonia and Lithuania, showed their desire for autonomy. The republics were supported by Yeltsin who believed that each republic should become a fully independent state before it decided to join a new union.

In every republic Communism was in retreat. In Russia, Yeltsin banned all political party activity in the work place, thus rendering Communists virtually impotent. On 19 August 1991 the hardliners in the party saw their last chance to "save" the union, and instigated a coup attempt while Gorbachev was out of Moscow. They declared that Gorbachev had taken a rest for health reasons. Yeltsin led the resistance to the hardliners, who soon surrendered. This failure illustrated how little support the conservatives had, and resulted in a great increase in the political standing of Yeltsin.

On 21 August Gorbachev was reinstated as president, but as most state bodies were involved in the coup, and as most of the republics soon

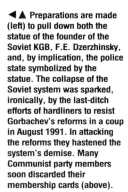

declared independence, there seemed to be little to be president of. Yeltsin had clearly emerged as chief power broker and on 24 August Gorbachev was forced to resign as general secretary of the Soviet Communist party. The party, in effect, ceased to exist.

On 1 December 1991 Russia, the Ukraine, and Belorussia formed the Commonwealth of Independent States and made the historic declaration that "The Soviet Union . . . ceases to exist." On 25 December Gorbachev resigned as president of the now defunct Soviet Union. In his resignation speech he summed up his achievements by saying that: "A totalitarian system which deprived the country of an opportunity to become wealthy and prosperous a long time ago has been liquidated". The new states were left to deal with ethnic conflicts, economic backwardness and quarrels over boundaries.

◀▲ Preparations are made (left) to pull down both the statue of the founder of the Soviet KGB, F.E. Dzerzhinsky, and, by implication, the police state symbolized by the statue. The collapse of the Soviet system was sparked, ironically, by the last-ditch efforts of hardliners to resist Gorbachev's reforms in a coup in August 1991. In attacking the reforms they hastened the system's demise. Many Communist party members soon discarded their membership cards (above).

◀ Ethnic conflict erupts in Azerbaijan. One of the major causes of the destruction of Soviet rule was an upsurge in nationalism, particularly in the Baltic states, where nationalist leaders struggled to regain independence lost during World War II. The Soviet leaders also faced the challenge of Islam in the south, where religious strife was added to economic and social discord. Western reactions to these movements were mixed. Inclinations to support the principle of self-determination were tempered by fears that Gorbachev would be undermined and hardliners restored to power.

THE
WORLDWIDE
NETWORK

Time Chart

	1974	1975	1976	1977	1978	1979	1980	1981
Industry	• Sep: 17 oil companies build a pipeline from the North Sea to the UK	• May: Peru nationalizes Gulf Oil de Peru • 11 Aug: British Leyland nationalized (UK)	• 26 Feb: Contract signed between the British government and oil companies Shell and Esso regarding North Sea oil	• Jun: Merger of French truck producers SAVIEM and Barliot with the Renault group (Fr) • Aug: French national control of the subsidized steel industry commences	• Apr–Nov: China buys US wheat in bulk • Aug: French motor company Peugeot–Citroën takes over Chrysler Europe, becoming Europe's largest car producer	• May: Renault builds a motor plant in Portugal for $400 million (Fr/Port)	• May: US government aid for Chrysler due to decreasing car sales • Sep: Discussion on a joint agricultural policy between UK and France	• Jan–Mar: Introduction of a quota system in the steel industry of the EC countries to reduce production surplus • Sep: Merging of Coneco and DuPont de Nemours (USA)
Technology	• West German–French satellite *Symphony* begins operation	• 1 Oct: US scientists warning about the environmental dangers of CFCs – refrigerant and aerosol propellant gases	• Development of glass fiber cable for use in telecommunications		• First demonstration of compact discs (FRG)	• 28 Mar: Accident at the Three Mile Island nuclear power station due to a defect in the cooling system (USA)	• 5 Sep: Opening of the largest road tunnel in the world, the St. Gotthard tunnel in Switzerland	• 12 Apr: Launch of the first space Shuttle *Columbia* (USA)
Finance	• Jan: French franc begins flotation for six months • Oct: General Arrangement to Borrow (GAB) of the "Group of Ten" renewed • Nov: Introduction of the currency unit Arcru by Arab countries to recycle income from sale of oil • Dec: US citizens are permitted to buy, sell and own gold for the first time since 1933	• Jan: US Treasury holds its first auction to dispose of a portion of its gold holdings • Feb: Central Banks of the Arab countries establish an Arab monetary fund • Dec: Meeting of the ministers of finance and the governors of the central banks of the "Group of Ten" countries in Paris. They agree to coordinate the sale and purchase of gold by their central banks	• Jun: The "Group of Ten" countries, Switzerland and the Bank for International Settlements (BIS) grant $5.3 million credit to the UK • Sep: Mexican government allows the peso to float due to precarious foreign exchange situation • Suspension of the official gold price by the IMF. Legalization of foreign exchange rate flotation	• 10 Jan: IMF grants the UK a credit of $3.9 billion. The central banks of the "Group of Ten", Switzerland and the BIS agree on a medium-term credit facility of $3 billion to the Bank of England • Apr: New fixing of foreign exchange rates by the Scandanavian countries. Sweden withdraws from the European currency system • Oct: Flotation of the pound (UK)	• Jan: Measures taken by the US government to strengthen the declining dollar and to counter increasing inflation, coordinated with the Federal Reserve Board and other central banks • Mar: Severe foreign exchange restriction in Japan • The West German Bundesbank and US Treasury agree on a duplication of the swap credit lines	• 1 Jan: Introduction of the European Monetary System (EMS) by the EC • Feb: Credit base of the IMF strengthened by the introduction of supplementing credit facilities (Witteveen facility) • May: GAB of the "Group of Ten" renewed for a further five years	• May: Meeting of 115 bankers and governors of central banks from 23 countries to discuss the financing of oil imports • Sep: New currency (shekel) introduced in Israel as a result of inflation • Sep/Oct: Annual meeting of the IMF and World Bank discusses the external debts of the developing countries	• Jan: European Monetary Fund (EMF) established • Jan: European Currency Unit (ECU) introduced • Mar: New fixing of the exchange rates in EMS. Devaluation of the Italian lira and the French franc and revaluation of the Deutschmark and the Dutch guilder
Economic Policy	• Oct: US president Ford publishes his economic program to counter inflation and the energy crisis • Nov: US secretary of state Kissinger proposes a "common loan and guarantee facility" by the OECD to recycle $25 billion income from sale of oil • Dec: Declarations of Ayacucho and Guyana demand the economic independence of Latin American countries and economic cooperation	• Jan: Establishment of an oil facility by the IMF to assist countries affected by the oil crisis and to recycle income from sale of oil • Nov: First economic summit of the six major Western industrial nations in France. Declaration on the need for recovery from recession • Dec: Conference on International Economic Cooperation in Paris • Sep: US government begins a $100 billion program to become self-sufficient in energy	• Jun: Second economic summit in Puerto Rico. Consultations and cooperation between the seven major western industrial countries pledged to continue • May: CIEC decides in Paris to establish a common fund to help stabilize the prices of certain commodities • Oct: Labor party demands the nationalization of banks and assurance companies • Sep: French prime minister Barre publishes a plan to counter inflation	• May: Third economic summit in London. Conference members pledge cooperation on economic problems • Bullock report on industrial democracy published. Industry does not accept the report, claiming it gives the trade unions too much power (UK) • Steel industry crisis begins in the EC countries	• Jun: Annual meeting of the OECD. International coordinated action demanded to stimulate the world economy • Jul: Economic summit in Bonn. Common strategy of mutually reinforcing action to promote world economic recovery • Dec: Increase in the oil price of 14.5% by OPEC, in the second round of increases	• Mar: 9% increase in the oil price by OPEC, with a further increase of 23.7% in June • Jun: Fifth economic summit in Tokyo of the seven major Western industrial nations. Secret agreement on trade with China • Jun: 33rd session of Comecon in Moscow. New methods of economic cooperation by the member countries proposed • Jul: US president Carter issues a report on the economic situation in the USA and announces anti-inflationary measures	• Jan: US president Carter imposes restrictions in trade with the USSR as a consequence of its invasion of Afghanistan • May: Sixth economic summit in Venice of the major Western industrial nations. Declarations on the world economy and on Afghanistan • Council of the EC confirms its intention of strengthening the EMS as means of reaching the aim of monetary integration	• Feb: US president Reagan presents his economic program of reducing the budget deficit and taxes, and increasing the defence budget (USA) • Mar: 26th party session of the CPSU decides on principles of further economic development • Aug: Declaration of Tegucigalpa. Middle American countries demand to be better integrated into the world economy
International	• Jul: Conference of Kingston held by 44 African, Caribbean and Pacific countries. Association with the EEC discussed • Sep: Agreement between the six major industrial nations on limitation of the governmental support of export finance • Sep: Comecon takes up informal contacts with the EEC	• Feb: Agreement between the EC and ACP (African, Caribbean, Pacific) countries to regulate trade, financial and industrial cooperation (Lome agreement) • Mar: Second UNIDO conference in Lima. Declaration on industrial development and cooperation	• Feb: COMECON publishes a plan for economic cooperation with the EC • May: UNCTAD conference in Nairobi. Problem of north–south dialog and a program for the use of raw materials discussed • May: Establishment of an $800 million fund for developing countries by the OEEC	• Jan: Agreement on financial cooperation between the EC and Egypt, Syria and Jordan signed • Mar: Opening of the UNCTAD conference on the establishment of a fund for raw materials • Nov: Beginning of dialog between the EC and ASEAN countries	• Feb: Agreement between EC and EFTA on the regulation of the steel trade • Mar: Vietnam becomes the tenth member of Comecon • Sep: Agreement between Japan and several Arab countries to regulate the oil trade	• May: OECD demands a greater use of coal from its members in order to reduce the consumption of oil • Jul: OPEC increases its fund for supporting developing countries • Jul: World agricultural conference discusses the UN development program on the problems of developing countries	• Mar: China becomes a member of World Bank, IFC and IDA instead of Taiwan • Jun: Meeting of the ministers council of the OECD countries demands restrictive monetary policy • Jun: UNCTAD conference in Geneva signs agreement on the establishment of an international fund for raw materials	• Greece becomes the tenth member of the EEC • Apr: Meeting of the "Group of Five" of the IMF. US criticism of government subsidies in Europe • Jun: Meeting of the minster council of the OECD. Demand for a liberalization of trade and economic cooperation with developing countries
Misc.	• Watergate scandal initiates impeachment proceedings against US president Nixon (USA)	• 30 Apr: Surrender of South Vietnam to the Communist forces of North Vietnam	• 2 Jul: Unification of Vietnam and its proclamation as a socialist republic		• New leadership in China proclaim a new economic policy of industrialization	• Beginning of the Islamic revolution in Iran under Khomeini • Military interention in Afghanistan by the USSR	• Wave of strikes in Poland. *Solidarność* trade union formed • Beginning of the Gulf War as Iraq invades Iran	• Martial law under General Jaruzelski proclaimed in Poland. *Solidarność* banned

1982	1983	1984	1985	1986	1987	1988	1989
Jun: New principles for mergers in the US. More control over mergers of competing firms	• Mar: Discussion on leaving farmland fallow because of production surplus and sale problems (USA) • Dec: Mass redundancies in Talbot motor company (Fr)	• Apr: Nippon Kokon (Jap) gains a half share in US National Steel Corporation • Dec: Toxic gas leakage at the US chemical company Union Carbide in Bhopal, India	• Feb: Discussion on the shutting down of the nuclear plant at Zwentendorf (Aut) • Jul: Greece signs a contract for 40 Mirage 2000 with the French company Dassault	• Apr–Oct: Food destroyed in Europe due to contamination following explosion at Chernobyl nuclear plant near Kiev (USSR) • Jul: Fish killed in Mosel River by cyanide poisoning (FRG)	• 18 Sep: Polish cardinal Glemp signs the foundation document of a benefit institution for agriculture sponsored by the Catholic church (Pol)	• Jul: 166 people killed by gas explosion on the British oil rig Piper Alpha in the North Sea • FAO conference in Rome discusses the locust problem in Africa and Eastern Mediterranean	• Strikes by Soviet miners in the Kuzbass and Donbass regions force concessions from the government over pay and conditions
Test of Pershing 2 missiles by the USA Ground boring in the USA and USSR reaches a depth of km	• Beginning of the Strategic Defense Initiative (SDI) program (USA) • Development of a microchip with 1 billion bits per qcm (Jap)		• Testing of energy production by means of laser-fired nuclear fusion in Japan and the USA	• 28 Jan: Space shuttle Challenger explodes on takeoff killing its seven astronauts • Toshiba/NEC (Jap) and Texas Instruments (USA) develop a four megabit memory chip	• Laying of a glass fiber cable (TAT 8) across the Atlantic Ocean • Beginning of boring of the Channel Tunnel at Calais (Fr/UK)		• Stealth bomber developed (USA) • 13 Nov: Opening of the LEP particle accelerator (Fr/Switz)
Jun: New fixing of change rates in the MS. Devaluation the Belgian and Luxembourg francs, the Danish crown, the Italian lira and the French franc, with valuation of the Deutschmark and Dutch guilder Dec: Medium-term mutual financial support between the C countries prolonged for a further two years	• Mar: New fixing of exchange rates in the EMS, with a revaluation of the Deutschmark, the Dutch guilder, the Danish crown and the Belgian and Luxembourg francs, and a devaluation of the French franc, the Italian lira and the Irish pound • Jun: Change of Argentinean currency unit from Peso Ley to Peso Argentino • Dec: New peak of the US dollar in Europe	• Feb: New legislation regarding the control of banks and the credit system (FRG) • Sep: New fixing of exchange rates in the EMS. New calculation of the European Currency Unit (ECU) • Oct: Medium-term mutual financial support between the EC countries prolonged for a further two years	• Jul: Bank of Greece joins the agreement of the European central banks on the EMS, but does not become a part of the exchange rate fixing • Jul: New fixing of exchange rates in the EMS, with devaluation of the Italian lira and revaluation of all other currencies • All international financial institutions allowed to hold ECU	• Jan: Currency reform in Israel. New shekel replaces the old shekel • Apr: New fixing of exchange rates in the EMS, with devaluation of the Irish pound and French franc, revaluation of the Deutschmark, Dutch guilder, Danish crown and Belgian franc • Oct: Annual meeting of the IMF and World Bank. Consultations on the situations of the developing countries and their external debts	• Jan: New fixing of the exchange rates in the EMS. Revaluation of the Deutschmark, Dutch guilder and Belgian franc • 19 Oct: Worldwide stock exchange crash due to disturbances in the international financial markets • 3 Dec: West German Bundesbank and other European central banks decide to reduce the head interest rates to avoid further financial disturbances		• Japanese yen overtakes the US dollar • 16 Oct: Worldwide stock market crash due to failed takeover bid. Markets steadied by US Federal Reserve • Dec: EEC agree schedule for economic and monetary union
Jan: Over three million unemployed in the UK Jun: Economic summit of the seven major industrial countries in Versailles discuss the reasons for and consequences of the world wide recession Jun: Beginning of a four-month price and wage freeze (Fr) Dec: West German government publishes a program toward the creation of work for the purpose of economic recovery	• Jan: British prime minister Thatcher publishes an economic policy aimed at curbing inflation and reducing the budget deficit (UK) • Feb: Soviet leader Andropov announces economic measures to counter the lack of economic discipline • Mar: US president Reagan announces his intention to procure $5 billion for the creation of work (USA) • May: Economic summit of the seven major industrial nations discusses measures for the recovery of the world economy	• Jun: China encourages foreign investment by the establishment of four special economic areas • Jun: Economic summit of the seven major industrial nations in London to discuss the world economic situation • Sep: US president Reagan refuses governmental support for the US steel industry • Consultations by the French government to counter the Lorraine steel crisis (Fr)	• Jan: Chairman of the EC commission J. Delors publishes a plan for the realization of European integration by the establishment of a European market • May: Economic summit of the seven major industrial nations in Bonn. Measures against inflation and a reduction of budget deficits agreed • Jun: Key speech by new Soviet leader Gorbachev on the future of economic development in the USSR. Announcement of the policy of perestroika (reconstruction)	• Jan: Sudden collapse in the price of crude oil. OPEC conferences discuss the new situation and demand a reduction in oil output • Feb: Arab League agrees on the establishment of a free trade area due to oil price collapse • Jun: Economic summit of the seven major industrial nations in Tokyo • Sep: Meeting of the "Group of 77" developing countries to discuss their external debt crises	• 22 Feb: Intensive economic cooperation and a reduction of differences in the balance of payments agreed by the major Western industrial nations (Louvre accord) • Feb: EC and the USA plan common measures against Japanese trade restrictions and trade policy • Apr: Conference on external debt among the developing countries discusses a possible suspension of those debts	• Apr: Conference of the "Group of 77" developing countries on the global system of trading preferences • Jun: Economic summit of the seven major industrial nations discusses international debt problems and reduction of agricultural subsidy • Aug: Conference of the "Group of Eight" in Rio de Janeiro on possibilities for economic growth in the Third World	• Polish external debt of $39 billion. Promise of US and EC aid. Solidarność prime minister T. Mazowiecki (elected in August after elections in May) in October invites Adam Smith Institute (UK) to advise on privatization
Jan: IDA reduces credits to developing countries due to lack of funds Oct: UN General assembly demands that no credits be given to South Africa by the IMF Dec: No agreement reached on quotas of crude oil output after OPEC conference	• Jan: Switzerland becomes a member of the "Group of Ten" of the IMF • Jan: EC countries agree on new fishing quotas • Mar: OPEC agrees on a reduction of the oil price to $5 and a limitation of the daily production	• Jun: Third summit of Comecon in Moscow. Declaration on intensified economic cooperation • Oct: New fixing of the quotas of crude oil production by OPEC in Geneva • Nov: Third Lome agreement signed on economic relations between EC and ACP countries	• Jan: Iran, Turkey and Pakistan agree on the establishment of an organization for economic cooperation • Sep: Special meeting of GATT demands a new round of tax and tariff negotiations • Oct: UNCTAD conference in Geneva publishes declaration on economic support for developing countries	• Jan: Spain and Portugal become eleventh and twelfth members of the EEC • May: EFTA demands the liberalization of international trade • Sep: Meeting of the GATT country ministers. Soviet Union requests affiliation with GATT	• 15 Feb: EC commission publishes Delors package, which includes reformation of agricultural policy, establishment of a structure fund and World Bank and the introduction of new budget principles • Aug: World trade conference UNCTAD demands cooperation between industrial and developing countries	• 25 Jun: Beginning of official relations between the EC and Comecon • Sep: Annual meeting of IMF and World Bank provokes an "anticonference" of those organizations' critics	• Nov: EC discussions on the new situation in Eastern Europe
2 Apr: Argentina captures the disputed Falkland Islands, but these are retaken by Britain six weeks later	• 21 Jul: Lifting of martial law in Poland • 1 Sep: Korean passenger plane shot down by Soviet air force		• Mikhail Gorbachev succeeds Constantin Chernenko as general secretary of the CPSU, and implements a widespread reform policy (USSR)	• US F-11s bomb Tripoli in reprisal for Libyan terrorist activities (Lib)		• UN ceasefire brings an end to the Gulf War between Iran and Iraq • Large earthquake in Armenia with great loss of life	• 4 Jun: Army crush demonstrations in Beijing (China) • 9 Nov: Berlin wall opened after leader E. Honecker ousted (GDR)

45

Datafile

So dramatic were OPEC's oil embargo and price rises of 1973–74 that they may be seen as the end of the long postwar boom under American leadership. Higher oil prices redistributed world income away from the West and inaugurated a long period of "stagnation", years of slow or zero economic growth coupled with rising prices. Gradually the industrialized world reduced its demand for oil and developed other sources, until 1986, when oil prices tumbled.

▼ Middle Eastern dominance of the world oil market was well established in 1980. The Soviet Union and China jointly, and Central and South America, owned larger extracted reserves because of the demands of their considerable populations, but their proved reserves were comparatively small.

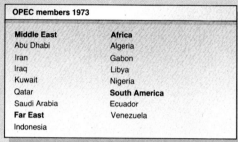

OPEC members 1973	
Middle East	**Africa**
Abu Dhabi	Algeria
Iran	Gabon
Iraq	Libya
Kuwait	Nigeria
Qatar	**South America**
Saudi Arabia	Ecuador
Far East	Venezuela
Indonesia	

▲ By 1973, almost as many members of OPEC were located outside the Middle East as within that area. The driving force had, however, been Saudi Arabia, with its huge proven reserves and small population, which had been willing to underwrite output restrictions in order to raise oil prices and OPEC revenues.

▼ Other primary commodities became more expensive in 1973 as well as oil. The price effects of the two oil crises in 1973–74 and 1979–80 can be clearly identified, as can the slump of 1985–86. Although commodity prices in general were more erratic than oil prices in the 1970s, in the 1980s their decline was more gradual.

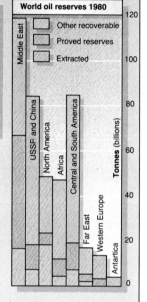

World oil reserves 1980

- Other recoverable
- Proved reserves
- Extracted

Tonnes (billions): 0, 20, 40, 60, 80, 100, 120

(Middle East, USSR and China, North America, Africa, Central and South America, Far East, Western Europe, Antartica)

Energy consumption 1976

North America: 6%, 2%, 29%, 27%, 18%, 18%

Western Europe: 6%, 2%, 15%, 7%, 50%, 20%

Japan: 6%, 1%, 2%, 3%, 15%, 73%

- Natural gas
- Oil (domestic)
- Oil (imported)
- Coal
- Hydroelectric
- Nuclear

World oil and commodity prices

Other commodities

Oil

Index (1982=100): 0, 40, 80, 120, 160

1973, 1976, 1979, 1982, 1985, 1988

◄ Japan, North America and Western Europe all drew upon coal, hydro and nuclear power, to supply roughly similar proportions of energy, but relied mainly upon oil. Japan was particularly vulnerable to disruptions of world oil supplies since about three-quarters of her total energy in 1976 came from oil.

North Sea oil ownership 1977

5%, 1%, 7%, 2%, 13%, 43%, 26%

- USA
- UK
- Norway
- Holland
- Belgium
- France
- Italy
- FRG
- Canada

► Vast experience in the application and development of oil extraction technology gave United States firms a competitive advantage in exploiting oil under the North Sea bed. Norway and Britain otherwise allowed their own companies the lion's share of the remaining sites they claimed.

The end of the long postwar boom might be dated to the rising unemployment and inflation of 1968–70, or it might be seen as coming with the explosion of primary product prices in 1972. In that year the pressure of demand caused by reflation of all the industrial countries' economies at once reversed the downward trend of the terms of trade between manufactures and primary products. More expensive food and raw materials cut back Western spending power. Measured by rates of economic growth, the depression associated with tight monetary policies and the oil crises of 1979–80 could be regarded as the end of the boom, for on average world growth continued at quite respectable rates during the 1970s. But the most dramatic economic events of the post-World War II years, those of the first oil crises of 1973–74, are the obvious terminal point of the boom. These years appeared to mark a turning point in the economic balance of power between the West and the poorer countries. In the United States the contraction of 1974 was the

THE OIL CRISIS

The end of the postwar boom

Oil producers and oil consumers

OPEC changes the balance of power

The search for new oil fields

Reducing demand

most severe since the Great Depression of the 1930s, even though it was far less deep and long-lasting. As in the Great Depression, 1973 and 1974 saw the collapse of major banks such as the United States National Bank of San Diego and the Franklin National Bank of New York.

Middle East oil and OPEC

By the 1970s, Western countries in general had come to rely ever more heavily on a regular supply of oil for energy – in heavy industry, transport, and even in domestic applications such as central heating. Britain and France had withdrawn politically from the Middle East in the years after World War II, but were still highly dependent on Middle Eastern supplies of oil, as were other industrialized countries in Europe, as well as Japan. But the new national governments of the Middle Eastern countries – whether under monarchs like the Shah of Iran or military rulers like Colonel Nasser – were determined to regain control over their own resources, especially oil.

▼ Control of huge oil refineries such as this, both of crude oil that was pumped into it and the distribution of the refined products, conferred enormous political and economic power.

The Organization of Petroleum Exporting Countries – OPEC – had been formed in 1960 by five oil-exporting countries: Iran, Iraq, Kuwait, Saudi Arabia and Venezuela. Its formation had been triggered by reductions in the prices that the "Seven Sisters" – the major oil companies' cartel which consisted of Standard Oil (New Jersey), Royal Dutch Shell, Mobil Oil, Texaco, Gulf Oil, Standard Oil (California) and British Petroleum – were prepared to pay for crude oil. Throughout the 1960s, OPEC demands for higher prices and greater participation in oil extraction and refining were deflected, deferred or declined. Tired of such exploitation, OPEC gradually acquired technical expertise and began – especially in Libya – to use cartel-breaking independent oil companies such as Occidental to supply outlets and information denied to them by the Seven Sisters.

A Saudi Arabian attempt at an oil embargo in 1967 had failed because the United States was then producing more oil than it consumed and could therefore supply any shortfall. But by 1973

the position had changed radically: the United States had become a net importer of oil. The opportunity for the OPEC countries to change the balance of power had arrived.

In early October 1973 the Arab–Israeli war began. Arab states reduced oil production and imposed embargoes on both the United States, as a supplier of arms to Israel, and The Netherlands, which was closely identified with Israeli foreign policy. World oil supplies fell by approximately seven percent in the following quarter. Within a month the European Community had taken a pro-Arab position on the Middle East, to which the Arabs responded by easing European oil shipments. The Japanese adopted a similar stance. However, oil was still in very short supply in the West, and American, Japanese and German companies bid up oil prices to a peak of $16–17 a barrel, compared with an official pre-crisis price of $3. Inflation in the West rose as governments reacted by implementing policies which were aimed at contracting demand – a completely inappropriate response since price rises were triggered by the external oil shock.

Economic reactions

High oil prices boosted the incomes of net oil producing economies at the expense of consumer states. Since countries measured their incomes in different currencies, redistribution created an international transfer problem. An oil-importing country was not only obliged to give up consuming some other goods and services in order to pay more to oil producers, but it had to pay in foreign currency – dollars. The demand for more foreign currency tended to drive down the exchange rate,

making all imports more expensive and exports cheaper, at least relative to the goods of oil-exporting countries. This balance of payments adjustment to the oil price increases varied in magnitude between countries, not only in relation to the scale of their reliance on imported oil but also in relation to their ability to borrow. Those oil importers with highly developed capital markets, notably Britain and the United States, were destinations for unspent oil money from OPEC members with low "absorptive capacities". Saudi Arabia and Kuwait owned enormous oil deposits but their populations were small, and, unlike Iran or Iraq, they could not immediately spend all their new income on development programs or armaments. So they placed their surplus earnings on short-term deposit in major world financial centers. The capital inflow to London and New York eased or deferred British and American balance of payments adjustment to the higher oil prices.

The switch in expenditure to pay for imports was not generally fully compensated by an increase in demand for exports by the OPEC countries. But the appropriate Western government response, a fiscal policy designed to encourage expansion and maintain output and employment, was not adopted. Western leaders were more worried about inflation than unemployment and so were willing to lose jobs in order to hold down price rises. They failed to realize that inflation in 1974–75 was not driven by too much domestic spending but by rising import costs.

Less developed countries with poor credit ratings were less able to ease the adjustment process by borrowing. Though they needed little oil

▲ Those political leaders in the strongest position to influence oil prices walked a tightrope. The Emir of Qatar was a traditional Arab ruler whose small state happened to possess vast oil deposits. Although such leaders themselves had little interest in alienating the Western world with oil embargoes and high oil prices, the joint threats of Arab socialism in other countries and of the Arab–Israeli wars pressed them into cutting back their oil production.

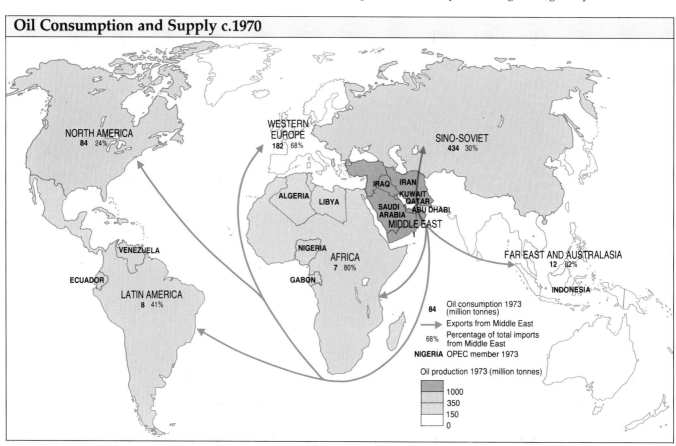

Oil Consumption and Supply c.1970

NORTH AMERICA
84 24%

WESTERN EUROPE
182 68%

SINO-SOVIET
434 30%

IRAQ IRAN
ALGERIA LIBYA KUWAIT
QATAR
SAUDI ABU DHABI
ARABIA
MIDDLE EAST
1

VENEZUELA

NIGERIA
AFRICA
7 80%

GABON

FAR EAST AND AUSTRALASIA
12 82%

ECUADOR

LATIN AMERICA
8 41%

INDONESIA

84 Oil consumption 1973 (million tonnes)
→ Exports from Middle East
68% Percentage of total imports from Middle East
NIGERIA OPEC member 1973

Oil production 1973 (million tonnes)
1000
350
150
0

Cartels and Commodity Prices

◀ Jamaican bauxite was mined by Western multinationals.

Various other commodity-producing countries tried to band together to emulate OPEC's success, with different results. Six American banana-exporting countries (Colombia, Costa Rica, the Dominican Republic, Guatemala, Honduras and Panama) formed the Union of Banana Exporting Countries in March 1974. An export tax percent on 42 percent of world banana exports, applied by four members of the group, was intended to raise prices. The banana companies reacted strongly. United Brands in Panama began a boycott and Standard Fruit of Honduras stopped buying and exporting from their plantations. In consequence, Panama, Honduras and Costa Rica had to reduce their tax percent by 70–75 percent.

Phosphate suppliers were more successful. Moroccan phosphate rock exporters raised their prices by over 400 percent in 1974. Four other members of the Institute of Phosphates (Algeria, Senegal, Togo and Tunisia) followed, as did the phosphate and phosphoric acid export cartels of the United States. Higher prices encouraged increased supply and reduced demand, however, and Moroccan and American prices fell back dramatically within four years.

Assertion of host-country power over copper resources began at much the same time as with oil. In 1966–67 the Intergovernmental Council of Copper Exporting Countries (CIPEC) had been formed by Chile, Peru, Zaire and Zambia. Five years later all the members except Peru had nationalized all or some of their mines, formerly owned by multinational companies. CIPEC gained confidence in 1972 when American copper companies attempting to block copper sales from nationalized Chilean mines were met by a CIPEC agreement not to provide an alternative supply of copper. Unlike OPEC, CIPEC members produced only just over a third of world output in 1976, although they provided over two-thirds of world exports. On the other hand, poor copper exporters like Zaire, Zambia, and Papua New Guinea relied on copper for 50–95 percent of their export earnings. Nonetheless CIPEC agreed first a 10 percent cut in exports and then a 15 percent reduction in production, though this was not strictly adhered to by members. The cartel was formally abandoned in 1976.

◀ Arab economic and political power in 1973 was based on substantial control of world oil supplies. Exports from the Middle East dominated Western European, Soviet, Chinese, African, Far Eastern and Australasian oil imports. Some of these areas, in particular the Soviet Union, were major oil producers and their oil imports were small. But most were entirely dependent on imports for their oil supplies. Any disruption to those supplies was a real threat to their transport systems.

compared with the industrialized countries, their transport systems had become dependent on oil imports and they were far less able to meet the higher prices. Compared with the maximum of $1–2 a barrel which the oil companies had taken before 1973, the payments now required by OPEC were enormously exploitative, amounting to $10 or more on production costs of 10 to 30 cents. Certain Middle Eastern producers aimed to cushion price rises for selected Muslim countries, and special facilities were made available by Venezuela and Mexico to Central American countries. But for some states the only way out appeared to be the replication of OPEC's coup in other commodities, and various other groupings were formed. The closest approach to another OPEC was the International Bauxite Association. Jamaica led the way in March 1974 by establishing that bauxite revenues should be linked to

aluminum prices. Jamaica's revenue jumped by almost seven times. All the other Caribbean producers and Guinea followed suit; only Australia among the principal bauxite suppliers remained aloof.

In general, such policies did not work very effectively because there were too many suppliers and their interests were too diverse. If they managed to agree to restrict output so as to allow prices to rise, it was always in the financial interests of individual countries to renege on the agreement and supply more of the commodity at the now higher price. If all the signatories did so, then the price would fall back to that of the free market. OPEC's unusual solidarity stemmed from the links of a common religion among the principal suppliers and a shared antipathy to Israel, together with leadership by the country most abundant in oil, Saudi Arabia.

▲ Among the larger industrial countries, Britain was unique in having achieved self-sufficiency in oil at the beginning of the 1980s. This position was established by people such as these welders shown at work on the link between two sections of BP's 175km (110-mile) pipeline from the Forties field to Cruden Bay. They are welding from a barge out in the North Sea.

▼ Believing that the economy could not develop solely on the basis of oil exports, Saudi Arabia embarked upon a massive development program intended not only to build oil refineries but other "downstream industries": those relying on oil or cheap energy. The Al Jubail industrial zone exemplified this strategy. Petromin, a Saudi Arabian government agency, and Shell were jointly engaged in the operation.

The response to OPEC

However, even that solidarity was not sufficient to maintain high oil prices for ever. First, recession in the West reduced oil demand; then efforts to economize on oil consumption, either by substituting other fuels or by employing more energy-efficient techniques, became effective. Coal and nuclear power provided alternative primary sources of energy that generated an increasing proportion of electricity during the 1970s. Cars were demanded and produced with smaller, more economical engines, providing a further opportunity for Japanese imports to the United States. General speed limits were introduced to save petrol, and incidentally saved lives. Non-OPEC sources of oil began to expand. The most dramatic development was in the North Sea, where high oil prices and new technology made possible the extraction of so much oil from under the sea that by the beginning of the 1980s Britain was self-sufficient in oil.

In an attempt to avoid a repetition of the events of 1973–74, 16 states formed the International Energy Agency (IEA) toward the end of 1974. The organization was intended to supervise a system for sharing oil in future emergencies and to reduce the likelihood of such emergencies by encouraging greater self-sufficiency in oil production. In return for sharing the oil of oil-producing member nations – the United States, Canada and the United Kingdom – during emergencies, non-oil-producers accepted in 1976 a minimum selling price of $7 a barrel to protect their investment in new high-cost oil sources.

None of these responses convinced the world that the oil problem had been solved. In 1978 Paul Erdman published his novel *The Crash of '79*, predicting a major war originating in the Middle East, precipitated by the Shah of Iran and the struggle for oil. Fiction proved more accurate than many less entertaining forecasts, for 1979 marked the onset of the second oil crisis, initiated by the overthrow of the Shah of Iran and the disruption of Iranian oil supplies. Oil prices doubled even though the world oil shortfall never exceeded four percent and OPEC production for the year at

tained a new peak. During the first crisis, oil companies had rationed oil supplies and so limited the price consequence of the scramble for oil. By the second crisis they controlled only about one-half of the oil in international trade and could not be so effective. The United States only ceased stockpiling oil in March 1979 and could not access the stocks subsequently because pumps had not been installed. The IEA's emergency sharing system was not activated, despite a Swedish request that it should be, on the dubious grounds that activation might increase the panic. A second opportunity for the IEA to prove itself arose in September 1980, when fighting broke out between Iran and Iraq. By early November oil exports from the two countries ceased, reducing world supplies by slightly more than in the 1979 crisis. Yet oil prices rose from $31 to $40, falling back to $35.5 by the end of the year. Markets were calmer because Saudi Arabia increased production, and the IEA encouraged members to decrease their stocks rather than add to them.

Using oil revenues

OPEC revenues increased to a maximum of $287 billion in 1980, but the new round of price increases stimulated further reductions in demand. OECD countries cut their demand for OPEC oil by 20 percent between 1979 and 1985. By this last date OPEC was supplying as little as 40 percent of the non–Communist world demand for oil, which yielded revenues of only $132 billion. The following year the price of oil fell by almost 70 percent in six months. By 1988 revenues were around $90 billion. Anxious to reduce the economy's dependence on oil, Saudi Arabia had embarked upon massive investment in new industries, such as chemicals, in some of which there was already world excess capacity. As a geographically large country with a small population and a traditional monarch, bordering on populous states with radical governments, Saudi Arabia also felt obliged to acquire the most

sophisticated defense equipment possible. So long as oil prices held up, oil revenues allowed the Saudi government to finance these plans. When oil prices fell again in 1986, Saudi domestic economic strategy became untenable. Saudi Arabia's willingness to adjust its own oil supply in order to maintain agreed prices gradually evaporated as budgetary stringency increased. With the collapse of this pillar of OPEC, the prospect of the cartel wielding market power almost disappeared.

As an oil exporter, the Soviet Union should have benefited from the rise in prices, but the delicate relationship with its oil markets in Eastern Europe made this problematic. The Soviet Union was subsidizing its buffer states by supplying oil at less than world prices. But poor performance by the Soviet and satellite economies made this subsidy an increasingly heavy burden.

▼ New sources of oil were sought and exploited, even in climates as inhospitable as Alaska's, where the oil pipes are covered in frozen snow and the oil-worker has to wear a face mask for protection against the extreme cold. Thanks to the construction of a 1300km (800-mile) oil pipeline, from Prudhoe Bay on the Arctic North Slope to Valdez harbor on the Pacific, Alaska became one of the richest places in the world.

Datafile

During the 1970s the Western world entered a new phase of development; inflation rose along with unemployment, growth of output and productivity slowed. By the end of the decade conservative policymakers were adopting tight monetary policies to deal with what they identified as the principal economic problem. Unemployment, it was increasingly believed, tended to settle at a "natural rate" which could not be shifted by demand management.

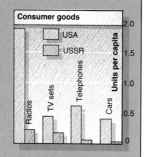

Consumer goods

USA
USSR

Radios
TV sets
Telephones
Cars

Units per capita

Inflation and unemployment

Inflation
Unemployment
Real GDP growth

Percent

1970 1975 1980 1985

◀ **Unemployment shot up as inflation began to decline in 1974. In 1979, unemployment rose sharply simultaneously with inflation, but continued rising long after inflation fell. The 1970s eroded the belief that governments could choose the level of spending that gave the desired balance of inflation and unemployment.**

▲ **One measure of economic performance is the ability to provide durable consumer goods. In this respect the Soviet Union showed itself far behind the United States in 1975. Radios, telephones and cars were in short supply. Only in television ownership did the Soviet Union remotely approach American levels.**

▶ **Inflation is generally an index of political, economic and social tensions. Sometimes these may be largely explained by war expenditures, as in Israel's case. The stability of the postwar settlement in West Germany can be judged by her low inflation rate, while British price increases may reflect the polarized social and economic structure.**

▼ **Unemployment was a waste of opportunity, both for the individual and for society. Sweden and Japan were successful in holding down unemployment rates during the 1970s and 1980s. So far as the official statistics may be believed, Italy was much less so. In almost all countries unemployment rose after 1973.**

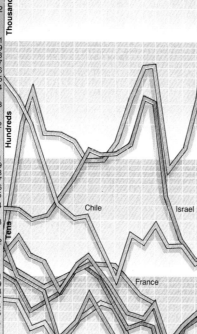

Inflation rates

Thousands
Hundreds
Tens
Percent

Argentina
Chile
Israel
France
UK
FRG
Japan
USA

1974 1976 1978 1980 1982 1984 1986 1988 1990

Unemployment rates

1973 1979 1985 1991

Percent

USA Italy UK France Sweden Japan FRG

Unemployment in the West rose in the 1970s and worsened further in the 1980s. Inflation also accelerated, contrary to what had become the accepted wisdom of the "Phillips curve", whereby it was believed that lower unemployment could be bought at the cost of higher inflation. After the first oil crisis a new term, "stagflation", was coined to account for the coexistence, previously thought impossible, of high inflation and high unemployment. The Keynesian doctrine that a government could spend its way out of a depression became discredited. Instead, monetarist ideas, which emphasized the existence of a "natural rate of unemployment", which could not be reduced by demand management without accelerating inflation, came to be accepted.

More than any other single figure, the American economist Milton Friedman was responsible for this change in attitudes. Friedman argued forcibly that the solution to unemployment did not lie in government policies which aimed to control inflation and unemployment through altering government expenditure and

CHECKS CASHED HERE

A NEW TECHNOLOGICAL REVOLUTION

taxes which had the effect of influencing demand for goods and services, but rather in "supply side" policies. These would remove "distortions" and "imperfections" in the labor market, such as minimum wage legislation and high ratios of unemployment benefit to wages.

The American recession of 1974–75 was allowed to take its course without any change in government policy to soften its impact. Monetary policy was tight, and fiscal policy was not used as a control mechanism. Unemployment averaged 8.5 percent in 1975 and remained above 7 percent in the following two years. Policy remained passive, primarily because inflation reached an unprecedented 12 percent in 1974. The entry of more teenagers into the labor force, a reflection of the high birth rates of the early 1960s, and their greater likelihood of experiencing spells of unemployment, account for some of the increase in the numbers of jobless. Nevertheless, the Humphrey-Hawkins Full Employment and Balanced Growth Act passed under the Carter administration in 1978, which enshrined in legislation the earlier target of four percent unemploy-

▼ ▶ **Recession in the West was induced by tight monetary policies. Former car-workers in Detroit queued to cash their unemployment cheques. A more attractive form of support was a public sector job. In Chicago thousands of people crammed the staircases of the Civil Service Commission to apply for such posts.**

ment, was clearly ambitious in aiming to achieve its goal by 1983 or even 1985.

As recession deepened, the typical pattern everywhere was for the numbers of those losing their jobs to increase, while those finding work continued to do so at the same rate as before. The average period of unemployment therefore lengthened. Those joining the unemployment register were likely to be young, unmarried people who had formerly held semi-skilled or unskilled manual jobs with earnings below the national average. In the United States, about forty percent of all teenage unemployment was accounted for by new entrants to the labor force. In Britain, the situation was particularly bad: by 1982 more than half the unemployed had been without work for six months. In the United States and most other countries, the duration of the unemployment was less serious, though very high levels of longterm unemployment were also found in Belgium, Italy and France. In Italy, youth unemployment was particularly high, and Spain and Ireland too suffered especially high unemployment levels.

One of the effects of recession and tight fiscal policies, which kept down wages in the public sector, was an acceleration in the loss of talented people from state-financed areas, especially in medicine, teaching and research, as a growing percentage left for secure employment and well-paid jobs abroad, especially in the United States, or moved to other employment. For the continuing rise in inflation hit consumers' pockets hard as wages and salaries in the state sector failed to keep pace.

▲ Although the Soviet Union's system of central planning ensured full employment, Mikhail Gorbachev's introduction of freedom of discussion and expression, coupled with an increased reliance upon market forces, prompted a public response to Soviet economic problems that would have been quite impossible under earlier Soviet regimes, such as Siberian miners' strike for improved working conditions and accommodation in 1989.

▶ Even in rich countries poverty was not hard to find. The accommodation of these squatters on Venice Beach in the United States contrasts starkly with the high-rise apartments in the background. Rapidly growing, competitive economies generated wealth, but not everybody shared the affluence. Disadvantaged individuals and groups found getting a foothold at the bottom of the social ladder difficult. Sliding down the scale was easy for many of those dogged by ill health, mental problems, addiction to alcohol or drugs, or for single-parent families. How the state social security system coped with such people varied from country to country. Controversy as to whether the benefits of such systems alleviated or perpetuated the poverty problem became intense during the 1970s.

Unemployment and social security systems

Among the reasons put forward for rising unemployment in the West was the form unemployment schemes took. These varied between countries and over time. For instance, in Italy and West Germany benefits were paid by the state; in the United States, employers paid all the cost of the benefit, according to their record of dismissing or laying off workers, so an employer with a good record paid a much lower tax.

Unemployment benefit not only prevented the incomes of the unemployed from falling too low, it was also intended to encourage them to be more selective in their search for work, in the hope that they would be well suited to the job they eventually took, which would improve productivity. But since unemployment benefit in the United States and Britain was around sixty to seventy percent of wages, critics of these allegedly high benefits maintained that, rather than encouraging a search for jobs, such high benefits encouraged idleness and stimulated further unemployment.

The British social security system was generally more comprehensive in providing for the unemployed than those of France or West Germany, but this did not mean that many of those receiving benefit in all three countries were not still very poor. In Belgium, France, West Germany and Italy social security support usually ceased after a given period whereas in Britain it was paid indefinitely. However, in these four

◄ In areas formerly dominated by heavy industry such as coal mining and steel, young people experienced considerable difficulty finding their first job. Traditional employers needed far fewer workers, especially in the recession after 1979. Instead of learning new skills on the job and acquiring work discipline, as they would have done a decade or two earlier, youngsters like these in Swansea, Wales, were inclined to fritter away their time in idleness, enjoying the sunshine whenever they could.

countries family benefits were paid on the basis of numbers of dependents, regardless of income, and tax rates continued to fall as income declined. In Britain, where family income was means tested so that as it increased, eligibility for benefits decreased and a "poverty trap" was the result. A formerly unemployed worker who took a job could find that the increased taxes he was obliged to pay and the benefits lost left him no better off than before.

It was no coincidence that Belgium and Britain experienced worse employment rates than elsewhere. Both countries paid a minimum flat rate benefit, which amounted to about sixty percent of earnings for the first year of unemployment. In 1981 a typical Belgian family with one-half of average earnings would have been 24 percent better off unemployed, and a similar British family would have been neither better nor worse off. France, Denmark and Italy, on the other hand, operated unemployment benefit/income ratio systems which ensured that there was no "unemployment trap", while Germany administered a hybrid system that created a trap only at very low incomes. In all social security systems there was some tension between the demands of economic efficiency, which required the abolition of poverty and unemployment traps, and the dictates of equity, which sought a minimum subsistence rate below which no one, employed or not, should be allowed to fall.

The Nordic bloc was much more successful at keeping down unemployment rates than other European countries: full employment was an important objective of state policy. Finland had the highest rate, of around seven percent in 1987. The rates of Norway and Sweden never exceeded 3.5 percent through the 1980s, and were rarely that high. The oil and gas industries developed in Norway helped, not only as employers but also, perhaps more importantly, in providing a tax yield which helped to fund state measures in

regard to unemployment. Sweden lacked this advantage, so it is even more impressive that the Swedish government helped in achieving the restructuring of the country's industry, and was very active in finding work for and in retraining the unemployed.

In Italy, unemployment benefit was paid as a proportion of lost pay, as in France, so the ratio of benefit to earnings could not reach the high levels of Belgium or Britain. On the other hand, the Italian unemployed might be required to subsist on a very low income indeed. Assessment is difficult, because Italy has a history of massive tax evasion, and the employers' social security contribution of 40.25 percent of wages, was so high as to be a positive encouragement not to pay. A former Italian finance minister has estimated that taxes amounting to seven percent of GDP and 25 percent of actual tax revenue were evaded at the beginning of the 1980s. The Italian black, or informal, economy is generally reckoned to be the largest in Europe, and contributes to enable people to survive, even though official statistics suggest severe impoverishment.

▼ Drug abuse was closely linked with both poverty and crime. Drugs appeared to offer an easier escape from poverty than the job market. Addicts often spent all their money on drugs, leaving nothing for food, clothing or shelter, and frequently turned to crime to pay for more. Their health tended to deteriorate quickly, even if they were not caught up in gang warfare over the supply of illegal drugs. Here a police drug squad in Washington DC picks up an unconscious youth at three o'clock in the morning.

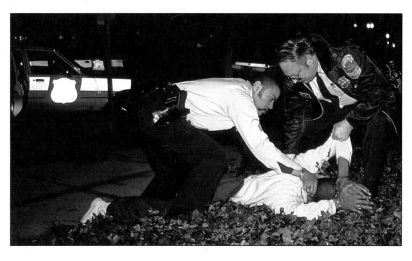

Black economies

Increasingly heavy taxation to support complex and comprehensive social security and defense systems gave rise in both East and West alike to expanding "informal" or "black" economies. In the West this manifested itself in the statistics as an increasing excess in the amount spent over the amount calculated from recorded (and therefore taxable) income as being available for spending. Originally the discrepancy was merely attributed to errors of measurement, but by the early 1980s the divergence had become too large for that explanation to be credible. Estimates for 1980 were that the alternative economy generated an output equal to 7.5 percent of GNP in Britain; in the United States the figure was ten percent, and the range of estimates for Italy was 15–40 percent. Although the institutions were different, black economies existed also in the Soviet Union and other Eastern bloc countries. That of the Soviet Union itself generated an output of perhaps ten percent of GDP. Soviet enterprise depended upon an army of illegal "fixers" to supply the resources necessary to fulfill plan targets, which were not available through official channels.

The performance of the Soviet economy

While the West suffered from increasing unemployment and inflation, the Soviet Union remained remarkably free of these ailments. Full employment was ensured by the centrally planned economy and the social waste of paying to support unemployed workers was avoided. Prices were fixed by planners on political criteria or on a cost-plus basis. Yet the Gorbachev reforms of 1987 onwards were based upon the Soviet view that their economy was inefficient and falling behind the West.

It is difficult to judge whether this view was correct, for comparison is not simple. One approach is to compute the amount of working time required to buy goods and services in different economies. With the exceptions of public transport and rent, all consumer goods needed more work in the Soviet Union than in West Germany or the United States in the 1970s and early 1980s.

► Since the first five-year plan, agriculture had been the weak spot of the Soviet economy, squeezed in order to release resources for heavy industry. Farm collectivization had been Stalin's bloody and none too effective means of forcing more work from the peasants. This agricultural show held in the Economic Achievement Grounds, Moscow, was intended both as an encouragement to Soviet farmworkers and as a showpiece. Judged by the Soviet Union's need to import food, exhortation was little more effective than brutality. Farms were too big for adequate management control and their workers, lacking identification with the goals of the enterprise, and any effective incentives, were not interested in boosting productivity.

▼ "We shall fulfill the decisions of the Party Congress" announces the "new" Communist man. Two passers-by take no notice and nor did most of the Russian economy on the eve of Gorbachev's reforms. The centrally planned economy in which the planning bureau, Gosplan, decided what was to be produced, how much and in what quantities, was generally conceded to have failed. Exhortation did not work. People wanted cash incentives and material rewards if they were to exert themselves, but these remained in short supply. On the other hand, unemployment was concealed by overmanning and underproducing.

In 1977 the average amount of house space per person was only 12 square meters, and ownership of consumer durables in the mid-1970s showed the Soviet Union well behind most European countries and the United States. On the other hand, social benefits such as pensions and the guaranteed minimum wage were fairly generous. There were more doctors per head of the population than in the United States or West Germany, and medical care was provided free by the state. Whereas a low-income British family spent 27 percent of that income on housing, fuel and power, a similar Soviet family needed to spend only 5 percent of their income on these items. Life expectancy in 1980 was comparable with that of the United States and Britain, at 70 years old as against 71 and 72 respectively.

The major problem for the Soviet economy was undoubtedly a heavy commitment to defense expenditure. Western estimates of Soviet defense spending in 1982, for example, ranged from 10 to 20 percent of GNP compared with 9.3 percent in 1968. At that earlier date the United States had been spending a similar proportion of a much higher income, but this was reduced to 7.2 percent in 1982. French defense expenditure remained steady at about four percent of GNP at both dates. Military demands on the Soviet economy always took priority over civilian needs and probably exacerbated materials shortages and production bottlenecks. Expenditure for military purposes neither made civilians better off nor enhanced the productive potential of the economy. As weaponry became more technologically sophisticated, an increasing proportion of GNP had to be devoted to defense, if the American effort was to be matched. But the Soviet planning system was increasingly unable to deliver. Hence Gorbachev's "second revolution" – a willingness to reform economic organization (*perestroika*), and in greater openness in the Soviet Union (*glasnost*). Gorbachev's 1987 law on state enterprises was intended to release production units from the clutches of state planners and allow some market

price setting. Seventy large factories were granted the right to trade abroad directly, joint ventures with Western companies were encouraged and cooperatives were allowed. But against the entrenched resistance of Soviet ministers and planing bureaux and against a deep distrust of profits, these reforms made little headway in the first few years, shortages of consumer goods continued and unrest began to mount.

Technological change: the Swedish experience
At the shop floor level, the same new technology that gave advanced Western economies the edge over the Soviet Union was often seen as a major cause of unemployment. Western workers were traditionally inclined to restrict the introduction of the latest techniques if they were able, and expected their trade unions to resist such aims. Economies that continued to grow in the long term either found means of allaying workers' fears or of rendering labor powerless. Sweden chose the first route. The country's centralized industrial relations system, established in 1938, had given Sweden a long period of industrial tranquility. The climate began to alter at the beginning of the 1970s. Technological change, especially computerization, began to give rise to industrial unrest. Information technology penetrated the Swedish economy early on. Sweden quickly developed process control systems, industrial robots, air traffic control systems and computerized office equipment. In the early 1980s computer-aided design and manufacturing systems spread rapidly. Engineering employed nearly half the country's industrial workforce and therefore these changes radically affected work patterns. A legislative reaction began in the early 1970s covering security of employment, the status of shop stewards, the right to board representation, the work environment and industrial democracy. Minimum standards, such as the 1981 regulations on working with VDUs, were laid down.

РЕШЕНИЯ СЪЕЗДА ПАРТИИ ВЫПОЛНИМ!

Sweden's high standard of living and sustained economic growth showed that these measures had been successful in maintaining industrial cooperation while absorbing new technology in the 1970s and the 1980s. Yet by the end of the second decade, large companies like Volvo and Saab were experiencing considerable absenteeism. Their work was not fulfilling and the sense of social obligation or discipline was starting to weaken.

The diffusion and impact of new technology

Although the fundamental breakthrough had been made in the late 1940s and early 1950s, the general public only became aware of microelectronics in the 1970s. The greatest potential lay in communications – in satellites and miniature television cameras and in improving the working of the telephone. But, as it turned out, microelectronics spread faster outside telecommunications, because it was not clear if there really was the demand for improved quality at a higher price. Even teletext and electronic mail, which welded together the techniques of computers and telecommunications, failed to penetrate Western markets as rapidly as had been predicted. Only in France, where the state decided that every household should have a Minitel terminal, did teletext gain much ground outside specialist uses, though it came to be widely used for airline booking in the 1980s.

Independent microelectronic and computer applications showed the most rapid progress. Pocket calculators came into existence using American chips, but in 1971 Japan imported American chips and captured 85 percent of the American calculator market by exporting them back within low-cost calculators. Prices eventually fell so low that calculators became almost throwaway toys, whereas in the 1930s a mechanical calculator had cost as much as two family cars. Digital watches were almost as spectacular and visible a sign of microelectronics but of little fundamental significance for the economy, despite the reduction in watch prices. Of greater significance was the rise of the microcomputer industry. With the falling prices and increasing sophistication of the mass-produced silicon chip, "micros" – computers that could sit on a desktop and needed no attachment with a larger processing unit – could perform many of the tasks of far more expensive mainframe computers. Often built by small companies at low cost, many of them taking advantage of innovations drawn from research and development done by the large computer firms, the rise of the micro bit heavily into the market of the established computer companies. One strategy adopted by the larger companies – among whom IBM remained pre-eminent – was to concentrate on mainframe computers and largescale business installations, but the need to provide industry standards in the fast-moving world of micros meant that IBM, at least, retained its central role, if not its domination, in this field too.

Microelectronics spread into the motor car industry far more slowly than in other areas since manufacturers at first resisted on grounds of

increased complexity. Only one percent of American Fords contained a microprocessor in 1978. Even so, a small penetration of a large market was worth a great deal. In American motor car production in 1980, the share of semiconductors was valued at $255 million.

The effects of microelectronics on employment were much debated from the mid-1970s. It was feared that mainframe computers would displace clerical labor, but in fact computers generated at least as many new jobs as they destroyed. They required an entirely new production capacity, and created new jobs in retailing, training and providing technical support, as well as creating many jobs in building software, both for mass-market purposes and for specialized tasks suited to individual customers. In general it was the same with the later word processors; there was little evidence of secretarial unemployment. The manufacture and maintenance of telephone exchanges were an exception to this generalization.

Even slower was the development of biotechnology. Biotechnology is a collection of techniques of which the most important is genetic engineering. Originating in Crick and Watson's working out of the structure of DNA in 1953, it was not until the early 1970s that gene transfers were carried out. Biotechnological techniques allow genes from one organism to be inserted into another. Human genes could be introduced into animals whose reactions then provided human growth hormones or other products like Factor VIII, which brought a revolutionary change in the treatment of hemophilia. Around six hundred biotechnology firms started up in the first 15 years after gene transfers became possible, most of them in the United States. The first patent granted for a biotechnology product was for a microbe which could digest crude oil. The first commercial drug, a form of human insulin, was produced at the end of the 1970s. The full impact of biotechnology was only just beginning to be felt in the late 1980s.

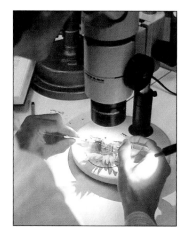

INSTANT INFORMATION

Telegraph and telephone provided instant information over any distance even in 1900, and to these was added radio, effective by 1914. Gone were the days when a fortune could be made by the possessor of a carrier pigeon who knew of the outcome of a battle before anyone else.

The telecommunication explosion of the late 20th century had at least three major aspects: the much increased quantity of information instantaneously available, on monitors and printouts; the enlarged numbers of people able to receive information broadcast on television; and the instant retrieval possibility of stored information. The number of "words supplied" in this way rose by 8 percent a year in the United States in 1960–80, and by almost 10 percent in Japan in 1960–75. By that time, one half of the economic activity of the United States was concerned with the processing of knowledge.

Inasmuch as the economic problem is the problem of uncertainty, the provision of instant information was a key factor. Since costs of knowledge do not vary with size, large firms derived greater advantage from the information revolution than smaller, and so did multinational concerns which, in turn, contributed materially to the international flow of information. For many purposes, the economic distance between countries depended increasingly on the quality and availability of their electronic links rather than on geographic proximity.

Instant information has had some dangerous effects, above all in the case of stock exchanges. These have now become highly volatile, thanks to computer-programmed selling which tends to accelerate price falls. This danger has had to be counteracted by an electronic "cutout", to stop transactions in New York when the fall in the Dow-Jones average (the prime indicator of stock prices) exceeds 400 points. Yet, in a typical instance of instability caused by instant information, on 13 October 1989 a sudden fall on the New York exchange by 190 points, or about 7 percent, on the Dow index left the financial world in turmoil; this was a Friday and the westernmost exchange, so nothing could be done until Monday. Then Tokyo opened first, and fell only by 2 percent. Frankfurt, next to open reacted most sharply, partly because many small investors panicked, and partly because foreign holders preferred this market. This left Paris and Brussels in turmoil; but when dealings opened in London, the worst was over, and after a sharp early fall, the Financial Times share index closed only 70 points, or 3.5 percent down. By Tuesday, things were back to normal throughout the world.

▲ ▶ The teleprinter operator works a machine that was near the technological frontier in the 1930s. Though a great advance over the earlier telegraph tape, it yet seems almost antediluvian compared with the electronic devices available to the office worker of the 1970s and 1980s.

▶ Before the massed monitors in the Hong Kong stock exchange sit operators who are in communication with dealers inside and out. Their access to information allows fast – hence sometimes unpredictable – reactions based on data or VDU screens (inset above).

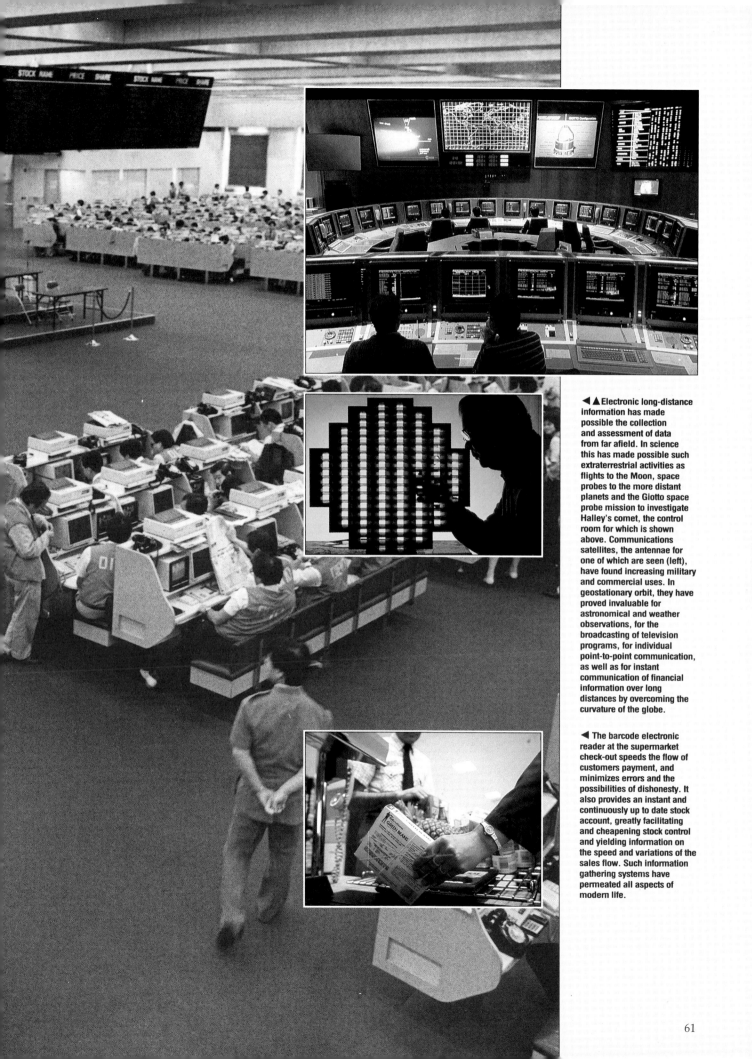

◀▲Electronic long-distance
information has made
possible the collection
and assessment of data
from far afield. In science
this has made possible such
extraterrestrial activities as
flights to the Moon, space
probes to the more distant
planets and the Giotto space
probe mission to investigate
Halley's comet, the control
room for which is shown
above. Communications
satellites, the antennae for
one of which are seen (left),
have found increasing military
and commercial uses. In
geostationary orbit, they have
proved invaluable for
astronomical and weather
observations, for the
broadcasting of television
programs, for individual
point-to-point communication,
as well as for instant
communication of financial
information over long
distances by overcoming the
curvature of the globe.

◀ The barcode electronic
reader at the supermarket
check-out speeds the flow of
customers payment, and
minimizes errors and the
possibilities of dishonesty. It
also provides an instant and
continuously up to date stock
account, greatly facilitating
and cheapening stock control
and yielding information on
the speed and variations of the
sales flow. Such information
gathering systems have
permeated all aspects of
modern life.

Datafile

Economic growth has it price. Given the high starting level after World War II, the growth of the world economy quickly led to serious pressure on the environment. In the developed world, this was caused mainly by the growth of consumption per head; in the less developed countries, it was caused by the unprecedented increase in population.

Many factors determine the point at which the environment is endangered. Population density is one factor, but soil, climate and the ability to trade also matter. Much of Africa is desert or semi-desert, which must be considered to be overpopulated. Many regions in Asia, too, were overpopulated.

Among the key issues in the debate over the environment were food and energy. Some areas which were traditional sources of food surpluses had now become dependent on imports, and that dependence increased. Energy consumption per head was much higher in the developed world; rising incomes elsewhere put even greater strains on the world's energy supplies.

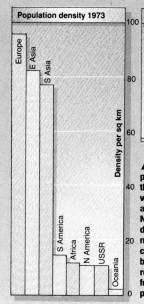

Population density 1973

Average crop yields 1975

- Developing countries
- USA
- World record yields

Maize, Wheat, Soy beans, Sorghum, Rice, Cassava

▲ A major problem for the poorer regions of the globe is the low agricultural yield for which inadequate techniques are partly responsible. Even North American farming did better with extensive methods. Intensive cultivation elsewhere has been able to achieve better results still, but it does not follow that such yields are possible everywhere.

▼ Total land surface is a poor guide to the agrarian possibilities of a region. The cultivable area may be only a fraction of the land surface. Intensive application of capital can make the desert bloom, and new strains can be developed to stand up to extreme conditions. The cultivable frontier is more flexible than is sometimes thought.

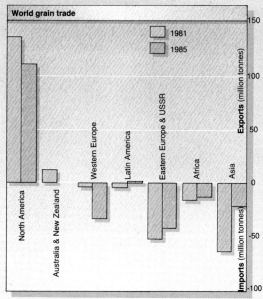

World grain trade

- 1981
- 1985

North America, Australia & New Zealand, Western Europe, Latin America, Eastern Europe & USSR, Africa, Asia

Exports (million tonnes)
Imports (million tonnes)

▲ Europe and Asia carry a much larger population per square kilometer than the other continents; parts of them are overpopulated on almost any definition. On the other hand, the low figures for Latin America, the Soviet Union and Africa are averages which hide large uninhabitable regions of desert, mountain or Arctic plain.

◄ North America, and to a small extent Australasia, are now the sole surplus grain regions. The formerly self-supporting or export regions in Eastern Europe and the Soviet Union are obliged to import increasing quantities. Elsewhere, rising population and stagnating technology have widened the gap between demand and supply.

◄ The developed market economies were able, after the oil price shock, to effect considerable savings in their energy consumption, mainly by the introduction of energy-saving techniques. The middle-income countries also did well. It was the poorest societies in which consumption continued to rise fastest, even on a per capita basis.

◄◄ A clear measure of the difference between advanced and less developed economies is their energy consumption per head. Climate may be partly responsible, but most energy is used in industry and transport. The high and rising consumption of the planned economies is due in part to inefficient use rather than to a high income.

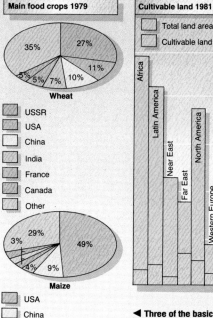

Main food crops 1979

Wheat
27%, 11%, 10%, 7%, 5%, 5%, 35%

- USSR
- USA
- China
- India
- France
- Canada
- Other

Maize
49%, 29%, 9%, 4%, 3%

- USA
- China
- Brazil
- Romania
- S Africa
- Argentina
- Other

Rice
35%, 29%, 16%, 7%, 5%, 4%, 4%

- China
- India
- Indonesia
- Bangladesh
- Thailand
- Japan
- Other

Cultivable land 1981

- Total land area
- Cultivable land

Africa, Latin America, Near East, Far East, North America, Western Europe, Eastern Europe & USSR, Oceania

Hectares (millions)

◄ Three of the basic food crops of the world are wheat, rice and maize (or sweet corn). Wheat is the main crop in the West, including the Soviet Union and North America, but it also grown extensively in China and other temperate regions. In Europe, its cultivation is labor and capital-intensive, and the area is self-supporting. Canada and the United States provide the export surpluses. Maize production is dominated by the United States, though China is another major grower. In the American economy, it is much used as animal feed in the meat-producing sector. Rice is the basic food of Eastern and Southern Asia. Its intensive production has kept pace with the huge population dependent on it.

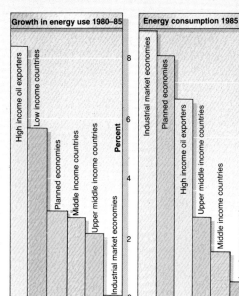

Growth in energy use 1980–85

High income oil exporters, Low income countries, Planned economies, Middle income countries, Upper middle income countries, Industrial market economies

Percent

Energy consumption 1985

Industrial market economies, Planned economies, High income oil exporters, Upper middle income countries, Middle income countries, Low income countries

Kg oil equivalent per capita (thousands)

THE RESOURCE CRISIS

The general feeling of depression and failure of this period was reinforced by the widespread emergence of fears about the environment and about economic resources on a worldwide scale. The dangers that began to exercise public opinion at this time were mostly of long standing, but had hitherto increased only slowly. Now their exponential growth took on alarming proportions in a number of fields simultaneously, and reinforced the pessimism engendered by economic stagnation and unemployment.

Possibly the most influential publication to catch the mood of the time was a volume entitled *The Limits of Growth* which appeared in 1972. Issued by the Club of Rome, a group of scientists and others called together and financed through the efforts of an Italian industrial consultant named Aurelio Peccei, it summarized in an apparently authoritative way virtually all the current fears about the depletion of resources and the pollution of the environment caused by unrestricted economic growth. An enormous flood of literature, both for and against, confirmed in the following years the widespread concern with the questions the book had raised.

Some developments affected mostly the richer, advanced countries, in which rising incomes caused the strain on environment and resources. Others were problems rather of the less developed or "developing" countries, in which the rapid increase in population gave most cause for concern. However, there were interconnections at many points.

The population explosion
The world's population was indeed growing at the unprecedented rate of 1.9 percent a year. It was not difficult to extrapolate this increase into the future with frightening results. Even assuming that the developing world would go through a "demographic revolution" of the same kind as the advanced countries, so that their falling death rates would be matched by falling birth rates, estimates of the figure at which the total world population would ultimately stabilize sometime in the 21st century ranged from 10.5 to 16.5 billion people – not "standing room only", as some were predicting, but serious enough. Most of this growth would take place among the poorer nations, since Europe, North America and Japan already had almost stationary populations. In some other areas, notably China and India, reductions in the birth rate that had been encouraged by government action were also beginning to have some effect. By 1980–85 world population growth had declined to 1.7 percent a year.

Even at that rate the world's population would double every 40 years, and this implied an un-

▼ "The explosive growth of the human population is the most significant terrestrial event of the past millennia." (P. R. and A. H. Ehrlich, *Population, Resources, Environment*).

precedented pressure on resources. This would be further aggravated by rising incomes as well as by rising urbanization. According to a United Nations forecast made in 1975, 81 percent of the inhabitants of the developed world would live in towns and cities by the year 2000, 41 percent in the developing world, and 50 per cent in the world as a whole; in cities of over 5 million inhabitants there would be 646 million people, of whom 464 millions would be in enormous conurbations in the developing world.

The problem of food supply
The rate of population growth brought the food problem to the fore. Much of the world's cultivable land, it was true, still lay fallow – estimates ranged to well over one-half – and productivity on many acres could still be raised by large amounts. Some estimates put the potential output at 20 times that achieved in the mid-1970s. Even

the United States, a country with plenty of land and a tendency towards extensive rather than intensive cultivation, recorded yields that were double and treble those of the developing world; results in the Far East, and peak performances elsewhere, promised even larger increases. But the necessary fertilizer, machines or drainage represented costs which farmers in the poorer countries could not as a rule afford, while the richer ones among them tended to invest their surplus outside agriculture. Governments, in their turn, frequently pursued perverse policies: they subsidized export cash crops, and kept food prices artificially low in the interest of the city populations, thus discouraging home food production. Food aid from abroad worked in the same direction. Moreover, the infrastructure, especially transport and technical expertise, was usually inadequate in the poorer countries.

In the 1970s and 1980s the developing nations as a whole only just managed to increase their output of food in line with the increase in population; in Africa output per head fell dramatically. Only in the industrialized market economies was output per head rising. These economies, hitherto the main providers of manufactures, were developing exportable food surpluses or sharply reducing their needs of imports of food, while the Third World and Eastern Europe, hitherto the suppliers of primary products, including food, were becoming importers of these commodities. Around 1960, about ten percent of the cereals consumed in Africa, Latin America and the Near East were imported. By the 1970s this had risen to 30 percent. The world still had enough, but the overall balance left unanswered the question of how the poorer countries in Eastern Europe and overseas were going to pay for food from the advanced regions of the world.

In 1979–81 it was estimated that about five hundred million people, including about a quarter of the population of Africa and Southern and Southeastern Asia, were suffering from malnutrition. On current performance, this would rise to one thousand million by the year 2000. In some areas, starvation was an acute problem already. In 1984 the world was shocked into immediate action by reports of starvation in Ethiopia, a catastrophe partly natural and partly artificial. In the Sahel region south of the Sahara, the desert was actually advancing. In the five years between 1968 and 1972 there were four years of drought, but the loss of fertility was made worse by human action. Formerly there had been a stable ecosystem, in which limited numbers of nomadic herdsmen had used the sparse vegetation on the edge of the desert, stocking up occasionally with food and

► Drought and the spreading desert have drastically reduced fertile land in Niger as in other parts of Africa in recent years. Climatic conditions may be to blame in part, but in many cases the calamity has been caused by human action, such as the disruption of traditional nomad patterns of pasturing. The countries concerned are too poor and technically too ill-equipped to deal effectively with the environmental disasters that have affected them. They have to be helped by aid from abroad.

The Spreading Deserts

The conversion of fertile land into desert happens in rich countries: the American "dustbowl" of the 1930s ruined many farmers. But in the 1970s and 1980s, deserts were made or grew larger mainly in poor countries, above all in Africa. Apart from climatic change, it was mainly the result of population increase and new technology. Overcropping and the reduction of fallow periods exhausted the topsoil. Rain might then wash it away. On pasture and shrubland, overgrazing and the collection of wood had similar effects. Elsewhere, the sinking of modern wells lowered the water table. Thus the desert advanced in North Africa, in Saharan Africa and in the southern part of the continent.

Famine in Africa drew the attention of the world to the problem. A conference on desertification in 1977 came down in favour of numerous projects designed to reverse the advance of the desert, on the basis of knowledge gained in the West, in the Soviet Union and in China. But by 1984, the United Nations Environmental Program (UNEP) reported that none of these had yet been realized. Some $10 billion had been spent in 1978–83, but almost all of it on infrastructure and preparation, virtually nothing on the desert itself.

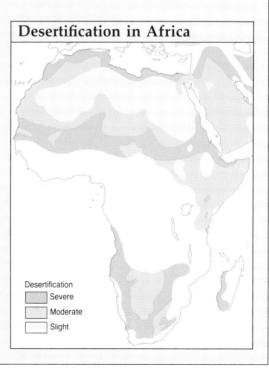

Desertification in Africa

Desertification
- Severe
- Moderate
- Slight

► Tigrayans from their famine-stricken province of Ethiopia journeyed on foot, carrying their meager possessions, over the mountains to the refugee camps in the Sudan. For those coming from the eastern region the journey took six weeks. Civil war has raged for many years in the area and has aggravated the problem.

In the course of 1985, millions of African children are likely to die of hunger-related causes. The immediate urgency of saving these children and their families tends to obscure the fact that the survivors of this crisis will inherit a massively degraded environment, barely capable of supporting them without extensive rehabilitation.

INDEPENDENT COMMISSION ON INTERNATIONAL HUMANITARIAN ISSUES, 1984

grazing among the settled farmers further south, whom they also supplied with manure from their animals, and with traded goods. This had been disturbed at both ends when the settled farmers were persuaded to turn to exportable cash crops, and the herdsmen had wells provided which allowed them to increase the numbers of animals beyond the capacity of the grazing lands. For both, the problems were aggravated during later drought years; the output of both groups was cut by half, and the region became a disaster area. By 1984, $14 billion had been committed in aid to eight Sahel countries – $44 a head per annum, equivalent to 17 per cent of these countries' GNP – but no effective method had been found to stop the desertification.

Energy

Next to food, it was energy that was pinpointed as a source of alarm because of the continuing growth of demand. One immediate cause of concern was the oil crisis of 1973–77 itself, but there had been repeated phases of fear over energy supplies, in particular the limited supplies of coal, since the 19th century. Here, though, there was a double potential threat: the exhaustion of supplies, in particular of oil, and the increase of pollution by the emission of carbon dioxide into the air, especially from motor cars, and by the heating up of the streams of water used as coolants for power stations.

Growing populations and their rising incomes did indeed cause the consumption of energy to rise. In 1980, the United States used around ten tonnes of coal equivalent per head a year, the rest of the advanced world around five tonnes, and the developing countries a quarter of a tonne. Yet technical progress also meant a saving in energy consumption: between 1950 and 1978, the consumption of energy per unit of real income had

Alternative Energy

Following the second oil crisis of 1979, efforts to find alternative sources of energy in the advanced countries were stepped up. In spite of the considerable savings in oil consumption in the years 1979–82, and falling relative prices, the momentum continued into the later 1980s. To supplement the traditional sources of water power, mineral fuels, peat, wood and nuclear power, the newly pursued alternatives included the direct conversion of solar power, the biomass, geothermal energy and extracting heat from the oceans, and the use of tidal energy, as well as the return to traditional wind power. Many of these involve enormous capital schemes. Research and development on renewable energy has therefore been largely undertaken by governments or with government support, to the tune of some 7 billion US dollars among the 21 member countries of the International Energy Agency in 1977–85 inclusive. Governments also provided subsidies, tax concessions, cheap loans and other incentives.

Direct solar energy, for example for water and space heating, is by now competitive in price in many countries, and its use is expanding. Wind power has proved viable, though only for small units. The biomass, in two forms (waste products, or crops specially grown), is used increasingly either by burning or by conversion into liquid or gaseous fuels. Sugar and maize have been most widely converted. The EEC sugar surplus could provide 2 percent of the countries' petrol needs, and there is a large potential in other crop surpluses, as well as in specially planted crops.

Among largescale schemes are tidal projects in Britain and France. Extracting energy from the oceans or from deeper strata of the Earth will require a great deal of further costly research, but may ultimately prove highly competitive.

◀ Solar power allows villages in Niger to receive television programs. A novel technology for using renewable energy sources is coupled with the most up-to-date electronic technology: the programs, which are broadcast from Niger's state-run television monopoly, are bounced off a satellite. As well as transmitting entertainment, the service is also used for educational programs.

◀▼ Wind-powered electricity generators in California are an example of alternative energy provision in the most advanced industrial countries. In poor countries without coal or oil but blessed with abundant sunshine, such developments offer hope for a breakthrough requiring relatively little sophisticated technology and relatively modest investments of capital.

fallen by 60 percent in the United States and Great Britain. Further, after the oil crisis of 1973–74, its consumption had been curbed very effectively in the advanced market economies, if not in the rest of the world.

The panic over supply was relatively short-lived. Even for oil, the energy source most likely to be exhausted first, the reserves measured in years increased rather than diminished with the passage of time, as rising prices and better technology led to new discoveries. Equally, as the price of oil went up, the exploitation of difficult and marginal sources became more viable. Similarly the estimated reserves of other mineral fuels also went up. Including shale oil, they quickly rose from 102 years to 500 years, not counting nuclear, tidal, solar, wind or other possible alternatives.

Similar revisions were also possible for the estimated reserves of other minerals. Some, like iron or aluminum, were found to exist in practically unlimited quantities; known reserves of others also tended to increase as time passed, through new finds and improved techniques of exploitation, recovery and recycling.

At the same time, some of the newly discovered supplies might need more costly or energy-intensive methods of refining before they entered the market. Optimism about their viability is based on the hope of continuing technical progress. Thus by 1970 the price of coal in the United States had fallen to almost one-fifth of its 1900 level in relation to real wages, that of iron to one-sixth, of copper to one-eighth, and of aluminum to one-thirtieth. Repeated attempts to create world monopolies in metals, like the government-sponsored tin agreement of 1975, seemed to be doomed to failure.

Environmental dangers

Yet the fact that the prophets of doom had so far proved wrong gave no grounds for complacency. At some point, a worldwide catastrophe might prove to be sudden or cumulative and irreversible, and mankind could not afford even one such miscalculation. At least three possible causes of catastrophe were discerned. One was the cutting down of tropical rain forests, particularly in Brazil, West Africa and Borneo: this might fatally interrupt the recycling of the world's oxygen, contributing to the second danger, the accumulation of carbon dioxide in the atmosphere to a point at which not enough heat was reflected outward from the earth, when a "greenhouse effect" would begin to heat up the earth's surface, melting the polar ice-caps. A third danger was damage to the ozone layer, especially that caused by certain ingredients in aerosol sprays. Action to curb this damage began to be taken in the late 1980s. Dealing with the greenhouse effect would require international action on a hitherto unprecedented scale, and there were some signs of agreement

between advanced nations on the need for this. As for the first, strict measures would have to be applied to governments which had hitherto been unable to enforce their environmental decrees, even had they wished to do so.

Other, less dramatic, forms of damage were also being brought home to the populations of the industrialized countries. They were largely responsible for the increased awareness of the dangers, and for rising demands for action. The threat to European forests from "acid rain" – acid pollution of the air, and consequently of the water cycle, by chemicals like nitrogen dioxide or sulfur dioxide – began to be noticed in the 1970s. Nitrogenous fertilizers, washed down the rivers, led to the eutrophication of lakes in North America and of large parts of the Baltic, through a complex chain in which oxygen shortage in the water ultimately killed off the fish population. Heavy metals also killed fish around the Japanese coastline and in North America. Rivers and coasts were polluted by the effluvia from the cities and from industry, and ever more European beaches

▼ Tashkent Heliostation illustrates the Soviet Union's interest in developing renewable sources of energy which do not harm the Earth's budget. Some of the southern republics enjoy climatic conditions which make the production of solar energy feasible even at the present state of technology. The efforts that have gone into solar energy research in the Soviet Union, as in the West, do not yet compare with the resources lavished on research on conventional and nuclear energy sources. However, there are indications that both East and West have been induced by signs of environmental damage, particularly the greenhouse effect, to increase their efforts in this direction.

became unfit for bathing. Elsewhere, dams altered the flow of rivers, their scouring action or the deposits they brought with them, In the 1970s, 700 dams a year were being built. Meanwhile, the world's water consumption had risen eightfold between 1900 and the early 1980s, and was estimated to be set to double again by the year 2000. In many areas, the water table was falling to dangerous levels.

Manmade disasters

Occasional disaster lit up a whole scene. One such was the Seveso accident in Italy in 1976, when the chemical TCDD (tetrachloridbenzoparadioxin) escaped from a factory, poisoning a large surrounding area and injuring numerous people. In 1984, escaping poison gas from an insecticide plant of the Union Carbide Company in Bhopal, India, killed over 2000 people. Another disaster was the explosion in a Soviet nuclear power station in Chernobyl in April 1986 which affected most of Europe. In the same year a fire at a chemical plant near Basle led to a massive pollution of the Rhine. These and other accidents in chemical firms led to the widespread allegation that it was unbridled profit-seeking that endangered humanity, but the danger was no less in noncapitalist economies. There the drive for maximum production at all costs was, if anything, even stronger than in the West. Also, the tradition of citizen initiative was lacking, while bureaucratic power was greater, especially

◀ Coal-fired power stations pollute the atmosphere and contribute very largely to acid rain, which has destroyed large areas of temperate and northern woodlands. Demonstrators in front of the Buschhaus power station in Germany, where damage to forests has assumed large proportions. express a widespread feeling of unease. Installations to reduce the chemical emission from conventional electricity works are expensive to install, but nuclear power stations, an obvious alternative, attract even more protest. Until solar energy becomes more widely available, alternatives are not easy to find.

▼ Effluent pollution in the Rio Martino National Park near Rome shows that progress to improve the environment is slow, even in European countries. Measures are taken more often to cure existing problems than in an effort to seek to prevent pollution occurring in the first place, and the cure is rarely sufficient. Pan-European measures on a cleaner water supply are being adopted, but will take some years to be put into effect.

Industrial Pollution

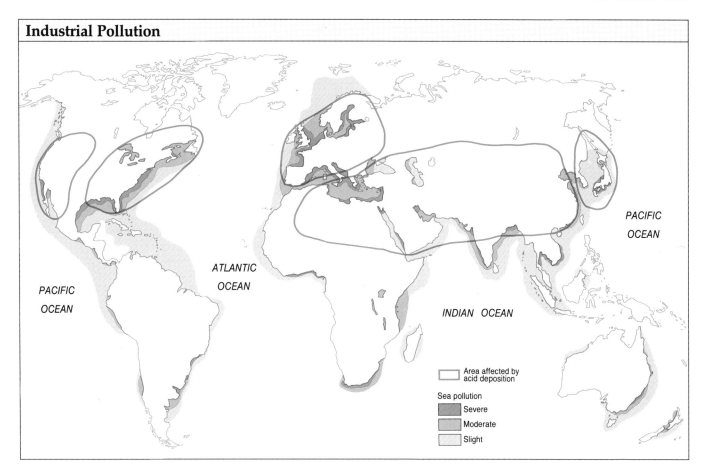

Area affected by
acid deposition

Sea pollution

Severe

Moderate

Slight

▲ Acid rain is a product of industrial civilization. Its main causes are the emissions from power stations using mineral fuels, from road vehicles, factories and domestic consumers. The worst concentrations are therefore found in the advanced countries, and especially in those not wealthy enough to afford corrective measures. They do not necessarily affect the exact spots in which the pollution occurs, since it is often carried elsewhere by the prevailing winds. In parts of Central Europe, up to one-half of the woodlands are affected.

► Checking radiation levels in the Chernobyl region. On 26 April 1986 one of the four reactors at the Chernobyl nuclear power station in the then Soviet Republic of Ukraine suffered a meltdown, following loss of fission control. Large amounts of radioactive material were deposited in the region around the power station itself and across Europe, producing the most serious threat to health arising from nuclear power in Europe to date. In the Soviet Union the accident was expected in the long run to produce thousands of cancer deaths. In the short run it strengthened demands for greater openness in public life – after the authorities at first attempted to keep the accident a secret.

if military production was involved. Moreover, Eastern Europe was as yet too poor to afford the costly resources necessary to protect the environment. Examples of environmental failure were the large-scale atomic poisoning at Cheliabinsk in 1958 which went officially unrecorded, massive soil erosion, the poisoning of Lake Baikal in the 1960s and 1970s by two cellulose plants, and, of course, Chernobyl itself. In the 1980s Upper Silesia and the Polish-Soviet Baltic coastlines were considered the most polluted regions of Europe.

The costs of containment

Given enough resources, most of these adverse effects could be contained. Britain's Clean Air Act of 1956 worked wonders in her cities, and the Thames was cleaned up sufficiently to carry fish again. The chemical DDT was prohibited in most countries by the 1970s. Some of the most destructive emissions from motor vehicles, it turned out, could be prevented by a catalyser, developed and applied first in the United States and introduced in the late 1980s also in Europe, though at different speeds in different countries and rarely compulsorily. Increasing numbers of cars were built to run on lead-free gasoline, and while in 1984 this was sold in only one percent of German filling stations, its use spread rapidly since it bore lower taxes and was therefore cheaper, by 1989 a filling station without it had become a rarity. Diesel engines emissions became limited in all European Community countries from October 1989. Finally, substantial reductions in the pollution of the atmosphere by sulfur dioxide from

power stations were agreed to by most Western European countries, with minimum reductions of 40 percent in 1993, 60 per cent in 1998 and 70 percent in 2003. New power stations were obliged to instal smoke-consuming apparatus.

Economists invented the notion of "Measure of Economic Welfare", MEW, in which pollution, congestion and other negatives were deducted from the usual measures of wealth and income, to symbolize the rationality of averting harm as well as of creating good. But the financial costs of counteracting the environmental threats often proved to rise exponentially, and could, in any case, not be afforded by the poorer countries.

Datafile

International economic relations are mainly those of trade and payments, to which, in recent years, has been added aid from richer to poorer nations. Trade, that is the delivery of goods and of the services associated with them, requires payments; if imports are not paid for, indebtedness results. The debt mountain of some countries arose because they absorbed imports without paying for them, or borrowed to finance imports.

Development aid 1980

Sweden, Netherlands, France, Australia, Belgium, FRG, UK, USA, Japan — GDP (percent) 0 to 1.0

Overall value of exports

Index (1980=100)

Developed countries

Developing countries

1975 · 1980 · 1985

▲ Development aid takes many forms. The totals for 1980 show that the smaller democratic countries of Europe have made greater efforts in this regard than the larger nations. From one point of view, the ratios seem small, especially when measured against the target of 3–4 percent of GNP of the donor country; but it is unique in world history.

▲ The 1970s saw a substantial rise in the price level of exports of the developing countries. This was largely due to the oil price increase which came in two big jumps, in 1973 and 1979. Since 1980–81 prices have fallen again, manufactured prices falling slightly faster than the food and raw materials exported by the developing countries.

▶ Between 1979 and 1987, there was a remarkable turnround in the developing, capital-importing countries. From deficit in 1979, there is a surplus even after debt charges.

Balance of trade
Net interest payments
Current account

Capital importing countries

US $ (billions)

1979 · 1987

Balance of payments

GNP (percent)

Japan

FRG

USA

1980 · 1982 · 1984 · 1986 · 1988 · 1990

◀ The three leading industrial market economies reversed their positions in the 1980s. The United States developed a large payments deficit, while Japan and Germany forged ahead. Both faltered by the end of the decade, however, and with the three leading economies all weakened, the world was plunged into recession.

▼ Some developing countries were growing so fast that they were moving out of that category into that of Newly Industrializing Countries (NIC).

Developing countries' annual growth rate 1973–89

GNP per cap. (percent)

Singapore, Hong Kong, Brazil, South Korea, Malaysia, Indonesia, Thailand, Sri Lanka, Pakistan, Tunisia, Yugoslavia, Bangladesh, India, Colombia, Philippines, Turkey, Mexico, Israel, Uruguay, Chile, Ethiopia, Sudan, Peru, Argentina, Nigeria, Bolivia, Ghana, El Salvador, Nicaragua

---

The Smithsonian agreement of December 1971, in which the major industrial countries (known as the "Group of Ten": the United States, Japan, Canada, Britain, France, West Germany, Italy, Belgium, The Netherlands and Sweden) had tried to stabilize the exchange rates of their currencies in relation to each other, proved only a temporary stopgap. By 1973, "managed floating" meant that central banks would, at best, try to minimize short-term erratic fluctuations of exchange rates, but that no longer-term stability could be expected. The dollar remained a kind of international reference point, but was itself subject to fluctuations.

Powerful forces made it hard to maintain stability. Large sums were flowing into the OPEC countries after the oil price rises of 1973–74 and 1979, and their recycling by the world's credit mechanism created problems, particularly for developing countries. The so-called Eurocurrency market, a mechanism for switching large short-term funds easily between major centers, added further sources of instability.

In this situation, the International Monetary Fund (IMF) resumed some of its original powers of evening out short-term fluctuations. Under the leadership of the "Group of Five" (the United States, Japan, West Germany, France and Great Britain), it strengthened the role of the dollar as the standard currency against which the others were measured. Gold, on the other hand, was reduced in significance, one-third of the IMF's gold holding being sold and part of the proceeds used to establish a Fund for the developing countries in 1976. In that year, the quota share of the OPEC countries within the IMF was increased, and the total of all quotas raised also. Further, the basis of the "special drawing rights" (SDRs), which had been created to enlarge the lending capacity of the IMF, was changed from gold to a basket of commodities in which the dollar predominated, but no new SDRs were created until 1979. In that year, as well as in 1980 and 1981, US$4 billion annually were added, bringing the total to $21.3 billion.

Towards a European Monetary System

Within Europe, a group of countries had agreed in 1972 to strive to keep their currencies more closely aligned with each other than the Smithsonian rules laid down, varying in effect by only 1.125 percent instead of 2.5 percent above or below par. In 1978 it was decided to strengthen that cooperation still further, and to move towards a full European Monetary System (EMS). Among the innovations were the creation of an European Currency Unit (ECU); an obligation on the central banks of countries achieving payments surpluses, as well as on those countries

INTERNATIONAL RELATIONS

in payments deficit, to take measures to preserve existing parities; and a European Monetary Fund to support the same objective. Though Britain refused to join, and Italy insisted on a wider "band" of six percent within which the lira could fluctuate, the EMS began its active life in March 1979. It had an uncertain start. Its relative exchange rates were changed seven times in four years before the major realignment of March 1983. The "stability" fostered by the EMS was at best relative. It did, nonetheless, provide useful experience for the closer monetary and economic cooperation planned for the future.

Expansionary policies in the United States
The dollar itself remained in a weak position, especially against the Japanese yen and the West German Deutschmark. Together with Switzerland, these countries collaborated with the United States to stabilize the dollar in 1978. Three years later, the United States struck out on its own

▼ The New York Stock Exchange is a highly sensitive indicator of events all over the world, sharp changes in share prices noted here send immediate shock waves round the world.

under its new president, Ronald Reagan. By a vigorous expansionary policy, fueled by a large budgetary deficit, American output was increased and the country's unemployment cut back. By 1983, the deficit had reached some $100 billion; by 1984 the figure was $170 billion and was still rising. It was approaching four percent of GNP, equivalent to about half the country's net savings.

Given the size of the American economy, such a drastic change of direction was not without significant effects on the rest of the world. Above all, the deficit (or shortfall of savings) within the United States led to a current account deficit in the external balance of payments of enormous proportions, met by a massive inflow (or repatriation) of capital from abroad. Much of this came from Japan and West Germany, where there were more savings than their less than fully stretched economies could absorb. The increasing foreign imbalance and the massive flows of capital be-

◄ The products of Western industry reach even the most distant consumers in the Third World. Here, at Senbatic market, in Ethiopia, housewives consider some of the discarded products of Western consumer industries. Perhaps goods will stimulate local initiatives and provide motivation for economic change; but it is difficult to see how the dumping of such cast-offs on the poorer markets of the world can help their development.

► China has not only accepted Western technology and American investment; it is considered a reasonable risk even for such advanced financial techniques as the American Express card. It may at present be available to a privileged minority only, but it may also be a sign of things to come.

▼ Brazil has some of the poorest people on Earth, but it also has rich and privileged citizens. It has been the inability of the Brazilian government to control the actions of the rich which has contributed to the country's position as one of the most indebted countries in the world. This enormous indebtedness has in part been caused, and is to some extent counterbalanced, by the capital sent abroad by rich Brazilians who distrust their own economy.

tween these three most powerful Western economies dominated international markets in those years and contributed to their uncertainties.

Any other country in deficit at home and abroad to the extent of the United States would have seen its currency drastically losing in value. Not so the American dollar. High interest rates, reduced inflation and reduced taxes in the United States made the dollar attractive for foreign investors, and far from losing in value, it began an astonishing ascent. By the end of 1983, it had gained 60 percent in real terms on a multilateral trade-weighted basis, and had risen by 40 percent even against the Deutschmark, and by 30 percent against the yen.

By early 1985, there was international pressure to reduce the deficit in the American budget and balance of payments. Some agreement in that direction was achieved at the meeting of the Big Five in New York's Plaza Hotel in September 1985 and in Tokyo in May 1986. Helped also by declining interest rates in the United States, the dollar fell from early 1985 onward as fast as it had risen: within a year, by April 1986, it had lost 20 percent and by May 1987, when the slide was halted, another 13 percent.

The high dollar had itself contributed to the American trade deficit which, in turn, helped to revive growth at least among the advanced industrial countries, though the flow of capital to the United States may have kept down real investment elsewhere. However, the high interest rates ruling in the United States as part of the package increased the burdens on the poorer debtor nations. These nations had taken little part in the deliberations on exchange rates and capital movements. Instead, their interest was focused almost solely on a single issue: how to transfer resources from the richer countries to themselves.

Rich countries, poor countries

Initiatives for what came to be known as the New International Economic Order (NIEO) had begun in the 1960s. Thereafter the developing countries used their voting strength in the United Nations (in 1960, 60 out of 104 votes, in 1980, 115 out of 151) and its agencies, as well as moral pressure on liberal opinion in the West, to keep up the

demand for more money from the West.

The first battles were fought out in 1964 within the United Nations Conference on Trade and Development (UNCTAD), itself the result of pressure by the poorer nations. In 1973 a summit conference of "nonaligned countries", politically rather a misnomer but comprising much the same countries, set forth their claims for more of the world's goods. A "Charter of Economic Rights and Duties of States", launched within the United Nations in 1974–75, emphasized the right of these countries to take over the property of multinationals and other foreign owners on terms decided by themselves. All these demands were broadly supported by the Independent Commission on International Development Issues, made up of distinguished political figures from "North" and "South" (the new synonyms for rich and poor countries). It met between 1977 and 1979 under the chairmanship of Willy Brandt, and early in 1980 issued its *North–South* report, which pleaded for concern for the poorest countries.

To some extent they pushed against open doors. The United Nations and individual Western countries were generally willing to continue aid, especially to the poorest nations. As a proportion of their own GDP, development assistance by OECD members changed very little between 1975 and 1985. In other respects, the political offensive to alter the distribution of the world's goods had, at best, an effect in limited specific areas only. However, in 1973 a major policy change was announced. Instead of as

before supporting projects mainly for improving the infrastructure of creditworthy countries, the Bank would increasingly lend to the poorest for the purpose of reducing their poverty. Using the mechanism of the International Development Association, the World Bank charged no interest for such loans which were repayable only after 50 years: in effect, they bore the character of free gifts and were based on grants by the wealthier nations. (Normally loans by the World Bank bore commercial interest rates and were repayable in 15–20 years.)

Most important of all were the actions of the IMF, which financed various innovatory schemes designed to make loans and credit available to the poorer countries. The result of these measures was that developing countries, which had received less than one-half of the Fund's credits in the 1950s and 1960s, accounted for over 90 percent in the early 1980s. By 1983, some $40 billion of cash flow had been provided for them.

Yet all these international official actions could not prevent serious repercussions from the oil price rises and the recession in the advanced countries on the developing nations. These can be divided into three phases: the impact of the first oil crisis and the consequent stagnation in the West of 1974–79; the second oil price rise and the international debt crisis of 1980–84; and the recovery from both from 1984 onward. It also helps to group Third World countries into three categories: oil exporters, middle-income oil importers and poor oil importers (though for some purposes, the centrally planned economies in Asia, Africa and the Caribbean are best considered separately).

While the OPEC oil price rise suddenly provided the oil exporters with a huge balance of payments surplus, it posed immediate problems for the other countries in the Third World. Not only did their oil imports go up in price, but so did their imported manufactures, since they came from countries which themselves began to suffer from inflation caused, among other things, by the rising oil prices. Further, as their growth slowed, the advanced countries reacted to "stagflation" by erecting obstacles to imports, which made it impossible for the primary producers of the Third World to raise the prices of their exports. Meanwhile rising interest rates were increasing the costs of borrowing. The result of all these factors

was an immediate sharp increase in the current deficits of the developing countries.

Nevertheless, with the exception of the African countries, they held to their policy of growth. This growth could, in view of their external deficits, be kept going only by borrowing ever more abroad, at a rate amounting in 1980 to about 5 percent of their GNP on average. The huge sums necessary to sustain that rate of borrowing exceeded the lending power of the international institutions, which were limited by their rules, as well as by the difficulties experienced by the advanced countries themselves, the ultimate source of these funds. The gap was closed by private banks which, facing a stagnating demand for their funds at home, were only too eager to place their investments abroad. With the sums obtained in this way, the borrowers were no longer building up the infrastructure or other productive units out of which interest and amortization could be paid, as they had been obliged by the World Bank to do in earlier years. Rather, they used them to maintain a level of income and rate of government expenditure which they were no longer able to afford out of their own efforts. Their annual interest and debt service bill rose, but nothing new was created out of which to pay it. The annual charges thus became an ever heavier burden on the export revenues.

Clearly this kind of economic policy could not continue indefinitely. From 1984, various solutions began to be found for the debt problem. For the very poorest nations, debts were canceled outright or much reduced. For the others, mutually agreed rescheduling lightened the burden without damaging credit standing too much. Between 1980 and 1986 there were 181 debt relief agreements. Above all, by drastic measures, frequently imposed by the international agencies, a basic turnround occurred. Annual new indebtedness was kept down, though at the price of slowing general growth and development, of unemployment and of runaway inflation in countries like Argentina and Brazil.

◄ Possibly the most effective direct help to the less developed nations has been medical aid. Here a nurse, one of only three medically trained people for 35,000 newly-arrived Tigrayan drought refugees in Eastern Sudan, examines a new arrival. In personal, human terms, this kind of aid should clearly have priority. Seen from a wider perspective such aid has contributed to the population increase which has helped to keep the poorer countries poor.

▼ Cattle ranching in Brazil. Many of the loans granted or guaranteed by the World Bank to the poorer and developing countries have been raised for agricultural development. Experience has shown that the careful fostering of sectors such as agriculture, though less spectacular, can be more effective than ambitious largescale innovatory schemes.

Latin American Inflation

Inflation was endemic in the postwar world, but the inflation rates which developed in Latin American countries in the late 1970s and the 1980s were exceptional and deserve to be regarded as a regional phenomenon. They were linked with the willingness of these countries to continue to accept foreign loans even after the price boom of their own exports, mainly minerals and raw materials, ended in about 1980. Much of this foreign capital went into the public sector: between 1973 and 1983, the private sector debt owed abroad increased only fourfold, but similar public sector debt increased tenfold. Many of the public sector utilities and "key" industries, financed in this way, were unviable from the start, and others became so as incomes ceased to rise after 1980.

The ever larger subsidies required to sustain them brought budgets out of control and public sector deficits soared. Once foreign borrowing ceased to finance them, such deficits were bound to trigger inflationary pressures. Inflation rates varied, with Brazil experiencing 100–200 percent a year in the 1980s, Argentina reaching 1,000 percent in 1984–85, and Bolivia 11,000 percent in 1985.

Such rates mostly hurt the working and lower middle classes, but there was no way of reducing them without serious inroads into standards of living. Neither were the methods of income squeezes recommended by the IMF and others politically easy to apply. If subsidies on basic food, electricity, fares and so on were ended, prices and thus wage demands would rise; if

◄ Argentineans protest against high prices. Argentina, in the interwar years among the more comfortably-off nations of the world, lost much ground when the high food and raw material prices of the postwar years collapsed. It also developed one of the worst rates of inflation and one of the highest debt mountains.

they were not, deficits would continue to fuel inflation. Only Chile, with its totalitarian government, managed to sustain a regime of austerity and slow growth. Brazil tried a drastic price freeze and a new currency, the cruzado, in 1986, but a consumer boom ensued, there was speculation against the price freeze as goods were hoarded and funds were sent abroad, and inflation was back in 1987. Argentina's drastic "Austral" plan of 1985, including a price and wage freeze, devaluation and a new currency, the austral, also failed. The Argentinean price index (1980=100) stood at 1,000,000 in January 1988, 5,000,000 one year later.

Instability in West and East

The world's financial markets experienced great volatility during the late 1980s. The first evidence of this was the crash of mid October 1987, when prices on most of the world's stock exchanges declined rapidly by 20 percent, or more. Subsequently the Tokyo Stock Exchange reached a historic high in December 1989, and Wall Street likewise in July 1990. Marked falls in stock market prices during the second half of 1990 had an explanation in the uncertainty caused by Iraq's invasion and occupation of Kuwait. Prices rose again with the expulsion of Iraqi forces from Kuwait in March 1991, but then collapsed: the Tokyo market fell from May, Frankfurt from June, and New York and London from November.

Some commentators saw an explanation of the 1987 world stock market crash in the burgeoning size of the US Federal budget deficit, although this had shrunk after being 5.5 percent of US GNP in 1985. Nonetheless it widened in the late 1980s. President George Bush was elected in November 1988, after pledging not to raise taxes, but in June 1990 was forced to renege, when faced with a projected deficit for 1990–91 of $160 billion.

Some in the US thought that the Federal budget deficit was sustainable, the fundamental problem being rather the growing international trade deficit. By 1989 this was mounting at $9–10 billion per month. During the summer of 1989 these anxieties increased as signs of a domestic recession surfaced, first in New England. Industrial production began to fall and unemployment

rose, although, as on the financial markets, the precise direction foreshadowed by national economic indicators was unclear. Growth continued during 1990, albeit sluggishly. Economic problems only became clearly evident during the autumn of 1990. An underlying factor was the fall in the rate of US investment from 7–8 percent of GNP during the 1960s and 1970s down to 5 percent over the 1980s.

Eastern Europe had experienced growing problems since the mid 1980s. The collapse of Communism was accompanied by the popular demand that the economies of Eastern Europe should quickly shift to "cut-throat" capitalism. This desire raised major political and economic difficulties – not to mention the practical problems of how to organize "privatization". Meanwhile Soviet supplies of oil and gas were reduced by 30 percent in July 1990, while from 1 January 1991 Eastern European countries were required to pay in hard currencies for their energy supplies. These shocks were coupled with the loss of their major markets within the Soviet Union as that economy began to disintegrate.

The initial euphoria arising from the end of Communism soon evaporated. The Polish and Czechoslovak governments, for example, embarked on liberalization, but the withdrawal of food subsidies and the freeing of markets soon resulted in mounting prices. Generally, Eastern Europe began to experience growing economic dislocation and inflation, which fueled political extremism and nationalist movements.

THE DEBT MOUNTAIN

International lending and borrowing became an accepted feature of the postwar decades. Total international indebtedness had been rising slightly, but so had prices, and defaults did not become an issue. This changed quite drastically with the rise in oil prices of 1973–74, and the slow reaction of the developing countries to this crisis. While the industrialized countries rapidly restored their balances of payments by cutbacks and economic slowdown, the developing countries reacted by borrowing more as their current deficits increased sharply.

They were encouraged in this course by the willingness of private bank consortia to lend; whereas in 1970 these had supplied only one-sixth of the lending, and in 1975 one-third, by 1985 they were responsible for well over half of the debts outstanding. By the early 1980s, the growing debt was threatening the trade balance of the poorer countries, and the solvency of the lenders – above all, the debt crisis hit the private banks in the advanced market economies, as well as in the OPEC countries.

The cost of servicing debts, as an average among all non-oil-exporting developing countries, rose from 16 percent of export revenues in 1977 to 20 percent in 1979 and 25 percent in 1982, in some extreme cases approaching half of the revenue from those exports. Drastic cuts reduced their rate of output growth, particularly in Latin America where indebtedness was especially high. Even so, the debts mounted up year by year. The chief creditors, who were by now banks rather than governments, could cancel the debts only at the expense of their shareholders, with negative effects on the economy of their own countries. Even "rescheduling" – stretching the period of repayment and reducing interest rates – harmed the creditworthiness of Third World countries which still needed ever more loans. Either way, catastrophe threatened. The debt issue thus became the major topic of international economic debate in the early 1980s.

Yet the picture was not altogether as bleak as it appeared to many. Much of the debt was owed by oil-producing countries, like Venezuela and the second largest debtor, Mexico, or by middle-income countries with rich resource bases like Argentina or Brazil, the world's largest debtor. Low-income countries owed only about three percent of the debt. Many of the debts were shortterm or renewable. In some countries, capital imports were matched by capital flight abroad: thus Mexican residents held about US$ 3 billion abroad in 1973 and US$ 64 billion in 1984, about as much as the whole of the public section of the country's foreign debt. Moreover, in view of the rapid world inflation in the 1970s, the real burden of debt rose much less than appeared at first sight. From 1984 on, however, the practice of rescheduling and also the complete cancellation of claims against the poorest countries slowed down the growth of international indebtedness, to hardly more than the rate of inflation.

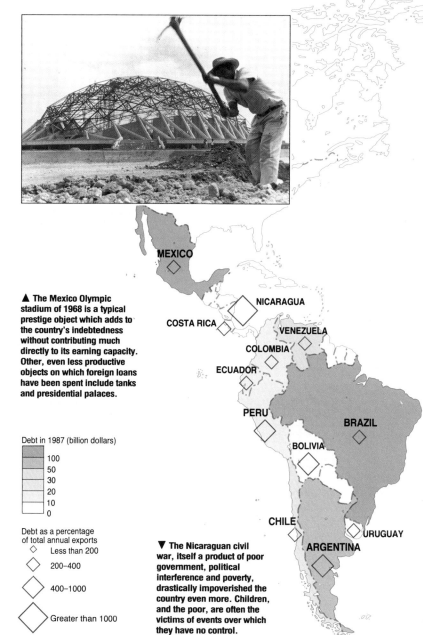

▲ The Mexico Olympic stadium of 1968 is a typical prestige object which adds to the country's indebtedness without contributing much directly to its earning capacity. Other, even less productive objects on which foreign loans have been spent include tanks and presidential palaces.

Debt in 1987 (billion dollars)
100
50
30
20
10
0

Debt as a percentage of total annual exports
◇ Less than 200
◇ 200–400
◇ 400–1000
◇ Greater than 1000

▼ The Nicaraguan civil war, itself a product of poor government, political interference and poverty, drastically impoverished the country even more. Children, and the poor, are often the victims of events over which they have no control.

POLAND

HUNGARY
YUGOSLAVIA ROMANIA

TURKEY

MOROCCO

ISRAEL

ALGERIA

EGYPT

SOUTH KOREA

INDIA

SUDAN

PHILIPPINES

GHANA NIGERIA

COAST

SINGAPORE

KENYA

INDONESIA

ZAIRE

CONGO

ZAMBIA

◀ The food queue before Christmas in Poland is a symbol for economies in which practically everything is in short supply – above all hard currency. Purchases from the West had to rely in part on loans.

▶ The levels of poverty in India are inconceivable to the Western mind, which cannot easily translate national income figures into human terms. In the cities, thousands sleep in the street; this Calcutta woman has made her home in a drainpipe.

▲ The amounts of outstanding loans rose most dramatically of all in Latin America. Unlike the very poorest countries, the region seemed to offer reasonable security for the lending national and international banks in the 1970s. At the time, not too many questions were asked about the purposes of the loans. In some cases, the sums outstanding were in part balanced by funds sent abroad for safety by rich citizens. Since the servicing and repayment of these loans have to come out of export earnings, the proportion which foreign debt bears to exports is significant if the loans are ever to be repaid.

▶ The joint meeting of the International Monetary Fund (IMF) and the World Bank held in Berlin in 1988 gave the many radical groups in the city the opportunity to protest about policies conceived in the West which they considered to have worked to the detriment of the poorer nations. Under its president, Robert McNamara, the World Bank has in fact gone far beyond the original concept of its founders to lay down easier conditions for Third World borrowers. However, international lending itself cannot end the world's poverty.

THE UNCERTAIN PATH

Time Chart

	1974	1975	1976	1977	1978	1979	1980	1981
Rural life	• Oct: India suffers its worst famine in 20 years	• Fighting in Ethiopia exacerbates continuing famine • Dutch elm disease begins to spread out from the Midlands and south of England; the disease has killed 6.5 million trees since the 1960s		• 19 Nov: In an effort to preserve wildlife, Jomo Kenyatta bans the hunting of big game (Ken)	• Apr: China purchases US wheat in bulk to supplement its supplies	• Jul: World agricultural conference to discuss the UN development program on the problems of developing countries	• Jun: Reports that ten million face starvation in East Africa; drought and wars create massive crop failures and refugee problems • Sep: Britain and France discuss a joint agricultural policy	
Industry and labor	• 6 Mar: UK miners' strike ends as miners gain a 35% pay increase • 18 Mar: Oil embargo on the US lifted by Arab states • May: Militant Protestants organize a strike which paralyzes Ulster (UK)	• Jan: UK wage inflation reaches 28.5%; in July the government passes a law to limit spiraling wage increases • May: nationalization of Gulf Oil de Peru • 5 Jun: Reopening of the Suez Canal • 11 Aug: British Leyland is nationalized	• 24 May: Concorde begins commercial transatlantic flights • Aug: 1.5 million reported unemployed in the UK • 15 Sep: 250,000 nonwhites go on strike in Capetown (SA) • 27 Nov: Four millionth Mini is produced (UK)	• 17 Jan: Workers in Cairo riot over increased prices (Egy) • Jul: "Social Contract" between the government and trade unions is destroyed by skyrocketing wage claims (UK) • French government takes control of subsidized steel	• 23 Jan: National strike is organized in opposition to the Somoza government (Nic) • Oct: Wave of strikes against the shah brings Iranian oil production to near standstill	• Jan: Britain's "winter of discontent" includes strikes by transport, hospital and local government employees • 28 Mar: Accident at the Three Mile Island nuclear power plant (USA) • 28 Jun: OPEC agreement to raise oil prices by 15%	• Aug: Polish workers strike and seize the Lenin Shipyard in Gdansk; two months of strikes and demonstrations bring concessions from the Polish government • 22 Sep: Polish workers launch *Solidarność* (Solidarity), a union led by electrician Lech Walesa	• 31 Jul: Strike of US professional baseball players ends after seven weeks • 3 Aug: Strike of US air traffic controllers • 7 Aug: One million Solidarity workers strike to protest at food prices and economic conditions in Poland
Government and people	• 15 Feb: Foreigners are banned from traveling within China • 1 Apr: Britain's NHS begins to provide free family planning service • Draft evaders and deserters during the Vietnam War are granted a limited amnesty by President Ford (USA)	• 1 Aug: US, Canada and 35 European countries sign the Helsinki Accord: a human rights agreement is signed; postwar boundaries recognized as fixed; USSR pledges to uphold human rights (Fin) • 29 Dec: Sex Discrimination Act and Equal Pay Act take effect (UK)	• Jun: Insistence that Afrikaans be an official language in Bantu schools leads to riots in Soweto (SA) • 4 Aug: 90% of political prisoners granted pardons by King Juan Carlos (Sp) • Sep: South Africa decides to allow multiracial sports teams to represent the country	• Jan: 240 Czech intellectuals, including playwright Václav Havel, sign Charter 77, a document proposing greater civil rights under the Communist government (Czech) • 17 Jan: USA restores capital punishment • 15 Jun: Spain holds its first democratic elections in 41 years	• Feb–Mar: Plans for moving Rhodesia toward black rule: all adult citizens enfranchised; Ian Smith and three black leaders sign an agreement to end white rule within a year • 6 Dec: Spanish referendum endorses the new democratic constitution	• Female prime ministers elected in Portugal (Maria Pintassilgo) and Britain (Margaret Thatcher) • 23 Jul: Ayatollah Khomeini bans the broadcasting of music, declaring it a corrupting force among the young (Iran)	• Feb: Margaret Thatcher recommends a 50% cut in strike benefits (UK) • 22 Feb: After anti-Soviet riots in Kabul, martial law is declared in Afghanistan • 30 Oct: Council tenants are now allowed to purchase their homes under the terms of the Housing Act (UK)	• 7 Jul: Judge Sandra O'Connor is the first woman ever appointed to the US Supreme Court • 18 Sep: France abolishes the use of the guillotine • 13 Dec: Martial law take effect in Poland
Religion	• 20 Apr: Sectarian violence in Belfast claims its 1,000th victim (UK) • Four Episcopal bishops disregard church law and ordain eleven women as priests	• Apr: Fighting begins in Beirut between right wing Christian Phalangists and Muslims (Leb) • 6 May: Cardinal Jozef Mindszenty dies in exile; the former Archbishop and Primate of Hungary was an outspoken opponent of Communism		• Feb: Idi Amin's troops murder the Archbishop of Uganda • Feb: Seven white Catholic missionaries massacred by guerrillas (Rhod)	• 6 Aug: Death of Pope Paul VI, succeeded by John Paul I, who dies 30 Sep, and is succeeded by John Paul II on 16 Oct • Nov: 913 followers of Jim Jones' religious cult, The People's Temple, commit suicide on the orders of their leader (Guy)	• 1 Apr: Khomeini declares Iran an Islamic republic • 20 Nov: Gunmen occupy the Grand Mosque in Mecca, Islam's holiest place; four days later, Saudi troops recapture the Mosque from the Shi'ite gunmen (Saud)	• May: South African police arrest 26 demonstrating churchmen • 19 Oct: Roman Catholic officials in Poland come out in open support of Solidarity	• 13 May: Turkish gunman attempts to assassinate Pope John Paul II in Vatican City • 12 Nov: Vote by Church of England General Synod allows women to become deacons
Events and trends	• Beginning of environmental fears about the condition and future of the earth's ozone layer • *Mariner X* satellite provides detailed views of Mercury and Venus • 11 May: Eleven million killed in an earthquake in China • 15 May: Dalkon shields contraceptive device is banned from the US market after fears about its safety	• 21 Mar: Monarchy is abolished in Ethiopia • Dec: US scientists claim to have established a link between oestrogen taken for period pains and uterine cancer	• 4 Jul: USA celebrates its bicentennial • 20 Jul: *Viking* spacecraft lands on Mars and sends back pictures to Earth • 24 Sep: Rhodesian prime minister Ian Smith announces a two-year plan to create black majority rule	• Sep: Study reveals that murder is the leading cause of death among young black Americans (USA) • 12 Sep: Black leader Steve Biko dies in police custody (SA) • Dec: Amnesty International human rights organization wins the Nobel Peace Prize • 800,000 people become refugees, "Boat People", from South Vietnam	• 29 Jan: Sweden is the first country to legislate against aerosol sprays which damage the ozone layer • 26 Jul: World's first test-tube baby born in the UK • 10 Dec: Millions of Iranians take to the streets in protests against the Shah	• 9 Feb: Fallopian tube successfully transplanted for the first time (UK) • 16 Jun: Exile of the shah of Iran • 11 Apr: Ugandan dictator Idi Amin deposed by a force of exiled Ugandans and Tanzanians • 4 Nov: US Embassy in Tehran captured by Iranians who take hostages (Iran)	• Jan: Surgeon General's report reveals lung cancer to be the leading cancer killer of women (USA) • 5 Jul: Iranian women protest in Tehran against the Islamic dress code for women • 4 Nov: Ronald Reagan elected president of the USA	• 16 Jan: National Cancer Research Institute in Tokyo reveals that the lung cancer rate is twice as high in women married to smokers (Jap) • Feb: Right wing of Guardia Civil attempts a coup in Spain • Dec: Alarm increases over a disease which affects the immune system and appears to be common among homosexuals in the USA
Politics	• Aug: US president Nixon resigns as a result of the Watergate scandal; vice-president Gerald Ford becomes the new president	• 16 Apr: Cambodia taken by the Khmer Rouge • 20 Nov: General Franco dies and is replaced by King Juan Carlos (Sp)	• 2 Jul: North and South Vietnam are united as a single socialist republic	• 5 Jul: Pakistani prime minister Zulfikar Ali Bhutto ousted by General Zia ul-Haq	• 18 Sep: Beginning of Camp David accords between president Sadat (Egy) and prime minister Begin (Isr)	• 7 Jan: Cambodia falls to the Vietnamese • 1 Feb: Ayatollah Khomeini returns to Iran after 14 years in exile • 26 Mar: Egypt and Israel sign peace treaty in the USA	• 4 Mar: Robert Mugabe is elected premier of Zimbabwe • Sep: Iraq attacks Iranian oil refinery at Abadan thus starting the Gulf War	• 6 Oct: Muslim extremists assassinate Egyptian president Sadat in Cairo • General Wojciech Jaruzelski declares martial law in Poland, and bans Solidarity

1982	1983	1984	1985	1986	1987	1988	1989
	● Mar: Problems created by production surpluses lead to discussions on leaving farmland fallow (USA)	● 2 Jan: Environmental report stresses the threat posed by acid rain to English lakes and countryside ● Global awareness of famine in Ethiopia; between 600,000 and one million die by the end of the year		● Apr–Oct: Food destroyed in Europe after contamination by fallout from the Chernobyl nuclear plant accident	● At current rates of environmental destruction, it is calculated that six animal and plant species are driven into extinction every hour	● Sep: Bovine spongiform encephalopathy (BSE) threatens British cattle in the West Country ● Oct: Measures announced in Brazil to end the destruction of the rain forests	● 1 Jan: Trade sanctions imposed on EC after it bans import of US hormone-treated meat
Jan: Unemployment the UK surpasses ree million 31 Jan: Two- to five-ld increases in prices ad to riots at the hipyards in Gdansk ol) Jun: Freeze on prices nd wages in France egins and lasts four onths	● Jan: Nigeria orders one million Ghanaian migrant workers to leave the country ● 14 Mar: OPEC members agree to reduce oil prices by $5 per barrel ● 20 Aug: Ban on sale of parts for the Siberian pipeline lifted by the USA	● 12 Mar: Beginning of a nationwide miners' strike (UK) ● Jun: With the establishment of four designated economic areas, China seeks foreign investors ● Dec: Leak of toxic gas from a Union Carbide plant in Bhopal, India, kills 2000	● 3 Mar: National Union of Mineworkers (NUM) votes to call off the miners' strike (UK) ● 1 May: Police and 10,000 Solidarity supporters clash during a march (Pol) ● US and Japan test process of energy production through laser-fired nuclear fusion	● Feb: Arab League agrees to establish a free trade area as the price of oil collapses ● 1 May: 1.5 million black workers go on strike in Johannesburg ● 30 Dec: Esso oil company announces that it will disinvest in South Africa	● 16 Jul: British Airways announces its intention to buy British Caledonian (UK) ● 7 Sep: Ford obtains the luxury sports car company Aston Martin (USA/UK) ● Boring of the Channel Tunnel begins at Calais (Fr)	● 8 Jun: Two million blacks go on strike to protest against apartheid (SA) ● 17 Aug: Polish coal miners strike nationally ● 7–12 Sep: Postal workers' strike causes tremendous disruption of the mail service (UK)	● Mar: Exxon Valdez tanker runs aground; 38 million liters of oil pollutes 160 km of Alaskan coastline ● Jul: 300,000 Soviet miners strike for two weeks in protest over conditions and pay ● 27 Nov: General strike brings Czechoslovakia to a halt
15 Mar: Constitution suspended in icaragua; ten days ter the Sandinista overnment declares a ate of emergency 8 Oct: Solidarity is utlawed by the Polish overnment although artial law is lifted in ec	● 7 Nov: Chancellor of the Exchequer announces cuts in public spending of £500 million (UK) ● 21 Jul: Martial law is lifted in Poland ● 3 Nov: Referendum among white South Africans favors sharing some power with Indians and Coloreds, but not Blacks	● 12 Jul: Democratic Party selects the first woman, Geraldine Ferraro, to run for vice-president (USA) ● 4 Sep: New constitution takes effect in South Africa, offering limited power to Coloreds and Asians but not Blacks, leads to violent rioting in Black townships	● 15 Apr: Racial sex laws are discontinued in South Africa ● 16 Jul: 10,000 women from around the world meet at a conference in Nairobi to discuss progress on women's rights issues ● 16 May: UK home secretary announces new police powers designed to control mob and picket-line violence	● 20 Jan: Martin Luther King holiday is observed for the first time (USA) ● Apr: Bishop Desmond Tutu asks the world to impose sanctions against South Africa ● 12 Jun: South Africa declares a state of emergency on tenth anniversary of Soweto uprising	● Jan: Soviet president Mikhail Gorbachev calls for greater democracy in the Communist party, his policies of perestroika and glasnost ● May: South African liberals lose numerous seats to militant whites in the Conservative party (SA)	● 5 Jun: Burma introduces a two-month curfew after antigovernment protests ● 29 Jul: Education Reform receives royal assent, introducing a national curriculum for schools in the state system as well as regular examinations (UK)	● 5 Apr: Communist officials agree to legalize Solidarity and hold democratic elections in Jun (Pol) ● 26 May: Martial law declared in China; roundup of young "rebels" begins in Jun ● 10 Oct: Hungary's Communist rulers vote to become social democrats
18 May: Sun Myung loon, leader of the nification Church, is ound guilty on charges f income tax fraud JSA) 17 Sep: Hundreds of alestinian refugees assacred by ebanese Christian ilitia	● Feb: Sectarian violence in Assam leads to the massacre of 600 Muslims refugees (Ind) ● Jun: In a return visit to his homeland the Pope openly backs Solidarity (Pol)	● Mar: Week of religious riots in Yola kills up to 1000 (Nig) ● May: Bombay is the scene of five days of bloody rioting between Hindus and Muslims (Ind) ● 6 Jun: Indian troops storm the Sikh Golden Temple to release it from Muslim extremists	● Jan: Israel ends its secret airlift of Ethiopian Jews (Falashas) ● 5 May: Jews angered by US president Reagan's visit to the Bitburg War Cemetery (FRG) which contains the graves of SS officers	● 12 Jul: Orange Day clashes between Catholics and Protestants leave 100 injured (UK) ● 6 Sep: 21 killed in an Istanbul synagogue by Arab gunmen (Turk) ● 7 Sep: Desmond Tutu becomes Archbishop of Cape Town	● General Synod of the Church of England votes in favor of ordaining women as priests ● Terry Waite, Archbishop of Canterbury's special envoy seeking hostage releases, is himself kidnapped in Lebanon	● 21 Feb: Leading US televison evangelist Jimmy Swaggart is disgraced ● 18 May: Siege of the Golden Temple at Amritsar ends when Sikh militants surrender (Ind) ● 15 Jan: Beginning of the Arab uprising (intifada) in Israel	● Feb: Ayatollah Khomeini issues a fatwa condemning to death British author Salman Rushdie for offence caused to Muslims by the latter's novel The Satanic Verses (Iran) ● Boston Episcopal church consecrates the first female bishop in history (USA)
1 Feb: US president eagan announces the JSA will provide mergency aid to the overnment of El alvador 2 Dec: Barney Clark eceives the first rtificial heart implant in n operation which asts 7.5 hours (USA)	● 14 Jun: Nationwide protests over the rule of Pinochet in Chile ● 18 Jun: Sally Ride, America's first female astronaut, goes into space as a crewmember on the space shuttle Challenger ● 1 Sep: South Korean airliner shot down by Soviet fighter; 269 passengers killed ● 22 Oct: Antinuclear protesters march in several European cities	● 18 Jul: Gunman shoots 20 people in a McDonalds restaurant for no apparent reason (USA) ● 16 Oct: Archbishop Desmond Tutu (SA) wins the Nobel Peace Prize ● UK scientists warn of the increasing threat posed by the "greenhouse effect" ● French and American scientists discover the virus which causes AIDS	● 2 Jan: USA officially withdraws its membership from UNESCO ● Live Aid concerts staged in London and New York to provide aid for the hungry in Ethiopia ● 19 Sep: Mexico City devastated by an earthquake ● Britain starts testing blood donors for the AIDS virus	● 28 Jun: US space shuttle Challenger explodes just after liftoff, killing its crew of seven ● 27 Aug: US report says a hydrogen bomb was dropped on New Mexico by accident in 1957	● Aug: One person per day reportedly dying of AIDS ● 10 Sep: 70 nations agree in Montreal to freeze current use of chlorofluorocarbons (CFCs) and to reduce their levels by 50% by 1999, in order to save the ozone layer ● 16 Dec: Largest Mafia trial ever brings 338 convictions in Palermo (It)	● 19 Mar: According to US scientists the ozone protection treaty has come too late to save the ozone layer ● 29 Apr: McDonalds announces that it will open 20 restaurants in the USSR ● Sep: Flooding in Bangladesh leaves 20 million homeless ● 10 Dec: Armenia rocked by an earthquake which kills up to 100,000 people	● 3 Dec: Presidents Mikhail Gorbachev and George Bush declare the end of the Cold War ● 25 Dec: Execution of Romanian president Nicolae Ceausescu after the Communist regime is toppled in a bloody civil war ● 28 Dec: Václav Havel is elected president of Czechoslovakia
2 Apr: Falklands conflict begins as JK territory; Argentina seizes the surrenders on 14 Jun	● 25 Oct: Operation Urgent Fury, as US troops land on Grenada after a Marxist coup there ● Dec: Yasser Arafat withdraws PLO forces from Lebanon	● Feb: International peacekeeping force withdraws from Lebanon as the situation becomes chaotic ● 31 Oct: Indian prime minister Indira Gandhi assassinated by Sikh bodyguards	● 10 Mar: Mikhail S Gorbachev becomes general secretary of the Soviet Communist party	● 25 Feb: Corazon Aquino drives Ferdinand Marcos from power in elections in the Philippines ● 26 Apr: Fire at Chernobyl nuclear power plant contaminates most of Europe	● May: Beginning of hearings on the Iran-Contra affair, "Irangate" (USA) ● 19 Oct: Black Monday: Wall Street share prices fall twice as far as in the 1929 crash; London and Tokyo are also affected	● 16 May: Soviet troops begin to withdraw from Afghanistan ● Aug: UN ceasefire agreement between Iraq and Iran	● 4 Jun: Troops crush demonstrations against Communist rule in Beijing, with 2600 killed (China) ● 10 Nov: Berlin Wall is opened, allowing free movement from East to West

81

Datafile

The sudden increase in oil prices in 1973 precipitated a crisis in the international economy which brought about a major restructuring. Features of this were the establishment of a "new international division of labor", involving the rise of newly industrialized countries led by Hong Kong, Taiwan, Singapore and South Korea. At the same time the old industrial countries saw "deindustrialization"; the further growth of services; and the introduction of new methods of work organization. "Flexibility" in labor markets meant greater insecurity for many workers and informal employment expanded. Decollectivization of agriculture in China heralded change in the socialist world.

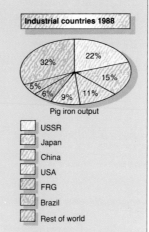

Industrial countries 1988

Pig iron output

☐	USSR
☐	Japan
☐	China
☐	USA
☐	FRG
☐	Brazil
☐	Rest of world

▶ At the beginning of the 20th century coalminers were the vanguard of the organized labor movement in Europe. In Western Europe they were no longer so. In Britain a strike lasting a year (1984–85) was unable to prevent large-scale job losses and pit closures. In France too the coalfields witnessed major job losses. In the Soviet Union and Eastern Europe, however, the miners of Silesia and the Donbas respectively were still able to force the hands of governments in the 1980s and 1990s.

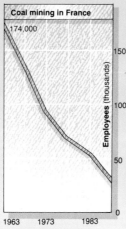

Coal mining in France

174,000

Employees (thousands)

1963   1973   1983

▲ The industrial structure of the world in the late 20th century is reflected here in the output of pig iron in 1988. The raw material of the first industrial revolution was now produced widely. The leading industrial powers shared production with large but backward industrial economies. The Soviet Union's preeminence did not equate with economic leadership as US preeminence had done around 1914. Heavy industries, such as shipbuilding, had largely moved away from the old industrial centers.

Information technology

Employment (thousands)

Massachusetts
California
New York
Illinois
Pennsylvania
Texas
New Jersey

◀ Knowledge became a key commodity and the means of handling it by information technology (IT) a competitive industry. Concentrations of "high-tech" industry grew up in America, based on big universities. Leading centers were the Stanford Silicon Valley (California) and the MIT–Boston Route 128 (Massachusetts).

▶ The change in the economic structure of the West by comparison with the state socialist bloc is shown in the greater importance of financial services in Germany as compared with the Soviet Union. This reflected the expansion of services employment and the reorganization of the global financial system.

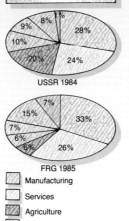

Employment groups

USSR 1984

FRG 1985

☐	Manufacturing
☐	Services
☐	Agriculture
☐	Transport
☐	Construction
☐	Commerce
☐	Finance

▶ Alongside the growth of "high-tech" industry there was an expansion in second jobs, often involving "moonlighting" and household-based work. It ranged from casual work by the unemployed to highly paid consultancy, design and craft work, and was one of the ways in which labor markets became more "flexible".

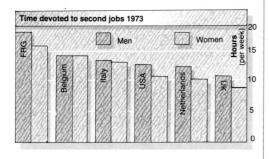

Time devoted to second jobs 1973

Men   Women

Hours (per week)

FRG   Belgium   Italy   USA   Netherlands   UK

The steep rise in oil prices in 1973 provoked an economic crisis that had been latent in the international economy for some time and brought to an end the long boom of the postwar period. The underlying causes of the crisis included the rigidity of Fordist large-scale methods of production and inadequate demand.

The responses that developed in the 1970s and 1980s saw a restructuring of the international economic system and of production methods. Labor was weakened by economic recession and employers made use of their greater power to make labor markets, production methods and patterns of consumption more flexible. The economies of scale that had been sought by Fordist mass production were countered by an increased capacity to manufacture a variety of goods in small batches, associated with more rapidly changing fashions. New production organization and the ability of firms to adjust rapidly to changing markets (to the point of adjusting markets) depended in turn on new information technology. This, for example, made possible the introduction of "just-in-time" production, whereby components were manufactured and delivered just as they were needed, which removed the need to lock up capital in the maintenance of large stocks of raw materials and finished goods. But the importance of information increased the advantages of large corporations even whilst often making production in smaller units desirable. At the same time more workers came to be employed on a variety of short-term contracts. This is what "flexibility" in the labor market meant – increased use of "informally" employed workers with few rights. The whole complex of changes was associated with aggressive neoliberalism in politics. It lauded the individual but its practitioners in government often proved to be centralist and interventionist. It was successful, however, in rooting a culture of entrepreneurialism deeply in Western societies and, in the early 1990s, extending it to formerly "socialist" countries.

The "new international division of labor"

The emergence of a new economic order involved the establishment of a new international division of labor following the rise of "newly industrializing countries". In the 1950s Hong Kong had begun to industrialize rapidly. For the first time, world demand for garments stimulated a poor city into frenetic growth. In the late 1950s Taiwan followed suit, and shortly afterward South Korea and then Singapore. In the last three cases – unlike Hong Kong – the process was initiated and supported by major state intervention. The process of rapid growth stimulated by the export of manufactured goods was not restricted to these

NEW DIVISIONS OF LABOR

four cases, although they attained higher rates of growth for a more extended period than many others. The phases of growth seen in South Korea – from garment exports in the 1960s to capital-intensive goods (ships, steel) in the 1970s to more skill-based goods in the 1980s (electronic, video and telecommunications equipment, vehicles) were replicated in some other developing countries in Asia and Latin America (though not successfully so in India).

The process did not so much indicate the peculiar merits of the four "little tigers" of Asia but rather a structural change in the world economy. In essence it reflected a decline in the comparative advantage of sectors of manufacturing in the more developed countries. By the 1980s the original Asian four had labor costs that were too high to compete in cheap garments, so other poorer countries took this over. China, for example, became a major exporter of garments. In Bangladesh employment in garment manufacturing for export grew to a quarter of a million. There was accelerated growth based on manufacturing for export in Thailand, Malaysia, Indonesia,

▼ The employment of young women, supposedly because of their "nimble fingers", is not confined to modern industries, such as electronics. Here in a factory in Java vulnerable women workers make cigarettes under conditions of low pay and negligible job security.

Mauritius, Botswana and elsewhere. Furthermore, while there was much fear that governments in more developed countries would block imports to protect their own manufacturing capacity (and, indeed, they did from time to time take such action), it seemed they had become increasingly dependent upon imports to produce their own output. To cut imports was thus to cut domestic employment, incomes and exports. Integration of a world economy had become a trend that could not be stopped at acceptable cost.

The process was seen most vividly in the burgeoning "offshore" production sites, particularly in the making of electronic components. In Southeast Asia and parts of Latin America, the same type of labor was involved: young women, literate, aged 15 to 22. Employers might say such workers were engaged because they had "nimble fingers" or were more conscientious and hardworking than adult men. A more obvious explanation was that, at a given level of education, this was the lowest-paid type of labor and it was subject in the factory to an extension of the patriarchal authority within the family.

Life in British Depressed Regions

In the 1970s and 1980s industrialized societies once again experienced high rates of unemployment. The burden was, however, shared unequally between regions. In Britain the gulf which had opened up in the 1930s between the North and South grew wider. This reflected the continued dependence of Scotland, Wales and the Northwest and Northeast of England on the old industries of the first industrial revolution. Now decline went so far as to represent "deindustrialization", and these regions knew persistent and long-term unemployment.

Those who had been vulnerable in the past were the least likely to escape unemployment now. Politicians urged people to move in search of jobs and, contrary to popular perceptions, many did. In 1980 600 workers a month were leaving the Northeast, mostly to look for jobs in Canada and Australia. But they were usually aged 25 – 35, and professional or skilled workers. For the least skilled who were most vulnerable movement was made difficult because of the availability of cheap public housing in the North, and the difference in house prices between declining and prosperous regions.

The hypothesis on "the psychology of unemployment", first developed in the 1930s, was borne out: "First there is shock, which is followed by an active hunt for a job during which the individual is still optimistic and unresigned: he still maintains an unbroken attitude. Second, when all efforts fail, the individual becomes pessimistic, anxious and suffers active distress. And, third, the individual becomes fatalistic and adapts himself to his new state. He now has a broken attitude". One Tynesider, now back at work but in a less well-paid job, described his experience in similar terms: "When I was unemployed I was very worried: I thought that was it, I didn't expect to get another job. I slept in late until about 11 a.m. I got very bored. Hours in the early afternoon were the worst – hours when I thought that I used to be working. I wasn't ready for retiring yet: I can still work, I wanted to work. I got very jealous of those who were working. My wife is right when she said it affects me *as a man*: it isn't the money so much as the feeling men have".

Reduced budgets and enforced contact between husbands and wives led to increased tensions within some families. There was disturbing evidence of violent rows and family breakups linked to unemployment in the depressed regions. Young people also suffered acutely, the risk of unemployment for them being greater than for the remainder of the labor force. More stringent conditions for entitlement to social security benefits finally drove some of these youngsters to search for a living in cities where they slept rough or in "cardboard cities".

▲ An industrial landscape in the Northeast of England. With its old coal-mining, steel and shipbuilding industries in steep decline as a result of international recession, competition from newly industrialized countries, and public expenditure cuts, the Northeast was one of the declining regions of the older industrialized world. Changes in mining technology also contributed to the decay of coalmining communities. The British government said in 1986: "The North East is in the unenviable position of having the worst combination of unemployment blackspots in the country."

Why did this shift of manufacturing capacity to parts of the Third World take place? There are several reinforcing factors: expansion in infrastructure and improvements in health and education in developing countries; the creation of export processing zones, free of the bureaucratic restrictions so common in many developing countries and with taxfree access to imported machinery and raw materials; the rapid decline in the cost of freight movement by sea, road and air; and reduction in the restrictions on imports in developed countries. All these were "permissive" factors; they facilitated growth only if demand was expanding. What caused demand to expand? Here a key factor seems to have been the price of labor in developed countries which, from the mid 1950s rose relatively rapidly, making it impossible for many lines of production to take place when cheaper imports were available.

As barriers to trade declined, the old assumptions about how capital and labor were combined were transformed. It had been assumed that there would always be increasing scale of production and increasing use of capital relative to labor, culminating in automation. But that assumed a particular price for labor. When a *world* labor supply became available, the calculations changed – small and petty units of production, with very little capital, could defeat the giant automated factory. Women working at home with their children on a sewing machine to produce shoes could defeat the shoemaking plants of the United States. Thus the informal sector could now become highly competitive in a world economy when it was not in an isolated national one.

The change in the structure of production resulted in striking social changes. New urban working classes were created. At various times they became politically significant in strikes and agitations. Labor parties were no longer restricted to the developed countries. Indeed, in the 1970s, under the impact of the first slump (1974–75), there was a wave of major strikes, including general strikes, that affected equally both the more and the less developed.

The same seems to have been true of business classes. When, in the Philippines in 1986, Mrs Corazon Aquino challenged Ferdinand Marcos in the presidential election she did so with the strong support of the majority of Filipino businessmen. The symbol of her movement, the yellow shirt, became something of an inspiration to the similar movement that developed shortly afterward in South Korea. There were other cases – in Brazil and Mexico – suggesting that in a number of middle-income countries significant business classes had begun to exercise more independent political power. They seemed no longer willing simply to act as loyal retainers to an all-powerful state, but demanded the right to participate in the determination of policy.

Social structures had been transformed. There was no longer a massive peasantry with a powerful state and tiny business and working classes. In the newly industrializing countries, the urban classes – the mass of workers, the large educated middle class, and a self-confident business class – had come to dominate society.

◀ This Turkish woman in Paris carries on a tailoring business at home, working as a subcontractor for a large establishment. Such "informal" employment reduces the cost of labor, partly by undermining worker organization. This is one of the ways by which Western economies have been "restructured".

▼ As the "young upwardly mobile professionals" (yuppies) of the Western world acquired more wealth in the 1980s, so sophisticated gadgetry such as this electronic diary came to meet their new market.

The onward march of deindustrialization?

In four of the six largest Western economies, real incomes fell between 1973 and 1975. Unemployment rates rose to what were, by postwar standards, unprecedented levels, such as had been thought incompatible with the postwar social order of a "corporatist" alliance of state, trade unions and employers. But it was not so. Indeed, unemployment rates resulting from the first slump, in 1974–75, were even exceeded by those of the second, in 1979–81. By then in many European countries there was little pretense of alliance any longer and governments were busy instituting market imperatives for all the supposed elements of the old social democratic pact – health, welfare and education.

The first slump, and even more the second, had particularly damaging effects in a major segment of manufacturing, much of it located in and around older industrial cities. The process, identified as "deindustrialization", was associated with another, "deurbanization" – the drift away from cities, especially large industrial ones. It was also associated with the further growth of service employment. The more advanced an economy, the higher the proportion of expenditure went on

▼ These Swedish automobile workers form a workteam, with responsibility for several stages of construction. Their employer argues that with such arrangements "the small workshop atmosphere is built into the large plant", and seeks efficiency by creating "meaning and satisfaction in work".

▲ Blocks of flats and rows of East Germany's Trabant automobile reflect the social regimentation of centrally planned economies. The Trabant, produced by inefficient and dangerous methods, was much sought after. Hard currency exports, such as cameras, were also produced by uncompetitive methods. It was calculated in 1990 that only 8 percent of the work force was employed in internationally viable enterprises.

public administration and defence (20 percent). These were the sectors in which, in the 1980s, so-called "yuppies" (young, upwardly mobile professionals) flourished in Britain and the United States. Implicit in the structural change in the economy was also a shift from full-time male employment in manufacturing to part-time female employment in services and a shift between regions.

There seemed to be another change of significance. For the black economy was said to have grown in a way similar to the expansion of the informal sector in developing countries. In the late 1970s Italy was famous for its major exports of garments, lace, shoes and some engineering products, much of which seemed to have been produced outside the statistical accounting of the Italian economy. The Los Angeles metropolitan region grew to be the largest manufacturing big city in the United States with one of the few competitive garment industries, based, it was said, on illegal Central American immigrants.

services, because people wanted to improve standards of relatively labor-intensive services – for example, health care, welfare and education. Even if they did not, the relative cost would rise because productivity in this sector does not increase as fast as it can in manufacturing.

The slump had the worst effects on old sections of industry, particularly heavy industry (steel, coal, shipbuilding, heavy engineering) which, with poor profit rates in the 1960s, had not received sufficient investment. Low-cost new producers with the latest technology, operating in the more advanced developing countries, scooped the markets.

Meanwhile, other sectors grew. In Britain the employment growth sectors between 1961/66 and 1976 were: insurance, banking and finance (52 percent growth); professional and scientific (56 percent); miscellaneous services (17 percent); and

Stagnation and restructuring in the Soviet Union
In the Soviet Union the long-term deceleration of economic growth culminated in 1979–82 in absolute stagnation of key sectors – the nadir of the so-called Brezhnev "years of stagnation". President Leonid Brezhnev died in 1982, opening the way for diagnoses of the Soviet malaise. The most influential of these was the 1983 "Novosibirsk Report", written by the Soviet sociologist Tatyana Zaslavskaya and secretly discussed and circulated among senior Soviet officials. In Zaslavskaya's view, "the national economy long ago crossed the threshold of complexity when it was possible to regulate it effectively from a single center" and "the system of production relations which has been in operation over the course of many decades has formed a predominantly passive type

▶ In Eastern Europe the "second economy" of self-employment was deeply entrenched. In Hungary, according to one authority, 70 percent of households earned incomes from the second economy in the mid 1980s. With the collapse of official distribution systems in Poland, farmers sold their produce directly in the street. Though still fined by the police (as here), their activity came to be seen as one of the bases on which a market economy might be built in a post-socialist society.

▲ Hard work in the fields in Yugoslavia. In 1986 under 4 percent of the work force in European Community (EC) countries managed about twice as much land as the 13 percent of the working population employed in farming in Eastern Europe. Yields of cereals and meat were 50–75 percent of those in the EC. Yet the idea of privatizing land was not universally popular because some farm workers (if not these Kosovo peasants) were cushioned in secure and undemanding jobs.

of worker", characterized by "indifference toward work performed and its low quality... and a rather low level of moral discipline". The system (in her view) needed complete reconstruction, not piecemeal reform.

This trenchant and daring report became a manifesto for "*perestroika*", for the "restructuring" of Soviet society under Mikhail Gorbachev, who became party leader in 1985. The program put forward at that time by Zaslavskaya included an expansion of autonomy for state businesses and of small-scale cooperative and private enterprise (particularly in retailing, catering and other services), full legal and financial accountability and the rule of law, greater openness and freedom of expression, a shift from vertical (hierarchical) "command" relationships to horizontal contractual relationships. There was to be "socialist pluralism" and "democratization".

The year of the report, 1983, was also a high point in the "new right" counterrevolution in the West and in the resurgence of Western capitalism. In the United States President Ronald Reagan was denouncing the Soviet Union as the "evil empire" and unveiling his "Star Wars" Strategic Defense Initiative which envisaged massive extra expenditure on weaponry. The Soviet

chief of staff Marshal Ogarkov, among others, voiced the growing anxiety in military-industrial and KGB circles that the existing Soviet system could not catch up with the West economically, technologically or militarily. The advocates of *perestroika* won crucial support from the military and KGB by promising to liberate creative and innovative energies and increase investment and imports of Western technology and capital goods in order to accelerate Soviet development.

However, Gorbachev and his adviser Abel Agenbegyan raised too many expectations and gave too many hostages to fortune, by promising not only "acceleration" but also greatly improved supplies of consumer goods, a doubling of the housing stock and increased health-care provision by the year 2000, not to mention drastically increased salaries and educational provision. They remained dangerously susceptible to gigantomania, to the cult of the leader and to the "great leap" psychology of the first Five Year Plans and of the Khrushchev era. They were unwilling to face up to uncomfortable choices. Their commitments to over-ambitious goals were bound to overstretch and overheat the economy, exacerbate imbalances, undermine market and financial mechanisms and thus finally to reaffirm the role of the party-state bureaucracy and encourage the eventual reversion to central allocation, rationing and controls – as happened in 1990. Gorbachev's entire team retained the mind-set of enlightened planners, technocrats, reformers "from above". When they were challenged "from below", by Siberian oil workers, Siberian and Donbas miners, by ethnic separatists, by groups and movements who were outside the "charmed circle" and who aspired to move rapidly beyond reformist and centripetal restructuring of the Soviet system (*perestroika*) to more radical dismantling of the Soviet system, the Gorbachev regime apparently floundered. It was much more adept in dealing with foreign governments and unrepentant bureaucrats than with Russian workers and ethnic separatist movements. By the 1990s the regime was no longer able to hold the Soviet Union together. A conservative coup against Gorbachev in August 1991 failed, and only hastened the final collapse of the Soviet system.

The economic squeeze in Eastern Europe

From 1973 to 1978, while the Western world went into economic recession, the East European economies grew even faster than they had done in the 1960s. This superficially impressive feat was made possible by the growing integration and interdependence of the Soviet and East European economies. In the long run this insulation from the recession further impaired their capacity to compete successfully in world markets. In addition, the East–West détente of the 1970s made available greatly augmented flows of Western capital and technology to the East European states. Intended to raise productivity and to expand the range of products available, it in fact increased reliance on Western capital and technology – Eastern Europe quickly ran up uncomfortably large hard-currency debts. It also had politically unwelcome social consequences. Increased contact with Western visitors, together with increased provision of amenities catering to their needs, helped to diffuse Western values.

▼ A Chinese peasant at a free market. Agricultural growth in China after 1978 reflected changes in the incentives offered to producers through the "responsibility system" and changes in prices and markets. The former effectively restored household farming, thereby tackling the problem of labor supervision in collective farming. The fact that periodic rural markets were again permitted led to resurgence of private marketing and facilitated increased specialization, but also provoked fears about increased inequality.

You townies don't know the first thing about the countryside – it's a lot more complicated than you think. Take this place: the land here was divided up only last year, but it's been redivided again this year. Why? Because the brigade cadres could see other people's crops doing well and were jealous of their land. That's why they had another share-out and got their hands on the best land.... We drew lots, but they fixed it. Nobody's going to have the law on them. That's village life for you.

CHINESE PEASANT, 1984

◀ A motorcycle repair shop in rural China. In 1984 land sales were effectively permitted again in China. One reason for selling would be to go into more profitable enterprises such as small manufacturing or (as here) services. Some 13 percent of households had given up farming to become "specialized households". "The days are gone", it was said, "when peasants boasted about their digital watches. The new rich are building bigger houses and buying Japanese vans".

The resulting "Westernization" of East European attitudes was, in the end, at least as dangerous and corrosive of party and state influence on the minds of the young as any formal change or "reform" in the socioeconomic system.

Increased reliance upon Western capital also proved to be economically hazardous. Debt service payments became very burdensome: in the late 1970s they began to exceed new inflows of Western capital. This time, moreover, the Soviet Union was unable to come to Eastern Europe's rescue. The 1979–82 world recession coincided with the nadir of the Brezhnev "years of stagnation" in the Soviet Union; Eastern Europe was thus caught in a two-way squeeze between a stagnating Soviet economy and a recession-bound West, from which it still had not fully recovered by 1989, when the "iron curtain" lifted and the communist dictatorships came to an end.

Between 1979 and 1991, with the possible exception of East Germany, the East European economies did not grow at all in real terms and, at least in the cases of Poland and Romania, experienced major reductions in living standards. Any prospect of economic development was made even harder by the fact that Eastern Europe, like the Soviet Union, had to a large extent "missed the bus" in the information technology, electronics and biotechnology revolutions.

Liberalization and decollectivization in China
After the death of Mao Zedong in 1976, the new Chinese leadership – increasingly under the direction of Deng Xiaoping – experimented with methods of overcoming the neglect of the years of Cultural Revolution in order to accelerate economic growth. In the late 1970s this increasingly entailed a liberalization of the economy, further decentralization and an orientation toward exports. The centerpiece of reform was the dismantling of the system of state-directed agriculture and the attempt to restore the close relationship between the cultivators and the soil.

The changes culminated in the abolition of the commune-brigade-team structure of agricultural organization and the effective restoration of a peasant-family-based system, with the right to acquire or dispose of land. The introduction of this "family responsibility" system went necessarily with the restoration of private markets.

The initial results were startling: agricultural output grew by 7.4 percent (and industry by 13.2 percent) in the 1980s. Village administrations were able to diversify into manufacturing, horticulture, services, transport and power. By the late 1980s there were said to be 80 million specialized rural manufacturing workers.

The pattern of decentralization made possible great diversification, but it also meant there were few flows between districts and provinces – poor areas stayed poor while rich ones grew richer. Furthermore, the stress on the need to make money allowed a rapid reappearance of unequal incomes and consumption. A new relatively rich social stratum emerged in the countryside, combining party cadres, rich peasants and rural industrial managers or businessmen. Corruption, never eliminated in China, grew at a prodigious rate. Loose controls on imports along with increasing demand for foreign goods, particularly from the newly rich, produced severe balance of payments problems.

In 1988–89 issues came to a head. After a run of good harvests that had sustained the success of the reform program, 1988 was a poor year. The total output of grain was well below requirements. Part of the decline was attributed to the government's relaxation of procurements and the introduction of more freely priced items while grain prices remained fixed and low. The peasants had therefore shifted cultivation out of grain to more profitable goods. The abolition of communes, it was said, had led to a neglect of rural infrastructure, particularly of irrigation and drainage networks and of rural roads, and this also had affected the harvest. It began to seem possible that decollectivization had brought only short-run benefits. "Noodle-strip", small-scale family farming might not lend itself, after all, to sustainable investment in land improvement.

Datafile

There were such major social changes after 1973 that some spoke of "the end of history". They referred to the triumph of neoliberalism and the collapse of socialist experiments. Throughout the West those who questioned the extent to which the state should intervene in social life were in the ascendant. Their ideas were found persuasive in Eastern Europe where communism was overthrown by risings in 1989–91 led mainly by the intelligentsia. Similar ideas motivated reformers in the Soviet Union. But amid the apparent failures of modernization in many countries, nowhere more so than in sub-Saharan Africa, Islam became an ideology of opposition to both socialism and capitalism.

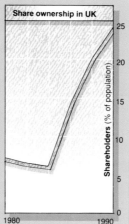
Share ownership in UK

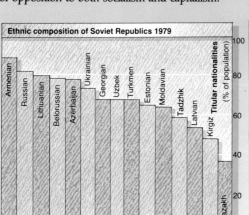
Ethnic composition of Soviet Republics 1979

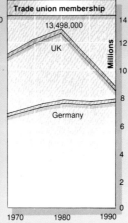
Trade union membership

▲ The increasingly strident nationalism of the Soviet republics, to which Gorbachev's reforms gave space in the late 1980s, was complicated by the fact that in nine of them 30 percent or more of the population belonged to a group other than the dominant one.

▶ The extent of Communist party membership in the socialist bloc in 1989 bore little relation to the effective support the party received when free elections were held. It emerged strongly in Albania and Bulgaria.

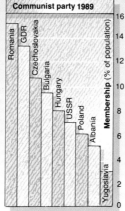
Communist party 1989

▲ In the 1970s social democratic parties appeared to be the "natural" parties of government in Britain and Germany. Trades union membership grew (above). This trend was reversed in the 1980s and in Britain especially private share ownership was expanded enormously (top), assisted by the privatization of nationalized enterprises. It was argued that now the relatively prosperous "haves" constituted a majority over the excluded "have nots", changing the whole nature of politics.

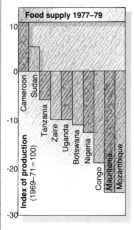
Food supply 1977–79

▶ The apartheid system excluded non-whites from government in South Africa, in spite of their numbers. Elaborated after World War II, apartheid was challenged in the 1980s, mainly because of the development of the African working class.

◀ Food production per head declined in a majority of sub-Saharan African states in the 1970s. This mark of economic decline was the result of attempts to subject agriculture to bureaucratic control, and its taxation through pricing.

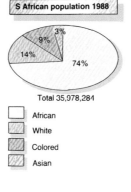
S African population 1988

Total 35,978,284

☐ African
▨ White
▨ Colored
▨ Asian

By the 1970s the integration of the world economy was well advanced. The process redefined not only the role of the state and its capacity to administer a domestic economy in some isolation from the disturbing forces of world markets, but also the old intellectual arguments about appropriate policies. From the 1960s the "Keynesian" orthodoxy which, it was claimed, had guided government policies in Europe and North America since the 1940s went into decline. With it went the centerpiece of European social democracy, the tripartite alliance of state, trade unions and business. The alliance had assumed that there was some point in allying, that governments could determine full employment, the number of the poor and standards of education and health. But in an integrated world it seemed increasingly difficult to do these things at acceptable cost; external markets increasingly determined domestic activity. There was therefore little point in the politics of alliance. Corporatism became unfashionable.

Neoliberalism in the West

In the 1970s government policy began to reflect a revival of faith in unrestricted markets for goods, services and capital. Unlike the Great Depression of the 1930s, the two slumps of 1974–75 and 1979–81 did not lead governments to try to limit their relationship with the rest of the world. Rather they continued the process of integration. They did not try to sustain high employment so much as argue that this power no longer rested in their hands (and imply that, in reality, it never had). Implicitly, governments abandoned responsibility for the poor and homeless, arguing that "communities" should take over.

While virtually all governments in the more developed countries began to shift their policy stance toward the new orthodoxy in the mid-1970s, two political leaders in the 1980s became champions of neoliberalism: President Ronald Reagan of the United States (hence "Reaganomics") and Mrs Margaret Thatcher, prime minister of Britain (hence "Thatcherism"). Neither added anything new to its doctrines. Nonetheless, in the popular mind, the two supposedly fashioned an ideology which in the late 1980s became one of the inspirations for dismantling the Communist economic regimes of Eastern Europe and the Soviet Union and replacing them with market economies and a key issue in the debates in developing countries. Their social importance lay perhaps above all in the way in which they led a shift away from the collective norms and values which were pervasive in the 1950s and 1960s toward competitive individualism as a central value, which has penetrated into many walks of life.

REVERSES OF MODERNIZATION

The end of socialism?

Socialism began in the 19th century as a doctrine of revolt by the mass of the population in Europe to create a society based upon collective cooperation rather than the competitive individualism of a minority. In urban industrial society it became the code of an industrial working class, which sought power in order to establish the cooperative society. "Collective cooperation" became identified, however, with state intervention. Indeed, for many communists and socialists, state action itself constituted the whole community in action, even when no means existed by which the majority could influence the state (as with dictatorships). The Stalinist achievement in swiftly industrializing the Soviet Union in the 1930s added enormously to the authority of the idea that the state could be an effective agent of modernization and social reform. Thus, the original libertarian origins of the socialist idea,

The new orthodoxy of neoliberalism

The collapse of socialism in Eastern Europe

Perestroika and its limits

Resurgent nationalism and antisemitism

Islam and modernization

The failure of development in Africa

Life in South African townships

▼ ▶ **Neoliberalism in Britain: corporate entertainment for the successful (right); the cold face of bureaucracy which confronted claimants of social security benefits at a government office (below).**

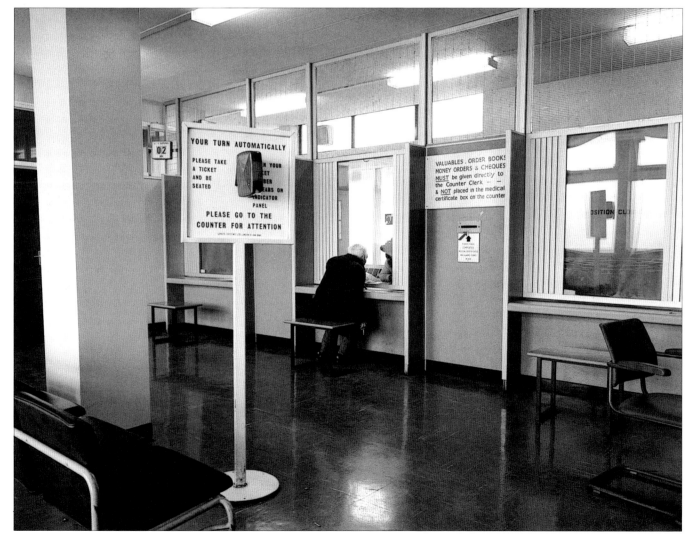

the common ancestry it had with the anarchists, disappeared. Indeed, socialism turned into its opposite: the doctrine of big government and bureaucracy.

In retrospect it can be seen that the emergence of Solidarity (*Solidarnosc*) in Poland in 1980 marked the beginning of the end of communist rule in Eastern Europe. Led by Lech Walesa, a shipyard electrician, Solidarity was born from the economic and social failure of Poland's so-called "United Workers Party" amid massive strikes in the shipyards on the Baltic and in the coal mines of Silesia. Elsewhere in Eastern Europe conditions may have been less grim than in Poland or (especially) in Romania. Nevertheless, there was widespread revulsion against all-pervasive corruption, concealment or perversion of truth, surveillance by internal security forces, police brutality and irksome restrictions. Citizens resented perennial shortages and hours spent queuing or searching for goods in short supply. Even in comparatively well-stocked East Germany, Czechoslovakia and Hungary, the spread of well-made Western goods produced a threatening escalation of expectations and discontent. Moreover, as growing numbers of nuclear weapons were stationed in Eastern Europe in the early 1980s and, more especially, after the nuclear power plant at Chernobyl in the Ukraine exploded in 1986, peace movements, green movements and Protestant churches intensified public concern about the military buildup, the growing reliance on Soviet nuclear technology and the environmental costs of neo-Stalinist industrial development.

By 1989 the programs of the East European communist dictatorships had lost all credibility and even the ruling Communist parties had lost faith in their capacity to lead their countries out of the impasse. The cataclysmic changes of 1989, which ended Communist rule in most of Eastern Europe, were in large measure a "revolution from above", stage-managed by the intelligentsia, "reform Communists" and the Soviet KGB, concerned to retain Soviet influence in Eastern Europe by changing its regimes. But KGB interventions merely unleashed changes which it was unable to control. Even the apparently spontaneous demonstrations of popular hostility to the dying Communist dictatorships were preceded and prepared by the cultural and political dominance of the intelligentsia. Through their control of the media and information services, the intelligentsia and "reform Communists" committed to pluralistic democracy were able to manipulate the symbols and ideology of the incipient East European revolution and even to indicate what was taking place, how pressure could be most effectively applied, and where mass demonstrations should converge or assemble.

At the end of the 1980s a business class was just beginning to emerge in Eastern Europe but it was not yet politically effective. Thus the intelligentsia remained the leading force in East European society, though it was apparently entranced by the idea of creating market economies.

A poet was grieving because in work camps... young people dance to rock and roll in the evenings. But why shouldn't these youngsters dance after a hard day's work? After all, what is rock and roll? Chiefly it's rhythm. Why accuse rock of every sin? It's like decrying iambics. You can write marvellous verse in iambics or you can write trash. It's the same with rock... Young people want a new culture.

A. VOZNESSENSKY, 1987

◀ Soviet economists estimate that economic growth in their country virtually stopped in the mid-1970s. The daily lives of Soviet citizens became steadily more bleak; more and more time was spent in queuing for goods of poor quality. The failures of the system were inescapable and Soviet society inspired little enthusiasm. Here people searching for a flat scan notices on a city wall. In the 1960s most Soviet families in urban areas had been able to move into two- or three-roomed flats, but the standard of housing remained low. The situation was better in Eastern Europe, though there were still between two and three times as many rooms per inhabitant in Western Europe.

The mainsprings of *perestroika*

In 1985 Mikhail Gorbachev became secretary of the Soviet Communist party and immediately called for more *glasnost* or openness in Soviet life. With this and his subsequent policy of *perestroika* (reconstruction) he tried to please and to mobilize the Soviet intelligentsia, in order to broaden the social power-base of the Soviet regime beyond the increasingly discredited Communist party. The white-collar intelligentsia had monopolized higher education opportunities, becoming in effect a hereditary self-perpetuating elite in control of key sectors of society. Unfortunately most of the intelligentsia was unprepared for change and incapable of providing new ideas. The leading ideas were directed toward the past – to a return to "true Leninism" or "Christian values" or 19th-century liberalism, combined with an exposure of Stalin's crimes and a rehabilitation of the victims of his purges and show-trials.

The struggle for *perestroika* was the outcome not only of official recognition of the urgency of economic reform, but mounting public concern over widespread corruption, soaring crime rates and major ecological crises (such as the shrinkage

of the Aral Sea). Other major concerns were the quadrupling of Soviet alcohol consumption in 1964–84, which led to the highest consumption per person of hard spirits in the world, increased crime, hooliganism, marital breakups and lowered life-expectancy. It was hoped that *perestroika* would reverse these and other adverse social trends. Except for temporary improvements in alcohol-related indicators, however, deterioration continued, contributing to various strands of the popular and official backlash against *perestroika* after 1988.

From 1985 to 1988 *glasnost, perestroika* and Gorbachev enjoyed considerable domestic as well as international acclaim. This helped Gorbachev to mobilize support and to surmount or outmaneuver conservative bureaucratic challenges, opposition and obstruction to a far greater degree than skeptics had thought possible. Legislation passed in 1987 and 1988 relaxed many economic restrictions. But economic changes were *smaller* in practice than they were on paper, due to the shortage of resources and the powerful inertia and passive resistance of central and local bureaucracies. Collective agriculture, command planning and

▲ Young people in Riga in Soviet Latvia. Such Western fashions were profoundly threatening to the old leadership of the Communist party. A counterculture of protest against bureaucratic regimentation had grown up. Some youngsters, however, followed Western fashions such as "heavy-metal" music while retaining a loyalty to the system which could bring them onto the streets to fight liberals.

central control of pricing, tax revenues and resource allocation were never really dismantled. The functioning of the command economy was gradually impaired, however, by the partial decentralization that did occur. In the political sphere, by contrast, the changes were much *larger* in practice than on paper. The whole climate was changed by the lifting of the veil of fear.

Contrary to the conventional wisdom that political liberalization was a *prerequisite* for successful economic reform, *glasnost* and political liberalization in practice became a *substitute* for successful economic reform. By unleashing forces that Moscow was finally unable to control, *glasnost* and political liberalization were the undoing of Soviet economic reform. Post-Soviet regimes were left to grapple with the problems of building market economies in the 1990s.

Socialism in the Third World

There were also sweeping changes throughout the rest of the erstwhile socialist world. After the Cultural Revolution China was radically different. It had highly decentralized local administrations which constituted competitive conglomerates. When liberalization was set in motion it thus produced – in contrast to the Soviet Union – rapid economic expansion with a proliferation of small-scale private firms. The economic transformation produced, however, demands for political change to which the Communist party, retaining sufficient cohesiveness, again in contrast to the Soviet party, reacted with violence in Tiananmen Square in Beijing in June 1989, when students demanding democracy were massacred.

Elsewhere the ruins of what was called socialism were only too apparent. Zambia and Tanzania, twin pillars of African socialism, had long since become immured in permanent economic crisis, with corruption replacing all the old hopes.

In Latin America socialism had made a spectacular advance in 1959 with Fidel Castro's victory in Cuba. In 1979 Sandinista rebels took power in Nicaragua and implemented far-reaching social reforms, only to be voted out of government in 1990. By now the Castro regime was beginning to feel a need to move to a less authoritarian system.

The origins of socialism had been in the savage social divisions which were created by the unrestricted operation of market capitalism. These not only remained but were likely to be enhanced in a liberalized and integrated world economy. Thus the prospects for the survival of some form of socialism were not entirely dim.

Questions of nationalism

In the late 1980s much of Eastern Europe embarked upon an unexpectedly rapid triple transition: from communist dictatorship to pluralist democracy, from centrally administered economies to market economies and from supranational Soviet hegemony to fully independent nation-statehood. Previous attempts to build a new order in Eastern Europe on the basis of fully independent nation-states (after each of the world wars) had provided abundant opportunities and a fertile breeding ground for extreme nationalism, and for fascist and communist authoritarianism.

▲ A desecrated Jewish cemetery in France. In the late 1980s the resurgence of antisemitism in Europe reflected fears about change at a time when national identities were in question. Ultra-right politics appealed to those bewildered by the changes taking place.

◀ In 1989 a demonstration in which thousands linked hands across the Baltic states revealed the strength of their demand for national autonomy. The Soviet Union had been held together more by coercion than by the creation of a "Soviet" citizen. Gorbachev's reforms allowed the expression of nationalism which was fed by the relative poverty of most non-Russians.

▶ Communist control submerged the ethnic patchwork of Central Europe. The stresses of the 1980s, associated with resurgent nationalism, finally erupted in 1991 in Yugoslavia, when Slovenia and Croatia declared themselves independent. Civil war later broke out in Bosnia.

Islam. In South Asia Muslim Kashmiris in India fought for their independence, as did some Sikhs in the prosperous state of Punjab following ill-advised meddling by the central government of Indira Gandhi. The events she unleashed, notably the storming of the Sikh holy places in Amritsar by Indian security forces, led to her assassination in 1984. Throughout much of India incidents of "communal" conflict between Hindus and Muslims became more frequent and more severe. Hindu nationalism (as opposed to *Indian* nationalism) became a force for the first time, threatening the secular principles on which Pandit Nehru had sought to build a modern India. In Sri Lanka Tamil-speaking people, as much "natives" of the island as the Sinhalese-speaking majority, fought a bloody guerrilla war for national sovereignty. In Africa there were comparable struggles as Eritreans and Tigrayans fought for independence in Ethiopia and black southerners fought Arabized northerners in Sudan. Almost everywhere in Africa the incidence of ethnically based conflict was high.

Such widespread events, occurring in very different contexts, have been associated with a variety of specific local circumstances. But there were common threads which help to explain the importance of nationalist and of other ethnic conflicts in the later 20th century. Nationalism, and other forms of ethnicity (such as "Hindu" versus "Muslim" or "Kikuyu" versus "Luo") which may indeed provide a base for nationalism, are to be understood above all as collective states of mind. They are, in Benedict Anderson's words, "*imagined* communities". The nation, Anderson says, "is distinguished as a community because, regardless of the actual inequality and

Unfortunately the changes set in motion in Eastern European countries rapidly and perilously created conditions and opportunities similar to those of 1918 and 1945. The national euphoria awakened by the ending of communist dictatorship heightened the importance of exclusive and potentially intolerant nationalism and national religions as the value systems and belief systems most capable of filling the void left by the demise of communism. Soon there was a resurgence of antisemitism, of discrimination against Gypsies and quite generally of tensions between majority and minority ethnic groups.

At the same time in the Soviet Union, as a result of *glasnost*, demands for national liberation began to be felt, especially in Latvia, Estonia and Lithuania, in Georgia, Armenia and Azerbaijan and even in the core republic of the Ukraine. Elsewhere in the world apparently similar forces were seen. In the West French-speaking Québecois in Canada again talked about parting company with Anglophone Canada; Basques and Catalans (in Spain), Flemings and Walloons (in Belgium) and Scots all sought greater degrees of autonomy or actual separation. Western Asia was a caldron of nationalist and ethnic conflicts, focused around the status of the state of Israel (founded in 1948) and the establishment of a homeland for displaced Palestinian Arabs, but exacerbated by old tensions between the Sunni and Shia traditions of

Ethnic Areas of Eastern Europe 1990

Ethnic majority over 50%
- Albanians
- Bosnians
- Bulgars
- Croats
- Czechs
- Germans
- Macedonians
- Magyars
- Poles
- Romanians
- Serbs and Montenegrins
- Slovaks
- Slovenes
- Turks
- Area of no majority

SWEDEN
DENMARK
Baltic Sea
USSR
Elbe
Vistula
Oder
Warsaw
GERMANY
POLAND
Prague
CZECHOSLOVAKIA
Budapest
AUSTRIA
HUNGARY
Po
Drava
Sava
ROMANIA
Belgrade
Bucharest
YUGOSLAVIA
Danube
ITALY
Sofia
BULGARIA
Black Sea
Scale 1 : 20 000 000
0   400 km
0   300 mi
ALBANIA
Tirane
GREECE
TURKEY

exploitation that may prevail in each, the nation is always conceived as a deep, horizontal comradeship. Ultimately it is this fraternity that makes it possible, over the past two centuries, for so many millions of people not so much to kill, as willingly to die for such limited imaginings". The idea of "nationalism" emerged in Europe in the 19th century in circumstances in which the old "face-to-face" communities, also imagined, but based on kinship and neighborhood, were eroded by the forces of modernization. The idea of the "nation", usually based on language, replaced older identities.

In the 20th century the small literate classes of colonial territories in Africa and Asia, mainly civil servants, professionals and some business people, for whom alone the idea of "the nation" could possibly have any meaning, sought to create independent nation-states in the pursuit of the political and economic goals of modernization. They had to build a sense of nationality among the mass of the people for whom "tribal" or religious identities had often been manufactured by the colonial powers. The failure of the elites in this effort, and the failures of modernization by industrialization, account for many of the conflicts considered here. There is almost invariably a crucial economic dimension: access to "good jobs" in the public sector (important in

building up ethnic/national tensions in Sri Lanka, for example, or in Uganda); or control over other assets. But this is only one dimension of a broader cause: the inability of the political class to live up to its modernist ideals. Like the void left by the collapse of communism in Eastern Europe, the strains created by modernization, by "development", or its outright failure in much of the Third World, provides fertile ground for sectionalism which is easily made intolerant.

Islamic fundamentalism
Another significant social phenomenon of the later 20th century was the rise of Islamic fundamentalism, commonly associated with the revolution in Iran in 1979 which swept the Shah from power. In fact this is a misleading notion, both because fundamentalist movements represent a very old tradition within Islam, going back to its foundations, and because Saudi Arabia – ally of the United States – was a fundamentalist state long before the Iranian revolution.

All of the great religions of the world establish social charters or designs for the organization of society – setting out standards and norms for all aspects of life. Islam, partly because of the circumstances of its foundation by a militarily and politically successful tribal group in Arabia, offers the most powerful of such designs, embracing all

Once we thought that western society had all the answers for successful, fruitful living. If we followed the lead of the West we would have progress. Now we see that this isn't true; they [the West] are sick societies; even their material prosperity is breaking down. America is full of crime and promiscuity. Russia is worse. Who wants to be like that? We have to remember God. Look how God has blessed Saudi Arabia. That is because they have tried to follow the Law. And America, with all its loose society, is all problems.

MUSLIM WOMAN

Islam and Women

In Islam women are regarded with a mixture of fear – as a source of evil – and of paternalism – because they are vulnerable and in need of protection. They are seen as being dominated by "unruly passion", in contrast with the "calm and orderly nature of men". Men have thus been given a status above women and authority over them. Women are thought of as being threatening to the stability and good judgment of men. For this reason it is extremely important that their sexuality should be under the control of men. They must be modest, their "adornments" concealed by a veil except in the intimacy of their own bedrooms. They should be married as soon as possible and then "give themselves unquestioningly to their husbands".

There is justification in the Quran for these ideas. Yet it also contains what amounts to a charter for marriage as a flexible contract between two consenting adults. In spite of this, after the revolution in Iran, Quranic justification was used for the reversal of rights which Iranian women had won – rights to education; to leave off the veil; to vote; to contest the custody of children in case of divorce; to abortion on demand; and a ban on polygamy. Women were required again to wear the veil; their rights in marriage were annulled while men were allowed up to four permanent wives and were given exclusive rights to divorce at will. Some religious leaders equated unmarried women with terrorists; their approval of polygamy was in spite of a Quranic injunction "to marry only one wife" because a man cannot treat a number of wives with impartiality. One ayatollah, opposed to polygamy, nonetheless approved concubinage as a way of preventing women from being led astray.

◄ Some Muslim women supported Iranian fundamentalism.

who have accepted the faith. They constitute a single community of believers, the *ummah*, who must maintain the solidarity of the faith against unbelievers. Christianity, associated at its foundation with a subordinate, rebel group of people, makes a clear distinction between state and religion. Such a distinction is not made in Islam. *Sharia*, the sacred law of Islam, based on the Quran and *sunna* – the sayings and doings of the Prophet as recorded in the *hadiths* – is the framework for polity and society. But there have been many disputes within Islam, throughout its history, over whether the Quran and the *sunna* are the law, or the basis for the law. Broadly, how much interpretation is permissible? There has always been a tension between more pragmatic and more orthodox tendencies, with the Sunni tradition inclined to the former and the Shia to the latter.

Islamic fundamentalism always aimed to protect the purity of Islam from adulteration by speculative interpretations. It was thus directed against internal threats, from the superstitious beliefs of peoples absorbed into Islam, or from scholastic debate, as well as against those from outside. The external threats were derived from Western influences, and Islam was riven by disagreement between those who, perceiving the gap between Western and Muslim societies, argued for modernization and those who argued for return to the fundamentals of *Sharia*. It is not surprising that the ideas of the fundamentalists should have been found persuasive by those threatened by modern economic change, or who have been uprooted by it – migrants from villages to towns and members of the urban petty bourgeoisie. Such people, led by often low- or middle-ranking clerics, provided the main backing for movements like the Muslim Brotherhood, which had great influence in Egyptian politics in the 1980s and 1990s, or the movement which destroyed the Shah's regime.

Attempts in the 1930s by Reza Shah to modernize Iran created distance between the increasingly

◄ Islam extends from West Africa, across Asia into Southeast Asia. This mosque is in Malaysia, which has experienced progressive political Islamization since the mid 1970s. By then the Malay language had become the language of social communication for all Malaysians (for Chinese and Indians as well as Malays). Islam therefore became the last symbol of Malay ethnic identity. The government has emphasized economic development with spiritual regeneration and aimed at proving that Islam is a dynamic and adaptable creed.

▼ Arabs in the Gulf state of Dubai playing bar football reflect the tensions within the Islamic world between modernization and Western influences and the defense of the faith. Arabs are also tugged between different loyalties, a general one to "Arabism" and a narrow one to region, clan or religious sect. These tensions and conflicts are set in a context of inequality. In 1986 GDP per head in the Gulf states was $16,500 (Qatar), while some 50 million Egyptians had only $1100 per head.

westernized upper classes and the peasants and the people of the bazaars who continued to follow the *ulama* (religious-legal scholars). Reza Shah's son's reforms in the 1960s, his authoritarianism and repression of the *ulama*, deepened these tensions in Iranian society. In this context Ayatolla Khomeini's arguments for the subordination of political power to Islar ic precepts, expressed in a simple and direct wa) and without any reference to western ideas, appealed to different social groups. He succeeded in welding together disparate forces – the urban working class and the traditional middle class of the bazaars, the modern middle class, which was by now resentful of royal authority and of foreign influence in the country, and the rural poor. Together they brought about the overthrow of the monarchy through massive demonstrations in 1978–79.

By the end of the 1980s Islam had become the central ideology of the Third World against the First. As the British political writer R. W. Johnson suggested: "In many parts of the world secular nationalism and socialism have failed in their project of modernization. The dream of surmounting poverty and drawing level with the West has, all too often, collapsed in despair and ruin. In that despair there is natural resort to a militant anti-Western ideology, to a creed that refuses the whole objective of 'modernization' – and Islamic fundamentalism has filled that need."

Crisis in Africa

In 1981 the World Bank published a major report which drew attention to the pervasive failure of economic and social development in sub-Saharan Africa. Four years later television viewers around the world began to become familiar with pictures of bands of emaciated refugees and of the victims of famine, especially (though not only) in northeast Africa. The hopes and expectations of independence had been utterly crushed. Of 34 countries described by the World Bank as "low income" in 1984, 21 were in tropical Africa. In the 1970s 15 African economies registered negative growth rates; population growth outstripped food production; life expectancy at 47 years was the lowest in the world; and in 1981 the region contained half of the world's refugees. Failure marked both those states which had espoused "socialism" and those which had explicitly sought a capitalist road. It was recognized that part of the reason for this situation was the way the continent had been torn apart by civil wars and other conflicts. In Uganda, for example, the atrocities of the regime of Idi Amin (1971–78) had ripped apart a society that had known relatively high standards of welfare and education. What had created this bloody turmoil and the "underdevelopment" of Africa?

When they became independent the states of sub-Saharan Africa were peasant societies. Their struggles for freedom had been won by small educated elites made up mainly of minor officials and teachers. There were few African businessmen; the most important traders were outsiders – Asians in East Africa, Lebanese in West Africa. The organized working class was generally small – less than 5 percent of the economically active

Life in South African Townships

Before dawn each day, streams of commuter trains disgorge black workers into South Africa's city centers. At dusk the workers are swallowed back into the trains and returned to townships such as Soweto, South Africa's largest township, situated outside Johannesburg.

South Africa's townships are the product of segregationist ideology. It defined cities as "white" and consistently sought to impede urbanization and to retain African workers in rural areas, where their employment options were confined to agriculture or factories and mines (as contract migrants). In 1923 the Natives (Urban Areas) Act provided for the establishment of segregated African townships by white municipal authorities on the principle that Africans "should only be permitted within the municipal areas in so far and for so long as their presence is demanded by the wants of the white population". African land purchase was curbed and, through the infamous "pass laws", a system of influx control was established.

Even so there remained only a grudging acknowledgment that a settled population of urban Africans was necessary. As late as the

▼ By the end of the 1980s overcrowding had reached crisis proportions in South Africa's townships, with densities of 15 people or more per four-room house. Those with jobs and housing accommodated unemployed relatives or took in lodgers to supplement inadequate incomes. Often they constructed makeshift extensions and corrugated shanties in their backyards. Even in the densely populated Witwatersrand area around Johannesburg, half the African population lived in informal rather than formal housing. Without electricity and adequate water supply, women's child-rearing and housekeeping tasks were burdensome.

1970s the state still attempted to restrict the proportion of urban African workers housed in family accommodation (as opposed to single-sex hostels) to 3 percent. It was even considered feasible to transport workers daily from new townships in the impoverished "homelands" up to 112km (70mi) away and weekly from points as far distant as 640km (400mi). In spite of the authorities' efforts a relentless inflow from impoverished rural areas continued.

By the mid 1980s 7 million urban people were housed in informal urban settlements. In Soweto alone, over 1 million people were subtenants. Moreover, juxtaposed with the makeshift extensions and tightly packed warrens of corrugated huts were middle-class suburbs, accommodating African bureaucrats, businessmen and professionals.

Township life has been characterized by resistance and struggle. In 1929 workers in Durban rioted against the municipal beerhalls whose monopoly over the sale of sorghum beer financed township administration. In the 1950s pass books were burnt countrywide. Education boycotts (as in Soweto in 1976) sparked off

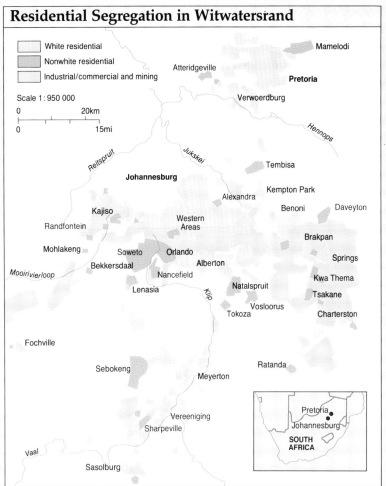

Residential Segregation in Witwatersrand

White residential
Nonwhite residential
Industrial/commercial and mining

Scale 1 : 950 000

0   20km
0   15mi

Mamelodi
Atteridgeville
Pretoria
Verwoerdburg
Hennops
Reitspruit
Jukskei
Tembisa
Johannesburg
Kempton Park
Alexandra
Benoni   Daveyton
Kajiso
Western
Areas
Brakpan
Randfontein
Springs
Mohlakeng
Soweto   Orlando
Kwa Thema
Bekkersdaal   Alberton
Nancefield
Tsakane
Mooirivierloop
Lenasia   Natalspruit
Klip   Vosloorus   Charterston
Tokoza
Fochville
Ratanda
Sebokeng
Meyerton

Pretoria
Johannesburg
SOUTH
AFRICA

Vereeniging
Sharpeville
Vaal
Sasolburg

organized campaigns, including bus, rent and consumer boycotts. In the 1980s township discontent was also directed against those who participated in black local authorities, many of whom used their positions to accumulate wealth and establish patronage networks.

During the 1980s the lives and property of the black accumulating classes came under attack by frustrated youths, intent on making the townships "ungovernable". Images of the charred bodies of "apartheid stooges" (victims of the "necklaces" of burning tires) flashed across the world's television screens. By the end of the decade township violence seemed endemic, with military and police occupation virtually the norm. Gangs of youth controled neighborhoods, entry to which was forbidden without the correct password or declaration of political allegiance. Workers reached their factories and offices exhausted and dazed, following sleepless nights peppered with sounds of gunfire and battles.

For all the horror of township life in the 1980s the townships continued to throb with assured energy. Popular civic associations had taken over as the effective instruments of local government; independent taxi services had replaced the state monopoly on transport; illicit "shebeen queens" had usurped the trade of the beerhalls; and a vibrant informal sector served consumption needs. South African townships have been isolated, but through this they have developed a language, music, culture and life of their own.

▲ By 1990 three-fifths of all South Africans lived in the country's urban areas. The mosaic of apartheid's segregated urban areas had been carefully designed and, moreover, designed to last. Spreading out from the central business districts were the affluent white suburbs, cocooned by buffer zones of vacant land or Indian and "colored" group areas. Flanking the peripheral industrial areas were the sprawling African townships, provided by the state to house its necessary but unwelcome urban work force.

▲ In the 1980s samples from the general population in eastern and central Africa showed levels of infection with Acquired Immune Deficiency Syndrome (AIDS) of up to 18 percent, representing a major social problem.

▶ There has been popular support for radical socialist policies in Africa as perhaps amongst these Angolan boys. Attempts to transplant Soviet methods to Africa have been disastrous however. Attempts to establish bureaucratic control over peasant agriculture have discouraged production in both socialist- and capitalist-style countries.

▶ Access to the luxury of an executive bed in Africa often depends upon being a bureaucrat, able to derive "rent" from control over regulatory activities and agencies of the state. These "haves" are among the favored clients of rulers, in systems of government which lack legitimacy and depend on force and a division of spoils through patronage. The members of the ruling classes, it is said, "respect the big belly squeezed under the steering wheel of a Mercedes far more than they respect talent, quality, and productivity."

population in most cases. In these circumstances the extent of organized, "civil society" beyond the state was limited. The political leadership was answerable to none but itself. The parliamentary institutions which had been transferred from the West were irrelevant in the absence of pressures from organized social classes, and in most cases they were effectively set aside quite soon. Power depended upon being able to command the personal loyalty of others, and this was secured through ties of kinship, "tribe" and region and by means of the distribution of patronage. "Jobs for the boys" meant the proliferation of bureaucratic roles which gave their incumbents the opportunity to appropriate bribes, or by using their powers to profit (for example, from the distribution of essential supplies like electricity). Because of these practices African bureaucracies no longer corresponded at all to Max Weber's model of the impartial, rational administration. In the absence of a secure legal framework and a working infrastructure, capitalism could not thrive.

It was also necessary for successful leaders to be able to use force and they needed either to have the army on their side, or to contain it by setting up rival forces. By the 1980s competitive party politics existed only in five countries and most of these were subject to personal rule by "strongmen" and were in practice dependent upon military power. The regular interventions, direct and indirect, of Western powers and their sales of arms only exacerbated the inherent instability of systems of personal rule. Public funds were looted; peasants were mulcted by taxation and by state marketing boards and tended to withdraw from the market; parallel or "black" economies thrived. These were the circumstances of decline in much of Africa. They proved generally resistant to the efforts of the World Bank and the International Monetary Fund in the 1980s to bring

about economic adjustment, but the packages of measures enforced by these agencies often had the immediate effect of causing further deterioration in living standards as welfare services were cut.

One crucial factor in the future of Africa remained the fate of South Africa, the continent's only major industrial society. The expansion of industrial capitalism there was for a time encouraged by the policy of so-called "separate development" for people of different races under *apartheid*. But it also created the conditions for the challenge to white supremacy which began to be felt in the 1980s, and which depended substantially on the rise of the African working class. Pressures for reform emerged even in the Afrikaaner white establishment in the 1970s, leading to the fall from power of John Vorster in 1978. The modest efforts of P.W. Botha thereafter to reform the instruments of white supremacy eventually encouraged more opposition. By 1990 his successor, F.W. de Klerk, had begun to negotiate the demise of apartheid, though tragically amid increasing violence between the supporters of the African National Congress and those of Zulu Chief Buthulezi's *Inkatha* movement. In spite of appearances, the savage killing which took place did not stem from "tribalism". Johannesburg's *Business Day* newspaper wrote: "Fear, hatred, vengeance and depravity drive this bestial process" – which had its roots in the envy and resentments which accumulated in squatter camps on the fringes of the townships. It was a conflict between "haves" and "have-nots", not between tribes.

The future of South Africa was a vital issue for the future of Africa. A progressive regime in South Africa, based on the African bourgeoisie and the working class, would have the capacity to bring about change elsewhere.

THE ROLES OF RELIGION

In its varied forms, religion seeks divine guidance to make sense of the confusion and contradictions of everyday experience and provides identity, guidance about behavior and, in most cases, the prospect of a new beginning after death. The rise of a scientific world view in the late 19th century and the growth of the belief that beneficial social change can be brought about by human agency might be thought to have challenged the place of religion in the world.

The first half of the 20th century did indeed see a rise in popular secularism. Disbelief received a powerful boost through the Bolshevik seizure of power in Russia in 1917. The Bolsheviks' Marxist-Leninist doctrine saw religion as an illusory distraction and offered instead a new social order, rules for achieving a good life and the prospect of improved living standards. In some ways communism was a religion without a deity. But religion has survived, sometimes because it has been useful for rulers, sometimes because it has been able to identify with the underdog, and sometimes because the need for religious powers of consolation have continued.

The use of religion as tool of conservative and authoritarian regimes is well seen in the state promotion of Shintoism in Japan until that country's defeat in World War II. In Spain the Catholic church was used as a means of securing order after the overthrow of the republican regime in 1939.

Religion as an element of resistance has been seen in numerous parts of the world in the 20th century. In Latin America the Roman Catholic church fought authoritarian states in the cause of the poor – often to the extent of coming into conflict with the papacy in Rome. In Poland the Catholic church helped to preserve Polish identity against communism and was at the core of the Solidarity movement in the 1980s. In the Middle East revivalist Islam has been at the heart of major social upheavals – from the Arab revolt against the Turks during World War I to the opposition to the Shah in Iran in the 1970s.

Among minority communities in Western Europe and North America – and for the majority black population of South Africa – pentecostal forms of Christianity have provided consolation and hope for the socially and politically marginalized.

Religion divides, religion unites. It may be revolutionary or conservative. Its strength lies in its unpredictability and flexibility, which suggests that it will long continue to resist the challenges of secularism.

▲▶ **Priests, generals and state power in Spain.** After his victory in the civil war in 1939, General Francisco Franco needed to unite a divided society. He looked to the church for assistance. Catholic organizations provided important support for his regime.

▶ **Church ceremony at the heart of the rural community:** a Lutheran church in Kansas, 1910.

▶▶ **Sikhs at the Golden Temple in Amritsar, India** – the focus for the sikhs' beliefs and their aspirations to be a separate nation.

◀ The old teach the young in the Jewish community in Morocco in the 1930s. Religious identity enabled this minority to survive in an Arab Muslim society.

▼ A newly baptized member of an evangelical Christian church in the United States emerges reborn in her new faith. Immersion demands commitment and symbolizes transformation.

▼ Desmond Tutu, leader of South Africa's Anglican church, inspires his followers (many of whom are not Christians) to fight for liberty from apartheid. Here religion moves from consoling the oppressed to becoming the vehicle for change.

Datafile

The late 20th century was a frightening time of increasing violence in cities, of rape and murder, drug abuse and drug-related crime, and of what seemed apocalyptic threats from AIDS and global environmental destruction. High divorce rates in the West, increased single parenting, and such phenomena as "dowry deaths" of women in India, resulting from the disappointment of bridegrooms at the size of the dowry brought by their wives, overturned cherished values. Yet there were also "new" social movements, depending more on mutual support than on hierarchy, reflecting deep moral concerns and which won wide support. They often depended especially on women who at last won greater individual freedom. All was not bleak.

▶ The largest cities in the world were now emphatically outside Europe and North America. World Bank projections showed that by early in the 21st century the populations of the developing countries would be more than urban than rural, suggesting the scale of the potential problems of urban management. In the industrialized countries increased inequality of this time is reflected in the fact that, for example, in large US metropolitan areas more than half the children were living below the poverty line.

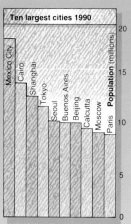

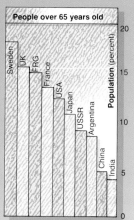

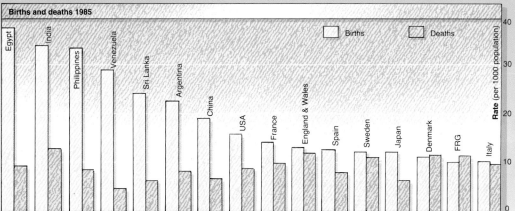

▲ In Western societies the problems of the "Third Age" – the increasingly significant period of people's lives spent in retirement – began to loom as large as those of youth. Between 1970 and 1990 the proportion of the population aged over 65 increased by more than 20 percent (36 percent in Japan). Already 15–16 percent of payrolls in America went in payments from the taxpayer to the elderly. How in the future, with costs rising to 25–30 per cent of payroll, would a smaller labor force pay for more care for the old?

▲ The disparity between birth and death rates meant that population growth was still high in developing countries, compounding the difficulties of welfare provision. One-fifth of their populations still went hungry every day. Yet a United Nations report on human development found that there had been improvement in levels of well-being in many countries, even in tropical Africa in the absence of economic growth. In most industrial countries population now grew only very slowly; in a few it even declined.

▶ In the industrialized countries the divorce rate was highest in the United States, followed by the Soviet Union, Canada and New Zealand. In the United States it declined a little in the 1980s, perhaps reflecting the renewed emphasis on family life in the ideology of the "new right". In times of economic insecurity it seems that the desire for stable values leads to greater emphasis on the authority of basic institutions such as family or religion, which it is possible to question or reject in "good times" such as those before 1973.

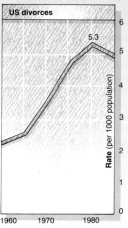

▶ Single parenting was a positive choice for some in the West, mainly in the middle classes. Among the poor it was less deliberate. In 1987 three-quarters of black babies in the big inner cities of America were born to unmarried mothers. Meanwhile, because whites had fewer babies a shift in the ethnic structure of the labor force was underway. By 2007 perhaps 30 percent of recruits to the labor force will be blacks or hispanics. Will such underprivileged workers pay through taxes for the care of elderly whites?

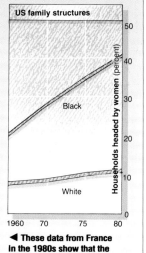

◀ These data from France in the 1980s show that the sharing of household chores or the undertaking of them by men was higher in households where there were no children. The work loads of women in employment thus increased when they had children. It was still difficult, therefore, for women to combine pursuit of a career and raising a family. Even where men did help with housework their contribution was small and tended toward social activities (such as washing up) rather than hard work (such as cleaning).

◀ High rates of crime in rich societies, especially of murder in the United States, of drug-related crimes (300 recorded cases for every 100,000 people in Canada, 276 in New Zealand), and rape (144 reported for every 100,000 women aged 15–59 in the United States, nearly 100 in Holland) perhaps reflected more accurate reporting. But there was no doubt of the distress in industrial societies, ascribed to "the weakening social fabric". Japan's low rates suggested a continuing sense of community and social cohesion.

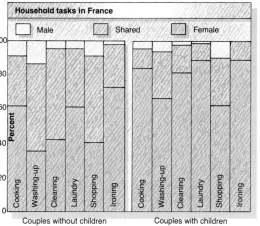

SOCIAL TROUBLES AND HOPE

Attacks on the family
Alternative family forms
Legal reforms and social relationships
Increasing violence and AIDS
New ways of responding to social problems

The 1970s and 1980s represented a major landmark in the public conception of the nature of marriage and the family, and of women's roles and their status. Extensive changes in marriage, divorce and family law were made in order to "modernize" what were thought of as traditional relationships. The legal status of women improved dramatically. Numerous laws were passed in support of equality.

Doubt about the role of the family

Amidst the eruption of so-called libertine values during the 1960s and 1970s, restrictions on the expression of sexuality were modified or ignored, conventional definitions of marriage were questioned and assumptions about sex roles were challenged. The long debate about the family and social change in the 20th century finally seemed to reach its culmination. The social unrest of the 1960s, which had brought forth the resurgence of feminism, had also thrown open many questions

▼ Members of the "Third Age", the period after retirement, which became more significant in the late 20th century. Care of the elderly became a major charge on funds.

about the family. Feminists attacked it as the bulwark of patriarchal society and the "new left" as a reactionary force that impeded progress. New research by historians and sociologists unfolded a whole host of misconceptions about the family and its history, which had been the premises of public policy for almost a century. There was now the new worry that the family might have become too self-contained – that in its intense privacy it had become "socially isolated", or as the British sociologist Ronald Fletcher wrote: "it seemed no longer to relate in a living way with the community". Others saw the community itself as but a "network of formal organization of people's wages, benefits, social services, rates and mortgages or taxation", while "being a person to others" had been lost. Why else would people have to turn to counselors or therapists?

There was new uncertainty, too, about the changed position of women and how that would affect family life – and new bewilderment when

▲ During the 1970s the single-parent family became a fairly common family pattern. Most of them were headed by women. But in the late 1980s there was an increase in single-father families (as here), due mainly to men's changing life-styles and desire to continue parenting. There is a general belief that single-mother families are "broken" and disorganized, the children deprived by their father's absence. This illustration seems to suggest that there can be warmth and deprivation irrespective of the sex of the parent.

▼ Homosexual wedding in Copenhagen. There have been a number of attempts by homosexual couples to obtain legal marriages which would give them the advantages of symbolic equality but also the usual social security or health insurance benefits due upon marriage. Denmark was the first country to institute homosexual marriage.

feminists attacked the myth of the happy home of patriarchal society and exposed wife-battering, sexual abuse and rape as the actual situation of thousands of married women. Others wondered whether the idealization of the family, the constant emphasis on love and sex throughout the 20th century had raised unrealistic expectations of marital relations – often leading to a breakup when not fulfilled. In the effort to raise women's awareness of their situation, feminist writing in the early 1970s indeed warned women against the pursuit of an ideal which was but a myth or a fantasy of fixed union and mutuality. The great anxiety over the rising separation and divorce rates certainly suggested a substantial gap between public expectations of marriage and the family and actual experiences. The emergence of more definite alternative family forms in the 1970s (usually associated with the emergence of the various countercultures of that period) similarly reflected this variance. The increase in single-parent families (which approximately doubled between 1970 and 1980) reflected to a high degree the steady rise in divorce rates but the number of people opting for "singlehood" also rose. The figures for one-person households also increased steadily, but mainly because of the higher proportion of elderly people living on their own – in Germany in 1982 they accounted for 31.2 percent of all households. "Cohabitation" (often seen as a temporary "trial marriage") became a preferred life-style for a significant minority of young or divorced people, though figures varied markedly from country to country (15 percent of couples in Sweden in 1979, 7 percent in Holland, 2.3 percent in the United States). Voluntary childlessness (in marriage), considered to be "atypical" until then, also made its impact in the 1970s. In the Netherlands in 1980 it was estimated that 20 percent of all marriages were deliberately childless. But although they were inconsistent with the patterns established in the "baby-boom" era, the lower marriage and high divorce rates and fewer children of the late 20th century were consistent with longer-term trends. They were not "abnormal" as was sometimes feared in the 1970s.

Life expectancy at birth 1991

CANADA

UNITED STATES OF AMERICA

MEXICO

CUBA
DOMINICAN REP
JAMAICA HAITI
BELIZE
PUERTO RICO (US)
GUATEMALA HONDURAS
EL SALVADOR NICARAGUA
COSTA RICA
PANAMA VENEZUELA GUYANA
SURINAM
COLOMBIA GUIANA
ECUADOR
PERU

PACIFIC OCEAN

BRAZI[L]

BOLIVIA

PARAGUAY

URUGUA[Y]
CHILE ARGENTINA

Life expectancy

70
65
60
55
50
0

☐ Data not available

Scale 1 : 115 000 000
0   3000 km
0   2000 mi

In the end it was this "deviance" from conventional ways of life and the rejection of old "proven" values, together with associated symptoms of social disorder (rising illegitimacy, juvenile crime, baby-battering, incest and so on), that forced governments into taking a new and critical look at the traditional relationships of authority in the family and marriage and at discriminatory practices elsewhere. The reforms that ensued were a deliberate attempt at reconstruction, departing from earlier notions of family relationships, of male dominance or of women's dependency, and of their exclusive role as mothers.

Public policy and family relationships

Upon marriage young couples in some countries were now given the option of using the bride's maiden name as an official family name. In many countries child-rearing allowances were introduced for either parent, or fathers were given the option to take parental leave to look after a sick

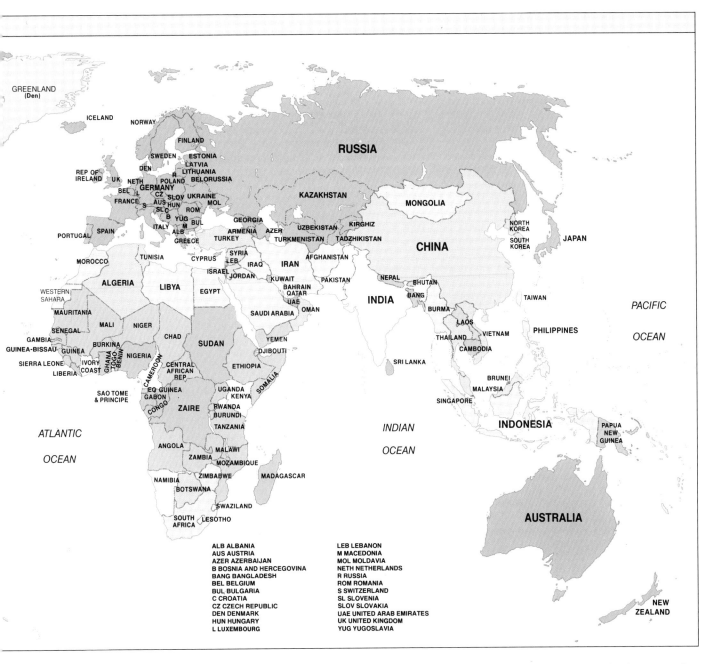

GREENLAND
(Den)

ICELAND
NORWAY
FINLAND
REP OF IRELAND
UK NETH
BEL L
GERMANY
FRANCE
S
B
AUS
SLC
HUN
ITALY
M
GREECE
PORTUGAL
SPAIN
SWEDEN
DEN
POLAND
CZ
SLOV UKRAINE
ROM
YUG
BUL
TURKEY
CYPRUS
ESTONIA
LATVIA
LITHUANIA
BELORUSSIA
MOL
GEORGIA
ARMENIA AZER
TURKMENISTAN

RUSSIA

KAZAKHSTAN

MONGOLIA

UZBEKISTAN
KIRGHIZ
TADZHIKISTAN

CHINA

NORTH KOREA
SOUTH KOREA
JAPAN

MOROCCO
TUNISIA
SYRIA
LEB
ISRAEL
JORDAN
IRAQ
IRAN
AFGHANISTAN
KUWAIT
BAHRAIN
QATAR
UAE
SAUDI ARABIA
OMAN

WESTERN SAHARA
ALGERIA
LIBYA
EGYPT

MAURITANIA
MALI
NIGER
CHAD
SUDAN
YEMEN
DJIBOUTI

SENEGAL
GAMBIA
GUINEA-BISSAU
GUINEA
SIERRA LEONE
LIBERIA
IVORY COAST
GHANA
TOGO
BENIN
NIGERIA
BURKINA
CAMEROON
CENTRAL AFRICAN REP
ETHIOPIA
SOMALIA

SAO TOME & PRINCIPE
EQ GUINEA
GABON
CONGO
ZAIRE
UGANDA
KENYA
RWANDA
BURUNDI
TANZANIA

NEPAL
BHUTAN
BANG
INDIA
BURMA
LAOS
THAILAND
VIETNAM
CAMBODIA

SRI LANKA

TAIWAN
PHILIPPINES

PACIFIC OCEAN

BRUNEI
MALAYSIA
SINGAPORE

ATLANTIC
OCEAN

ANGOLA
ZAMBIA
MALAWI
MOZAMBIQUE
NAMIBIA
ZIMBABWE
BOTSWANA
MADAGASCAR
SWAZILAND
SOUTH AFRICA
LESOTHO

INDIAN
OCEAN

INDONESIA

PAPUA NEW GUINEA

AUSTRALIA

NEW ZEALAND

ALB ALBANIA
AUS AUSTRIA
AZER AZERBAIJAN
B BOSNIA AND HERCEGOVINA
BANG BANGLADESH
BEL BELGIUM
BUL BULGARIA
C CROATIA
CZ CZECH REPUBLIC
DEN DENMARK
HUN HUNGARY
L LUXEMBOURG

LEB LEBANON
M MACEDONIA
MOL MOLDAVIA
NETH NETHERLANDS
R RUSSIA
ROM ROMANIA
S SWITZERLAND
SL SLOVENIA
SLOV SLOVAKIA
UAE UNITED ARAB EMIRATES
UK UNITED KINGDOM
YUG YUGOSLAVIA

▲ Economic development, social reforms, improvements in hygiene and social welfare together with advances in medicine have all contributed to the conspicuous increase in life expectancy in the 20th century. In developing countries average life expectancy increased by over one-third between 1960 and 1990, to 63 years (though only 52 in sub-Saharan Africa), even though 1.5 billion people still lacked basic health care.

child. Family law codes granted women equal rights in decision-making, in property and in work. Social policy was no longer to be punitive for working mothers but recognized women's right to work, attempting to ease rather than obstruct their dual role. Already by the 1970s women in Europe made up on average 37 percent of the labor force and 42 percent in North America – married women often outnumbered the unmarried. At the other end of the spectrum, women's "social invisibility" in the home (as "non-working" mothers who did housework) also received attention. Voluntary social security benefits were introduced for housewives, as for example in Germany. If things still went wrong, divorce was made easier too. Changes in existing laws generally replaced marital offenses as grounds for divorce with the principle of "irrevocable breakdown". Even in Catholic Italy the reforms of the Family Law Code (1975) granted spouses legal equality, permitted separation by

mutual consent and brought the long overdue equalization of the status of all children, legitimate or otherwise. In Ireland, however, divorce remained "unconstitutional".

After centuries of encouragement of childbearing, motherhood began to lose some of its centrality in public policy planning during the 1970s. Women were finally given leave substantially to control their own fertility, freeing them, as feminists saw it, from the tyranny of their reproductive functions. The wider availability of contraceptives and reform of abortion laws suggested that the separation of sex from procreation was now more generally accepted.

While reforms were intended to achieve greater justice in family relationships, allowing for greater "personal growth", rather than attempting to maintain family cohesion and fertility rates at all cost, the family's importance as the heart of society was never really questioned. The reforms were expected to strengthen the family once

Governor George Wallace in 1968; it provided the source of John Hinckley's infatuation with its star Jodie Foster – and in imitation of the film's central character, Hinckley shot United States' president Ronald Reagan.

The movie brats

From the mid-1970s the new bureaucratic and corporate style of Hollywood combined with the enhancement of the status of the "director as superstar". In the work of Coppola, Scorsese, Steven Spielberg, George Lucas, Brian de Palma, William Friedkin and John Milius there appeared a body of films which demonstrated a "personal cinema" through their mannerisms yet also fueled the entertainment machine. Storytelling no longer mattered. Disaster movies demonstrated the packaging possibilities of incident without narrative – the plot of *The Towering Inferno* (1974) was summarized by one critic as, "A building catches fire, some people die, some people don't"die – while the movie was sold on its spectacle and the array of stars who appeared in cameo roles. Later variants of the package took the phenomenon to even greater extremes. As the technology of special effects proliferated, the films that employed it did so at the expense of narrative complexity. One critic accused *Star Wars* of reducing "the rich philosophical possibilities of science fiction to a galactic pinball game," and the Disney Studios actually located its science fiction fantasy adventure *Tron* (1982) inside a computer video game.

The most successful of the new wave of "Movie Brat" directors, Spielberg and Lucas, were particularly attracted to fantasy forms, expressing a naive faith in space as the new frontier. In an increasingly conservative world, the *Star Wars* saga of a group of rebels restoring an old patriarchal order seemed appropriate. The late 1970s and 1980s saw several large-budget juvenile male fantasies such as *Superman – the Movie* (1978) and *Flash Gordon* (1980), which disguised their patriarchal attitudes with a veneer of knowing self-reflection. Other science-fiction films, such as *Alien* (1979), *Blade Runner* (1982) and *The Thing* (1982) owed their appeal more directly to the horror films of the early 1970s. Some critics argued that, in their brutal assault on their audience's sensibilities, films such as *The Texas Chainsaw Massacre* (1974) offered a critique of the patriarchal family as the monster in the American home, but few found much to defend in the "slasher" movies, which drew their prototype from *Friday the 13th* (1980), and alternated bouts of teenage sexual activity with the brutal destruction of those who engage in it. It was to teenagers themselves that these movies played most successfully.

The ironic, self-aware element in all these films, their willingness to step outside their fictions and disarm their spectators with a self-deprecating acknowledgment that no one is really supposed to take this seriously, has remained a persistent feature of Hollywood in the 1980s. The counterculture of the early 1970s was contained by the second half of the decade within a form of comedy that Hollywood took from television. The frenetic comic formula of many of the most

successful Hollywood films of the 1980s was inherited from the television of *Saturday Night Live* and *SCTV*, as were some of the most successful 1980s stars: John Belushi, Dan Ackroyd, Chevy Chase, Eddie Murphy. Their movies catered to the dominant American movie audience: young and mobile, preferring to find their entertainment in the smaller cinemas built in large numbers in suburban shopping malls.

Other critics saw in the horror cycle a response to the Vietnam War, which Hollywood was, at least for the war's duration, unable to address directly. Hollywood could not manufacture fictions about defeat on such a scale, any more than other areas of American life could easily accommodate the failure of the liberal technological dream in southeast Asia. Nevertheless, the trauma of Vietnam was reflected in the pervasive uncertainties of every aspect of film production in the decade, and more overtly in the recurrent appearance of heroic psychopaths who offered the simple solution of successful American violence to urban disorder. However ambivalent these heroic figures, such as Clint Eastwood's *Dirty Harry* Callaghan, appeared to be, their movies always showed the violent repression of disorder as successful.

When, at the end of the 1970s, Hollywood began to consider Vietnam nore directly, it was still ambivalent. Michael Cimino's *The Deerhunter* (1978) and Coppola's *Apocalypse Now* (1979) seemed to argue that anything undertaken in the name of survival was justified. During the 1980s it became possible almost to pretend that the war had not been lost. Sylvester Stallone emerged as the archetypal representative of the American white working class in the *Rocky* movies. His *Rambo* character directed the psychopathic individualism of the Clint Eastwood–Charles Bronson vigilante cop movies at the Vietnamese, who had demonstrated the inferiority of American technological heroism. Muscle-bound and loaded with military hardware, he went back to fight the war single-handed until he came out with the right result.

Amid the ironic and knowing films of the 1980s, *Rambo* was one of the few to take itself seriously, innocently proclaiming that might must be right. *Rambo* encouraged a second wave of movies about Vietnam, which, unlike the first, found ways to incorporate the war within something very close to the conventional rhetoric of the war-movie genre. *Platoon* (1986) and *Full Metal Jacket* (1987) resembled earlier war movies in telling stories of the sentimental education of young men under duress. The politics of the war itself, like the Vietnamese, were nowhere in sight.

After Vietnam real wars were treated differently in the media. Western democracies had learned significantly from the media coverage of Vietnam: whatever its effects were on the home population, no-one suggested that this coverage enhanced support for the war. When the British Task Force invaded the Falkland/Malvinas Islands in 1982, they did so without benefit of live television coverage. Preventing television journalists from reporting on the sinking of HMS Sheffield, an officer explained, "Don't you realize that you are

◀▲ After Vietnam, it was difficult to depict American heroes. Clint Eastwood's cop *Dirty Harry* (1971) looked like a hero but behaved like a psychopath (left). In *Taxi Driver*, (1976) Robert De Niro was a psychopath taken for a hero (above).

with us to do a 1940 propaganda job?" Such attitudes were by no means confined to the British military: German television, superior to the British system in terms of its accountability to the public and its representation of community interests, also came under increasing attack from Christian Democrats, long hostile to the concept of public service broadcasting.

Television and everyday life

Media analyst Marshall McLuhan once described television as lacking in intensity as a medium. Because television has become central to our domestic environment, it does not appear a very "heroic" medium; its most appreciated personalities celebrate their "normality". It is in its domesticity that it reveals its difference from the cinema, the appeal of whose stars always contained an element of the exotic. Television characters

seem most capable of generating audience identification when they are at their most mundane
and vulnerable, caught up in the predicaments
of everyday life. Whether nominally fictional or
not, television characters have become familiar
figures, inhabitants of our domestic environment,
and often more readily tolerated than those with
whom we actually share our lives. They rehearse
our recurrent emotional encounters, and acquire
substance through our acceptance of them into
the fabric of our daily lives, as a means through
which we express our own otherwise unspoken
fears, desires and memories.

Television, in this way, serves as company not
simply for the lonely but in its sense of familiarity
within the home. Alongside the proper disquiet
at the dangers inherent in television's role as "the
keystone in consumer capitalism", we do well to
remember that, as critic David Marc points out,
"Television is made to sell products but is used
for quite different purposes by lonely, alienated
people, families, marijuana smokers, born-again
Christians, alcoholics, Hasidic Jews, destitute
people, millionaires, jocks, shut-ins, illiterates,
hang-gliding enthusiasts, intellectuals…in spite of
all demographic odds."

Critics of the media often see the audience as
passive consumers in a one-way communication
process. Television executives, who live in terror

◄ Director Francis Ford
Coppola wanted *Apocalypse
Now* (1979) to be "a film
experience that would give
its audience a sense of the
horror, the madness, the
sensuousness, and the moral
dilemma of the Vietnam
war." Nearly three years in
production, the film was
spectacular, extravagant, and
incoherent, reveling in its
surreal images of the war as
the biggest show on earth,
and displaying Hollywood's
inability, at the end of the
1970s, to come to terms with
defeat.

▼ Was it his rabid
anti-communism or his
ape-like masculinity that
made John Rambo popular
enough to have a bar named
after him in Lhasa, Tibet?
The character who had begun
life as the inarticulate victim
in an anti-war novel became,
in the hands and pectorals of
Sylvester Stallone, an
Italian-American Tarzan,
a strutting, muscle-bound
apologist for American
foreign policy in the Reagan
presidency. Rambo was
as brutal an image of the
warrior-savage as any
culture had produced.

◄ By the late 1980s, the
Vietnam war had become
history, and Vietnam war
stories could be told
according to the conventions
of earlier war movies.
Platoon (1986), which
advertised itself as the first
film to tell "the truth" about
the war, in fact told a familiar
story about a young man's
education in the hell of war. It
was as much about only the
American experience of the
war as every other Vietnam
movie had been; the
Vietnamese were merely
extras to be raped, killed,
pitied and not understood.

The soap-opera formula – the serial drama with a small cast and limited studio sets – was an almost inevitable choice for any television service aiming to attract large audiences with low-cost programming. Latin American soap operas, called *telenovelas*, originated in Mexico and Cuba in the 1950s and were later also produced in Brazil and Puerto Rico. Daniel Filho, Brazil's most prolific maker of popular drama, suggested that, under military rule in the 1970s, his soap operas provided, with football, the only permitted topics of conversation: "In Brazil we believe in miracles, and all soap operas have a character who is going up in the world, making it." Like their Indian and Chinese equivalents, these variations on the basic American formula could easily accommodate local cultural requirements. However, the *telenovela* formula was devised to fill time cheaply – and this need itself arose from the adoption of the values of the multi-channel all-day commercial television, suitable for a rich country, by a much poorer one.

In the developed world further expansion of the media involved the exploitation of increasingly specialized markets for higher-priced media commodities such as financial information or "quality" television. These appealed to the more privileged social groups. A 1979 survey identified 14 separate audience groupings among the consumers of American television. MTM sustained

◀ For a brief period in the mid-1970s Hong Kong television production included some of the most innovative programming in the world, but when the writers and directors responsible for the innovations moved back to film, the television stations reverted to the production of formula costume drama serials that proved more popular with the viewing public. Ironically, the innovators found their film work was equally restricted by a combination of censorship and the conservative tastes of their audience.

of the hand on the channel switch, envisage a much more active viewer who chooses to watch something else, or not to watch at all. They may, perhaps, be closer to the truth.

The new communications media
The first worldwide television satellite link-up opened in 1967, with the Beatles performing their new song *All You Need is Love*. Benign promises about the "Third Age of Broadcasting" were made in the early 1970s – about the ways in which the media might change the world, or in which the media themselves might change – but few were kept. Other promises, concerned with developments in communications technology, took their place. Computer data processing, electronic news-gathering equipment and satellite transmission made the Global Village that media theorist Marshall McLuhan had heralded in the early 1960s a reality; by the mid-1980s the news agency Visnews expected to have a news story from the other side of the world on American television within 90 minutes of its happening.

The revolutions in information technology expanded the media and made their impact more immediate. In the West, network broadcasting reached its maximum potential in the mid-1970s, as watching took up more time than any other activity apart from sleeping and working, on average six hours a day per person in the United States. But there were more possibilities of expansion for the media companies than increasing the consumption of Western audiences. One involved the development of television services in the Third World. In 1986, 83 percent of Chinese households had a television set, and the most popular programs drew audiences of 100 million. In 1975 an Indian experiment in educational broadcasting to the rural population made use of direct broadcasting by satellite (DBS) for the first time anywhere in the world. But Indian broadcasting otherwise followed the familiar Western pattern: introduction of color in 1982, commercial sponsorship of programs in 1984. The audience encompassed 70 percent of the population but programming was aimed at the middle-class audience sought by the advertisers. One result was the development of Indian soap operas.

Indian Cinema and Television

the most impressive record among American producers of "quality" television, aiming series such as *Lou Grant* and *Hill Street Blues* at a liberal professional audience, who preferred programs that they felt were more sophisticated, stylistically complex and psychologically "deep" than ordinary television fare. "Quality" programs such as M*A*S*H* could reach "quality" social groups (the metropolitan, the upwardly mobile, the wealthy), and this offered advertisers an alternative strategy to the constant quest for a larger share of the ratings.

What such systems of scheduling demonstrated is that in an increasingly diverse media economy there can be profit in supplying products aimed specifically at the upper end of the market. As the hardware costs of broadcasting continue to increase, however, many analysts argue that only the pursuit of international mass audiences can sustain the investment in both equipment and programming. This leads to the prospect of a diet of least objectionable programming, sport, music, videos, news and reruns. They point to the Italian experience, where deregulation of broadcasting multiplied the number of stations, lowered program quality and drastically reduced cinema attendance. The introduction of commercial television in France has similarly been held reponsible for the decline in film production, while some Indian film-makers

Doordshan, the single government channel of Indian television, remained highly resistant to American imports, but its emphasis on low-budget development programming led to frequent complaints about its dullness.

The story in Indian cinema is strikingly different. Since 1930 India has been one of the four top film-making countries, and into the 1980s it produced 800 films a year, in 23 different languages. Adapting the conventions of traditional mythology, literature, theater, dance and music, Indian films developed quite different narrative practices from Western films, telling their familiar stories through a system of stylized expressions and abrupt changes of mood and tone. These distinctive forms have kept the Indian cinema dominant in its home market and hardly known outside that market. The Indian cinema best known in the West is the "parallel cinema" of Satyajit Ray, Ritwaik Ghatak and Mrinal Sen, which, although rooted in Indian tradition, has taken much of its cinematic esthetics from European models, and has been acceptable in Western "art cinema" markets.

On the other hand, the Indian commercial cinema has demonstrated an adaptability comparable to that of Hollywood. Although their forms are rooted in Sanskrit drama, Indian films use plots which would not be out of place on American television.

G.P. Sippy's blockbuster production *Sholay* (*Embers*, 1976), the most successful movie in Indian film history, took elements of its plot from Westerns such as *The Magnificent Seven* and *Butch Cassidy and the Sundance Kid*.

◀ On location in the Himalayas.

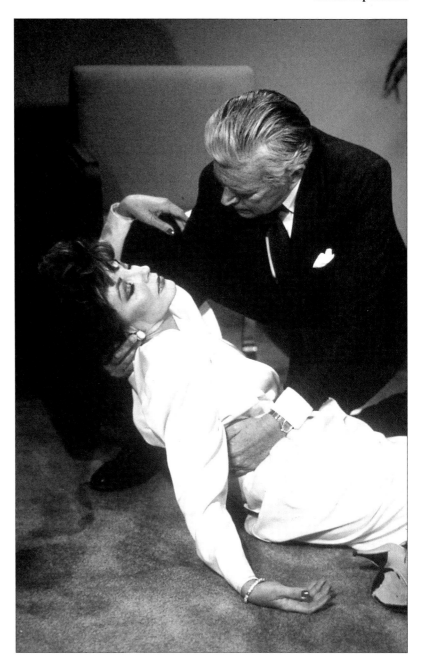

argue that there, too, television will end the "parallel cinema" of Satyajit Ray, Mrinal Sen and others.

For those who can afford it, High Definition Television (HDTV), using twice the number of horizontal lines as the present 525-line and 625-line systems, offers a sound and picture quality and size previously available only in the cinema. But, as with previous innovations in broadcasting and sound reproduction, rival systems compete to be adopted as a world standard, or tenaciously retain their share of the potential market. HDTV appeared first in Japan, the "television society" whose citizens watch more television than anywhere else in the world, and where most of the technology in HDTV has been originated. Satellite distribution, dominated by powerful multinational corporations, is gradually changing the nature of television, from a nationally regulated medium to one that is fundamentally unregulated. Whereas the American Federal

▲ Launched on CBS in 1978, *Dallas* and its arch rival *Dynasty* (shown here) brought the melodramatic excesses of American daytime soap opera to high-budget prime-time television. Following the improbably eventful lives of a constantly feuding Texas oil family, *Dallas* achieved extraordinary popularity in the early 1980s, first in the United States and then almost everywhere throughout the world except Japan. *Dallas* was American television at its most extreme: vulgarly opulent in its decor and costumes, never far from self-parody in its plots. "*Dallas* is crap", remarked its executive producer Lee Rich, "but it's good crap, done with a great deal of class and a great big wink".

VOICE OF AMERICA

▲ Novelist Gore Vidal called him "the Acting President"; more sympathetic observers "the Great Communicator". Ronald Reagan and his image-makers embraced radio and television as the media in which American politics were conducted.

▼ Television did what Hollywood had done before it – sold American culture around the world; but even on isolated Pacific islands, it did the job more cheaply and quickly than Hollywood ever could.

Communications Commission once upheld the Fairness Doctrine, which required broadcasters to provide balanced coverage of issues, this has been abandoned as the technology of international media distribution makes the effective regulation of the content of the broadcasts ever more difficult. However much the range of choice available to consumers is increased, the ever-higher costs of hardware will inevitably produce greater inequalities in access to electronic information, between nations as well as individuals.

In some respects the new technology has threatened the existing power structures of the media industry. American cable systems (whereby a consumer subscribes to a broadcasting service, which is then transmitted via an underground cable) and deregulation produced new rivals to the broadcast networks – among them Home Box Office (HBO), the first pay-TV channel in the United States, and Ted Turner, who expanded his Atlanta television station WBTS into an international operation based on the first 24-hour news channel, CNN. By a combination of conglomeration and diversification the major American companies have protected themselves from demise. Thus the world's largest media corporation was formed in 1989 by the merger of HBO's owner, Time Inc., with Warner Communications to form Time Warner Inc.

Some of the new technology freed the audience from the control of distributors. Video made films and television programs much more like books or records, objects to be enjoyed at will, and distributors strongly resisted this. Universal Studios and the Disney Corporation fought a prolonged but unsuccessful legal battle to have home video recorders declared illegal, because of their potential for encouraging breaches of copyright. There was a move to impose a levy on the sale of blank audio and video tape. Conglomeration of the new media companies with the old, and the merging of hardware and soft-ware concerns, provided a more circuitous remedy: in 1987 the Japanese electronic corporation Sony established a trend by buying CBS Records; in 1989 it also bought Columbia Pictures. These moves guaranteed Sony a library of musical and video products to play on any new audio-visual equipment it might introduce in the future.

Broadcasting and imperialism
Satellite television has presented issues of national sovereignty and censorship in Europe, but the impact of international broadcasting, whether radio or television, on areas of the Third World, has been considerably greater. By the late 1980s the Voice of America was broadcasting in 42 languages to an audience of 120 million, and buil-

ding 66 "superpower" 500kW transmitters to extend its service. The Soviet Union had 32 such transmitters, France 12, West Germany 10, while Britain, the only major power planning to cut back its overseas broadcasting, had eight. In all, 31 countries had external radio services spreading their ideologies beyond their borders cheaply and efficiently. The United States also transmitted *America Today* by satellite, providing two hours a day of arts and sports programming free to any cable-television system.

In 1984 there were 24 satellites providing programs for the domestic American market, and many of them cast their "footprint" over the Caribbean. The availability of American television asserted powerful cultural and political influences: much fuller coverage of American domestic politics was available to the islanders of St Lucia than news of their own internal political affairs. The fear was that dependence on American television would eventually displace national cultural values.

The concern was less with overt propaganda than with the proliferation of a transnational, homogeneous "world culture", produced by the politically and economically dominant countries and distributed as an instrument and badge of their dominance over the Third World. The argument has changed little in substance from the complaints against Hollywood's influence in the 1920s. As the mass audience in the West for radio and television began to fragment, broadcasting became internationalized through co-production arrangements, seeking its audience in many countries simply to pay the bills. The media have been important forces in maintaining Western influence and interests in Third World countries after independence from colonial rule: into the 1980s the majority of journalistic and technical staff continued to be trained by American or European agencies and partly as a result of this, to adopt Western values with regard to program content. Equipment and programs supplied at cut rates have made possible the establishment of broadcasting services, but have inhibited local production because of its high cost by comparison with American programs of much more ostentatious production qualities. These programs also cater to the status requirements of Third World metropolitan middle-class groups, the first consumers of the new media.

The availability of television is one of a number of attractions luring Third World populations to exchange rural poverty for a makeshift life on the edges of sprawling cities. Its main function even here, however, is to deliver viewers to advertisers. In most of South America television is entirely financed by advertising and sponsorship. In 1974 advertisements took up more than 35 per cent of programming time on Venezuelan television, while Brazilian TV Globo's *telenovelas* were often sponsored by manufacturing companies or banks as promotional devices.

The Third World is not only vulnerable to the economic power of the West, whose political authority insists on the "free market" in goods and television programs as evidence of the "democratic" nature of Third World govern-

The News in East and West

Soviet television, strictly supervised by the state, constructed "news" as a quite different commodity from its Western counterparts. By comparison to Western news, its main news program *Vremya (Time)* was humorless and undramatic, emphasizing industrial or agricultural production achievements. Watched in 80 percent of Russian homes, Soviet television openly acknowledged its role in forming taste, opinion and ideology. It reflected the multinational and multilingual structure of Soviet society through cultural diversity, in contrast to the cultural homogeneity purveyed by American television; nevertheless its rigid moral standards, which excluded the representation of sex, violence or corruption, were regarded as excessively puritanical by many Russians.

In part Soviet news programming fulfilled functions carried out elsewhere in Western television. Some researchers have suggested that much of the pleasure viewers derive from television comes from, for example, the spectacle of large numbers of people enjoying themselves provided by game shows and sitcoms recorded before a live audience. In this Western experience of television, news is consumed for negative reasons, to make sure that nothing has happened which might affect the viewer's life adversely.

▼ Broadcasting in 70 languages within the borders of the Soviet Union, Soviet television's news programming was unlike Western news. Undramatic in presentation, it often reported on achievements in agricultural or industrial production, as here. *Glasnost* led to substantial changes in program format, as Western media styles were imitated.

ments. It is also subject to the tyranny of a largely one-way flow of information. The Associated Press news service transmits 90,000 words of news a day from New York to Asia, and receives 19,000 words back. News from the Third World is even more vulnerable to a process of stereotyping than domestic news output. In the West, events become television news according to a predictable set of criteria: they must be phenomena of the moment – dramatic events rather than trends, big, apparently unexpected, preferably negative in character, and if possible focused on an individual already known to the audience. By these criteria little that happens in the Third World qualifies as news except war, natural disasters, and political instability.

What is taking place quietly in the living rooms of thousands of Caribbean family units as they sit innocently before their television sets frightens us. It is a process of deculturization, which is painless, but also very thorough and long-lasting.

CARIBBEAN PUBLISHING AND BROADCASTING ASSOCIATION

Datafile

In the 1980s sport became a business: the search for prize money and marketing opportunities drove the stars to greater achievement, while the appeal of many sports to a wider market lay in the television companies' ability to find an audience. In that respect, the 1988 Seoul Oympics were a disaster, with American and European television companies finding viewers – and advertisers – hard to come by.

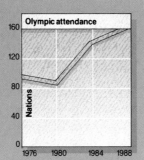

Olympic attendance

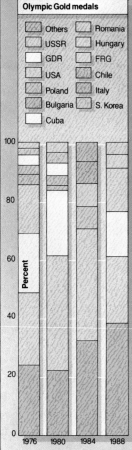

Olympic Gold medals

- Others
- USSR
- GDR
- USA
- Poland
- Bulgaria
- Cuba
- Romania
- Hungary
- FRG
- Chile
- Italy
- S. Korea

◀ Although the United States, the Soviet Union and East Germany (GDR) continued to bring home the bulk of the medals for those Olympics in which they chose to compete, the remaining medals were shared out between a much more diverse range of countries than previously, including many Third World nations.

▶ Boxers were by far the highest paid sportsmen in the early 1990s, although Mike Tyson's conviction for rape brought the sport to a new low in public perceptions. Basketball star Michael Jordan, by contrast, used his celebrity to campaign for AIDS awareness. Some sporting superstars cashed in on their status through promotional activities: including golfers such as Jack Nicklaus and Arnold Palmer whose heydays lay well in the past.

▼ Tennis became highly professionalized from the late 1970s, with an established circuit, computer rankings and ever-growing prize money. The best women rivalled the earning-power of the men.

▲ Despite financial problems at the 1976 Montreal Olympics, and political boycotts at Moscow and Los Angeles, competition to stage future Games remained strong. The success of the Seoul Games overrode the doubts of those who had claimed, in the 1970s, that the day of the mega-event was over.

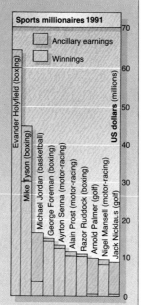

Sports millionaires 1991

- Ancillary earnings
- Winnings

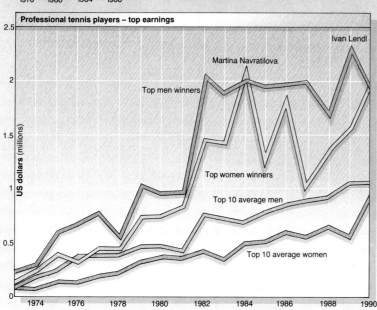

Professional tennis players – top earnings

In the 1980s sport increasingly defined itself in every advanced industrial nation as part of a leisure industry, and passed this seductive description on to other, less affluent, countries. As the "leisure economy" expanded, sports-related consumer expenditure increased, on building sports halls and stadia, on participation, ticket admissions, gambling, clothing and equipment, food and drink, television rights and advertising. In the hands of multi-million-dollar corporations, and inextricably linked to the international television market, sport became big business. Together with television, advertising, sponsorship and modern marketing procedures transformed the character of sport.

Sport and commerce

The 1984 Los Angeles Olympics – "The Corporate Games" – celebrated with unashamed commercialism a notion of sport subservient to marketing requirements. Thirty corporate sponsors, including Coca-Cola, Levi Strauss, and McDonald's, each paid between $4 million and $15 million for the exclusive right to market their products under the Olympic logo. They refurbished the LA Coliseum, built the velodrome and Olympic pool, supplied equipment, communications, transport and the "official" clothing. For the first time since 1936, the host nation's commitment to staging the Games as a demonstration of its ideological superiority was not measured by the scale of its financial commitment. However, this represents more a recognition of the cultural, economic and even political authority of American multinational corporations than it does any easing of the entanglement of sport and politics. The government of South Korea, where the 1988 Games were held, was keen to use the Olympics not simply as a means of legitimizing its existence politically, but also for its long-term economic effects. As Lee Young Ho, South Korean Sports Minister, explained: "Hosting the Olympics gives us international recognition and a psychological boost for our next step up to join the advanced countries within the next decade. Look what happened to Japan after the 1964 Olympics."

The Los Angeles Games also promoted the idea of sport as a form of entertainment to be consumed passively by its spectators; it is not accidental that many of the leading corporate sponsors of sport are food, drink and tobacco companies, things to be consumed while watching rather than playing. Far more people are now involved in sport through the press and broadcasting than in any other way. The Los Angeles Olympics were watched by 2,000 million viewers worldwide.

Sport has become central to the function of television as entertainment, acquiring the trappings of show business in its presentation. In the

THE INDUSTRY OF LEISURE

Sport and commerce
Sponsors and television audiences
Professionalism in modern sport
Sport and politics
Sport for all

United States there are now sports events organized specifically for television while the schedules of many other events are increasingly dictated by the need for sport to accommodate itself to the requirements of television. Other sports have been transformed into new forms of entertainment by changing their rules: shorter snooker matches, round-the-city cycle racing, World Cup athletics and World Cup rugby have all been developed to make these sports more attractive for television and sponsors.

The popularity of televised sport ensures that escalating sums of money are involved. At the 1976 Montreal Olympic Games, ABC acquired the American television rights for $25 million, and made three times that amount selling advertising. By 1984 American rights went to ABC at a cost of $225 million for the Summer Olympics and $90 million for the Winter Olympics; the sales of advertising netted over $300 million. The bulk of the income of the International Olympic Committee (IOC) derives from American television, whose networks also spent $1.4 billion in television rights to the American National Football League between 1987 and 1990.

Similarly, in 1977 Australian television mogul Kerry Packer saw the potential of using traditionally popular sports with a mass following to increase the numbers of spectators, increase players' incomes and attract huge sponsorship. To do this he changed the traditional format of cricket, played floodlit matches for the first time and even abandoned the familiar white clothes of the cricketer. He contracted 35 of the world's top players, dubbed "Packer's Circus", to play a series of international matches in Australia to be shown exclusively on his Channel Nine television

▲▶ **The more popular and profitable the sport, the higher the level of sponsorship in return for advertising space. Not only soft drinks' corporations and cigarette companies sponsored sport in the 1980s; the computer industry, banks and insurance companies all saw sports sponsorship as a good form of advertising.**

▼ **Every nuance of the athlete's experience of victory is captured by the camera, as British runner Sebastian Coe wins Olympic gold for the 1500m at Moscow in 1980. Its vicarious pleasures and sorrows have made sport an increasingly profitable form of entertainment, a development which the media have not been slow to exploit.**

network. A crisis in international cricket was provoked by this injection of commercialism into its self-definition as a game for gentlemen; this was as severe, if not as long-lasting, as that engendered by the banning of South Africa from international cricket competition.

Sponsorship is attracted to already buoyant sports, which in turn encourage the creation of special events to attract media coverage and more sponsorship. Lack of media attention results in a relative lack of sponsorship; this is a common fate for minority and female sports. Only those minority sports with an obvious televisual appeal have broken through this barrier and television has artificially promoted interest in some sports, concentrating heavy coverage on them simply because they are easy and cheap to televise. One result of this is the "discovery" of sports by TV channels excluded from the most popular – sumo wrestling has been one such import to the West by television companies and sponsors anxious to catch the next wave of popular interest.

Sport's vicarious excitement, built on the controlled unpredictability of rule-bound competition, makes it an ideal television commodity. The agony and ecstasy of athletes, the gestures and facial expressions of the spectators, confrontations, accidents, victory and defeat, fill broadcasting time with spectacle and excitement. Sport becomes continuous drama, presenting heroes and villains, highlighting beauty and brutality. The techniques of presentation "construct" a game for us through the selection of camera angles, the use of close-ups and action replays to repeat and emphasize key moments. Together with this visual presentation, the commentators' analyses as well as their value judgments convert the television spectator into an armchair expert on players' technical abilities and on umpiring decisions.

Radio, newspapers, specialist magazines and books reinforced television's discourse on sport as entertainment, personalizing and dramatizing it. Popular sports journalism used the language of

▼ Canadian athlete Ben Johnson's victory at the 1988 Seoul Olympics was short-lived. His winning time of 9.79 seconds set a new world record for the 100m but within 48 hours he had been stripped of his gold medal for taking Stanozolol, an anabolic steroid. These drugs were used illicitly by many athletes during training to speed up the body's recovery rate, thus permitting extra-hard training. The use of potentially dangerous drugs to enhance performance has often been described as widespread. This is a measure of the immense pressure to win that the commercialization of sport has produced.

the battlefield, where rivals and enemies are demolished or humiliated by a blast or a charge. As sport has increasingly assumed the characteristics of other forms of television, its performers have been obliged to adopt the mannerisms of celebrity, and, equally, have become victims of its terminology of hyperbole: every top athlete becomes a "legendary superstar". Like pop stars and film stars, they are required to distil a lifetime of acquired skill into moments of consumable spectacle for sport competition and show business to procreate profit. The celebrity they acquire opens their personal lives to the prurient gaze of the secondary media of gossip columns and talk shows. "Superbrats" as well as superstars are manufactured for our consumption as an integral part of media sport. Individuals such as John McEnroe and snooker-player Alex Higgins are characterized as unstable and irascible, versions of an entertainment personality archetype identified as talented, unpredictable and ultimately self-destructive. For the entertainment such figures produce they are paid vast amounts of money: the Argentinian footballer Diego Maradona cost Napoli a staggering £6.9 million,

and his basic salary was a million dollars annually.

The complete integration of sport as entertainment into the leisure industry has finally rendered the "amateur" concept obsolete. The values permeating modern sport come from the commercial model and percolate down from top professionals. Sports organizations as substantial as the International Amateur Athletic Federation depend increasingly on sponsorship for their survival. Even "amateur" athletes, the exemplars of amateur sport, are now able to command enormous fees from sponsors, take what is required for "expenses", and invest the remainder in a trust fund, which is, at least, an improvement on a previous situation in which top sportsmen and women received under-the-table payments, prizes and gifts, or else were covertly sponsored by their governments. The 1988 Olympics were the first in which this sham amateurism was replaced by open professionalism for the athletes.

The commercial model of sport emphasizes competition, an obsession with winning and an endless quest for records, all of which puts tremendous pressure on individual players and athletes. The myth of "rags to riches" inducts

▲ Synchronized swimming joined the official list of Olympic events in 1984. Other sports are still considered less than "ladylike" – female athletes are banned from the hammer, pole vault, triple jump and steeplechase.

▶ British Olympic medallist Fatima Whitbread is among the many women who have been subjected to clichéd analysis at the hands of male sports journalists, who continue to churn out copy on the looks of female athletes rather than discussing their skill and technique.

▲ The massive amounts of money generated out of television coverage of sport have resulted in equally massive fees for exclusive rights, putting crowd-pullers such as baseball or boxing beyond the means of all but the largest and wealthiest of the television companies. The smaller channels have responded by generating interest in the more esoteric sports, such as Japanese sumo wrestling.

youngsters into a world of aggressive, competitive sport where most of them will not make it to the top. The ordinary rates of pay for sports professionals are unremarkable, and most professionals are bought and sold like commodities, with little control over their conditions of work. Abuse of the body is intensified by success: in order to enhance performance, sporting superstars are impelled to overtrain, to take dangerous drugs, and to undergo extreme diet manipulation. The pressures on athletes in the Eastern bloc were similar, even though their sports system was non-commercial. Contemporary athletes mock

human physiology; champions are "produced" rather than "born".

Media sport remains one of the strongest bastions of male chauvinism. Televised sport belongs, almost exclusively, to the male gaze, and much of its appeal to sponsors and advertisers results from its being the form of television most likely to secure a male audience. In traditional male sports, such as American football and Australian-rules football, men are celebrated as 20th-century gladiators and warriors. In contrast, the most popular women's sports covered by the media are those seen as "feminine appropriate". A sportswoman is portrayed first as female, then as an athlete: popular journalism discusses her sexuality – how "lithe", "leggy", "pretty" or "graceful" she is, or her performance of other female roles – that she is a "housewife and mother of two" – as much as on her sports skill and technique.

Sport and politics
Such commentary is reserved for Western women: East European women athletes, particularly those from the German Democratic Republic (GDR), were castigated for their "masculine" appearance as well as their ideology. In 1972, the GDR competed in the Olympics for the first time, and by 1976 did so well that, together with the US and the USSR, it became one of the three "Olympic Superpowers". With a population of only 17 million, the GDR's performance was extraordinary, but if Olympic successes are calculated per capita of the population, Finland and

Trinidad are outstanding as well, while the United States and Soviet Union actually fall below other countries.

The GDR's achievement resulted from the active intervention of the state in sports provision and promotion; it gave a higher priority to sport than anywhere else in the world.

In contrast, in the West, among nations which have a liberal democratic ideology and where a market economy prevails, it is generally assumed that state intervention is minimal, and that individuals can participate without undue pressure and harmful effects. However, in all Western countries, there is greater government intervention than ever before, and sport is being managed now more consciously, though less overtly than in centrally organized societies. From the 1960s, commercialism has interacted intimately with nationalism and the role of the state. National governments of every political complexion have poured vast amounts of money into sport to gain international prestige.

The 1976 Montreal Olympics highlighted the financial implications of hosting sports extravaganzas. Reputed to have cost a staggering $2 billion, the games left massive debts for tax payers.

The Soviet intervention in Afghanistan, which led to the United States team withdrawing from the Moscow Olympics in 1980 and the subsequent refusal of the Soviet Union to go to Los Angeles in 1984, changed the character of the Games and demonstrated the hypocrisy of Western denials that sport was a form of international politics. Although, for the first time since 1952, the United States and the Soviet Union were not confronting one another in Olympic competition, ironically, Cold War politics between East and West were accentuated.

Sport has also become a vehicle for protest by individuals against oppression by their own governments. The anti-apartheid sports movement continued to use international sport as a means to oppose the South African government, despite the piecemeal amelioration of apartheid in sport through "multinational" sports events and the occasional appearance in South Africa of "rebel" tours by cricket and rugby players, who were well paid by their South African sponsors to compensate them for being banned from international competition by their own national sports associations. By 1990 it was clear that the sports boycott had contributed to the unraveling of the apartheid regime, and by 1992 South Africa had been readmitted to the international sporting community.

Racism and violence continue to be depressing features associated with some spectator sports, and nowhere more so than in Britain, where football hooliganism, insidiously linked to right-wing groups, has burgeoned in recent years. The simplistic explanation, couched in terms of moral outrage at the individual troublemaker and the need for firmer instruments of repression and punishment, has persisted as the political analysis, even in the face of the deaths of Italian fans as a result of the hooliganism of English football fans at the Heysel stadium in Brussels in May 1985.

◀ The distinctive appearance of Ruud Gullit, the Dutch soccer star of the mid 1980s, gave rise to a new cult image among his fans — a cult that emphasized the links between the position of the sporting star and the pop-star in modern society. For many of the new breed of soccer superstars, their national clubs are no longer enough. A "superleague" of clubs able to afford huge fees for the best players in the world has made soccer skill an internationally marketable commodity.

The dramatic and brutal nature of the Heysel disaster made it newsworthy, particularly since the scenes of the horror of the dying were seen live on television across the world. As a result English clubs were banned from international competition.

In the Western media, nationalism and sport seem to be linked when convenient, and separated when not. An athlete is always represented as winning for his or her country, but losing for him or herself. National rivalry between countries within the same political sphere and of comparable economic development – within Western Europe, for example – has been a useful way of retaining chauvinism without the need for military expense. The xenophobia evident in Britain during the Falklands/Malvinas war had been in part maintained and kept available by the displacement of nationalist sentiment into exchanges with bat or ball.

But one hopeful sign might be noted. If sport has now become "the continuation of politics by other means", as von Clausewitz described war, it is yet not war. If the gladiatorial combats between ideologies are played out in Olympic arenas, no-one dies in their enactment. Sacking the manager of a national football team for a humiliating defeat is less disruptive than overthrowing a government. When Diego Maradona scored a dubious goal for Argentina "with the hand of God and the head of Maradona" in a game which knocked England out of the 1986 World Cup, it did not prove necessary to resume the war between Britain and Argentina over the incident. Sport is neither innocent nor safe, but it is less dangerous, as well as more manageable, than war.

◀ Germany won the Jules Rimet football World Cup in Italy in 1990 with displays of flair and discipline. Nevertheless, many observers felt that the most significant trend of the competition was the emergence of a new generation of footballing countries, spearheaded by the Cameroons whose vitality, skill and enthusiasm was said to presage the entry of many other African countries onto the world footballing stage.

Sport For All

Despite the contemporary philosophy that sport is not a luxury, but an essential part of life, few Western governments recognize that flourishing grass-roots sport depends on state intervention, and that the best state policies are those that seek to ensure that sport is for everyone. Those who criticized sport under communism ignored that it was accessible to ordinary people free of charge. In comparison, in most Western countries many sports are still out of reach of the pockets of the majority. In America, the poor have few opportunities to participate in sport. One solution to the dominance of competition in sports ideology may lie in alternative forms of sport which stress cooperation and playfulness, such as fun-runs and mini-marathons.

In recent years many Western governments have channeled concern about national health into the promotion of fitness schemes and community sport. The Australian "Life – Be In It" campaign includes a light-hearted media promotion of new sports and fun for everyone, while the British Sports Council recruitment drive, "Ever Thought of Sport", identified groups with special needs, such as unemployed ethnic minorities and women.

▶ The Paraplegic Olympics, 1984.

Datafile

In the later 1970s and 1980s mainstream music has reverted to a formula dictated by the requirements of the international market-place: although the adult-oriented rock of the mid-1970s was much criticized, the music dominating the American charts 10 years later owed it a large debt. The radical drive of the rock bands of the sixties was much subdued; Bruce Springsteen, who took over the role of "the boss" of rock 'n' roll, was hailed by President Reagan as the embodiment of the ideal young American. Formula-driven disco dominated black music, although at least the work of Michael Jackson transcended many of the limitations of the formula while achieving huge international sales.

It remained true that American and, to a lesser extent, British music dictated style. After the passing of punk, a new breed of bands flourished that relied on synthesizers for their music and a high degree of marketing to promote them as image.

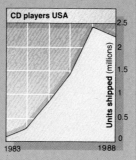

▲ Compact disk (CD) players became the most popular sound systems of the late 1980s, providing high-quality sound reproduction and offering great flexibility in playback. The development of portable and in-car systems maintained the momentum of the new medium, despite the relatively high cost of the discs.

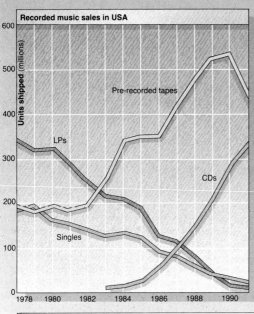

◀ Sales of recorded music in the United States in the 1980s failed to sustain the growth of previous decades, and the corporations relied increasingly on promoting their established stars. The popularity of portable music systems made the cassette, and later the CDs relatively more attractive than the more fragile vinyl disk.

▼ The Sony Walkman, a tiny portable cassette player, provided the most exciting marketing opportunity for recorded music in the 1980s until the advent of the CD player. Nevertheless, sales of sound systems remained fairly static. One result was the decline in the number of new releases across the range, though LPs and singles suffered most.

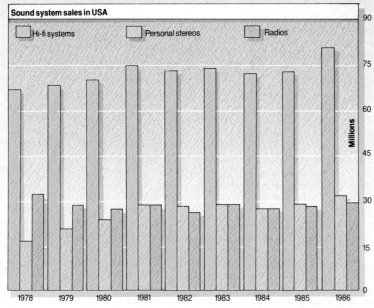

Popular music in the seventies and eighties was bewildering in its variety and rate of change and the critics frequently make the confusion even worse. But beneath the surface it may be possible to discern the broad movement – sometimes moving in parallel, sometimes in conflict – of two fundamental approaches to popular music. One, the "ecstatic", persisted from earlier eras: it continued to celebrate raw emotion and values inherent in the musical moment, and saw style as an expression of those values. Though still present in this period, its role was far less dramatic than before. The old confrontations with established authority and traditional values were not repeated (moral panic was directed to new regions of youth culture, rather than music) and their absence no doubt contributed to the appearance of a "steady state", which seemed to be reached by the late seventies.

The other approach, which might be termed "extrinsic", was rooted in the self-consciousness of postwar consumerism, in particular in the distinction between the commodity and its image. In music, this approach created a division between the art and the style. This separation seemed to permit some musicians cynically to exploit the popular music system, creating styles and fashions without being fully committed to them. More generally, though, it gave a new twist to some longstanding problems of expression in consumer culture – the relationships between "high" culture and "low", between authenticity and artifice, between creativity and commerce. Different solutions or part-solutions to such questions lay behind many of the constantly shifting patterns of much popular music in this period. In all of them, music seemed to serve style, not style music.

Adult-oriented rock

The early- to mid-1970s had seen a compromise between the two approaches. Earlier white rock had felt its way into the celebratory nature of black music (without fully reaching its spiritual core) and black music, in turn, had been influenced by the inventiveness of rock. Much music-making along these lines persisted, but elsewhere the so-called progressive rock of Emerson, Lake and Palmer or Jethro Tull, and singer-songwriters such as James Taylor or Carly Simon aspired to a Romantic ideal of art, which was interpreted as being true, first and foremost, to oneself. Preoccupied with the self, their "adult-oriented rock" (AOR) was ambivalent toward other functions of music. Although dependent on a notion of the need for "authentic" roots, and finding these in particular in rock's debt to the emancipating influence of black music, AOR musicians, critics and consumers began to regard

MUSIC, IDENTITY AND PROPERTY

Adult-oriented rock
The decline of black music
The challenge of punk
Style, image and art
Music from Africa

that music, and its derivatives, as emotionally and esthetically immature. Determined to appear equally stern toward commerce, they also looked askance at the growing tendency to celebrate consumer culture for its own sake. The irony of many rock stars, accumulating great wealth was not recognized; instead, their wealth confirmed them in the eyes of the public as independent, powerful figures, with whom consumers could identify.

These attempts to marginalize black music had relatively little impact on black music itself, or on its audience. But as the expressive power of black performers such as Curtis Mayfield or Marvin Gaye gave way to "formula soul" in the mid-seventies, there was a sense that black American music might, finally, have few more major revelations to make. Some looked to Africa or the Caribbean for a continued vitality in black music; others accepted the predictable and mechanical sound of the disco beat. In the past most changes in black music had come about either because of changes in the relationship between the black tradition and white approaches to culture and commerce, and in the subtle variations within that relationship, or because elements within black music reacted to each other in new ways. Soul had grown from the interaction of the sounds and rhythms of gospel, rhythm & blues and white pop, in the context of a successful black attempt to emulate white commercial ownership of the product. The Motown label, on which a special form of soul developed, produced the basis for the emergence of a closely related group

▼ In marked contrast to the drabness of the world outside, the strobe lights and impenetrable sound levels of the disco seem to create a special territory; and this territory helps to explain the music. Mechanical sounds and rhythms have little appeal in an everyday world itself marked by predictability; but in the disco that predictability is turned, temporarily, into a means of release. But what liberates the body in this context takes the music prisoner.

of highly charged musical styles. The Four Tops' 1966 hit single, *Reach Out, I'll Be There*, epitomized the way in which gospel message and secular emotion flowed into each other to produce a "utopia of feeling".

Although a utopia of urban life remained a remote prospect for blacks in the United States, music had helped to push the black consciousness movement into the public arena and into wider acceptance by blacks themselves. Following after this high point, the drift into formula soul, succeeded by the mechanical qualities of most disco music, seems almost inexplicable. It may have been that what black music represented had now become part of the musical common heritage and, as such, had forfeited something of its ability to surprise and shock.

The challenge of punk
Meanwhile in Britain – still the world's mainspring of popular music after the United States – developments were taking a different turn. Black music had developed its riches through being grounded in self-acceptance and affirmation, though paradoxically at its most intense it had opened up the possibility of self-surrender. By contrast, mainstream rock had become obsessed with the need for self-identification. Now came an entirely new approach in which the self contemplated itself, objectively, as "other". But in contrast to the classical legend of the self-absorption of Narcissus, the image of the self was not reflected in the comforting pastoral of water,

but projected on to the cold, shiny surfaces of commercial artifice. What was important now was not the internal self, but the self as a construct of consumer capitalism.

The roots of this change can be traced in part to the sixties' Mods, who were fascinated with commodities and determined to undermine the most idealistic side of pop and rock culture. But the principal source was to be found in the art-school connection. Art schools had exerted a persistent and powerful influence on the course of British popular music in particular, from the late fifties on. In the fifties and sixties, art school had been the first to see that popular culture, especially rock 'n' roll, offered the chance to challenge the control of high culture, either by demonstrating that rock, too, could be "high", or by a bohemian denial of the common assumption that "high" culture eventually touched everyone in some way. What distinguished the late sixties, and seventies, approach was the central perception that, in commodity culture, arguments about "high" and "low" were specious: all was commerce and all was art.

Although the central movement of thought and practice in this regard was most closely associated with Britain, an important impetus came from New York, from the ideas of Andy Warhol and the music of the Velvet Underground. In a society where mass communication ultimately appropriated and trivialized everything, and in which individual expression as the basis of art was irrelevant, what became important, in Warhol's view, was surface spectacle. For the Velvets, and especially for Lou Reed, that spectacle was urban decadence, viewed through the "streetwise cynicism of the Big Rotten Apple". The harsh, blighted New York sound of the Velvets contrasted most obviously with the optimism of the West Coast's counter-culture. But its celebration of impersonal urban monotony also obliquely challenged the fundamental principle of most of the century's popular music, which derived from the role of the offbeat – confidence in the existence of alternatives.

Ironically, their basis in what they saw as a value-free mass-culture esthetic failed to make Warhol and the Velvets commercially successful, and created instead a cult audience. In Britain, however, the situation was rather different. The familiarity of many musicians with pop art theories provided a more responsive environment for this idea. Equally important, however, was the fact that, from the consumer's point of

THE GLOBAL VILLAGE?
Music, Identity and Property

view, in mid-seventies Britain the relentless march of commodity culture had affected everyone, but had left untouched many of the country's "traditional" inequities and done little to erase the increasing sense of the loss of historically rooted identity. The self in daily life seemed constricted socially and undernourished historically. A new self could be created, by using commercial culture in a way that seemed to erase all memory of social and historical inhibitions. The opportunity was widely accepted, in the deliberate artifice of "glam rock".

Through all the confusion caused, especially in the mass media themselves, by the glam rock of David Bowie, Brian Ferry and bands such as Queen, it was their way of affording this opportunity that provided the most persistent thread. Bowie became "a blank canvas on which consumers write their dreams, a media-made icon to whom art happened". These "dreams" largely revolved around ambivalent images of sexuality, and it was here that moral outrage, seeking an outlet for a renewed bout of authoritarianism, focused its attention. But glam rock's display of sexuality achieved a result far from the perversion in which convention hoped to see the final dénouement of the permissive society. Glam rock challenged the male heterosexual domination of conventional society and the counter-culture by pointing, not to female repression, so much as to the false premises of that masculinity. It also insisted that sexuality was not part of an individual's essential being, but a role that could be chosen and enacted: "A display that was intent on demonstrating that the assumed 'privacy' of

sexual matters ... was an illusion. Sexuality was as much part of the public domain as politics, class, and subcultures."

The disturbing qualities of glam rock were to some extent tempered in the public mind by its obvious artfulness; punk, on the other hand, which followed, in the short period beginning in 1976, seemed by contrast to be a systematic denial of the merit of any kind of skill. Yet punk, like glam rock, had a deep acquaintance with ideas of image and artifice.

The most common interpretations of punk proceed along the lines of a defiant outburst from frustrated proletarian youth, or of a resurgence of democratic culture in the face of commercial appropriation. But punk's many art-school connections placed it, too, in the tradition of art-school experimentation. More extensively than had been done before, punk applied avant-garde artistic concepts, with only limited previous exposure in the visual-arts world, in a much more public arena. When attempting to assess the overall effect of punk what stands out is the *knowing* employment of subversive concepts, the *calculated* assault on traditional expectations, and the *self-conscious* use of alienating effects to create conditions in which the process of commodity culture could be re-examined. Punk achieved its effects by confusing distinctions, by standing relationships on their heads, by turning codes of practice against themselves. Audience expectations of performers were negated: the Sex Pistols sang *You Don't Hate Us As Much As We Hate You*. Concepts of gender were undermined, not by extremes as much as by the removal of overt sexuality. Rock's worried

▲ Jamaican reggae star Bob Marley was known in the mid-sixties as a Kingston "rude boy", one of those whose ska records provided Britain's black youth with its first real chance to identify culturally with the Caribbean. In the seventies, reggae, linked with Rastafarianism, provided a sense of hope – and Marley symbolized this above all others. Reggae's impact on pop remained spasmodic. The success of rap in the eighties, however, owed much to the "dub" techniques of the ska and reggae "sound system" disk jockeys.

African Music

From Algerian rai to Zairean soukous to South African mbaqanga, Africa is home to an unparalleled diversity of popular-music styles. Deep in their history the complex meeting of cultures under conditions of colonial domination was crucial; no less important was the legacy of the slave trade. When the various sounds of exile transformed by their New World experience (into jazz, rumba, calypso) returned to Africa in the fifties, the effects were dramatic – not a fusion with indigenous styles, so much as a series of combustions.

The "discovery" of African music by the West was one of the most distinctive developments of the eighties. Although European record companies were present in Africa from the 1910s, African music's popularity outside Africa had always been fitful. The changes in the eighties were due partly to determined efforts by individual African musicians to reach a wider audience, and partly to the increasing numbers of musicians basing themselves abroad. But "mainstream" success remained elusive. For many devotees this was not a matter of regret. They suspected the existing level of popularity was being a musical sightseeing trip with post-imperialist overtones – a tendency exemplified by Paul Simon's incorporation of *a capella* vocal sounds by Ladyship Black Mambazo in his best-selling album *Graceland* (1985).

▶ Nigerian juju band Sunny Adé in 1982.

compromise between art and commerce was vilified in the same breath as the industry itself; the Sex Pistols took EMI's handout, *and then* recorded a blast against the company. Meanings bestowed by history were systematically cut up, rearranged, re-used, just as punk fashion did with clothes. Musical "labels", like graphic symbols were stolen, divested of significance, often brutalized. Punk pointed to the failure of categorization to mean anything in contemporary commodity culture.

Music after punk

In punk, the position of music as sound was a paradoxical one. Music was no longer the energizing force behind change; the full effects, and effectiveness, of the "extrinsic" depended on the role of visual images, or of their memory. Yet, for the vast majority of customers, aural perception still provided the foundation of their likes and dislikes, and hence of their ability to respond in any creative way. For all its sophisticated approach, glam rock had been, by its own admission, a musical thief; while "the biggest mistake of the punks was that they rejected music" (according to ex-punk musician Mick Hucknall, in 1987). The comparatively short life of both may be attributed above all to the audience's boredom with the sounds.

Pure punk lasted only for a year or two after 1976, but its influence was out of all proportion to its longevity or its record sales. In the wake of punk a diversity of styles have co-existed. Various factors would appear to militate against this situation – corporations requiring a transnational product; commercial radio stations requiring the broadest possible audience to satisfy advertisers – yet, once again, it is the paradoxes which catch the eye. Swept up as never before in international commerce, popular music has become most valuable as a "property" not when it is sold itself, but when it helps to sell something else (sometimes, in charity festivals, even selling the needs of the poor in the Third World to the affluent Western young). But the success of music used this way depends entirely on its distinctiveness; put the other way, the commodity's success depends on a piece of music's individual autonomy.

Pop video, by contrast, which seemed intended to stake a claim for the absolute distinctiveness of each musical item, usually had the reverse effect. Whereas pop videos aimed to bring pop music into the realm of art, they more often drew attention to its kinship with advertising. Despite the global reach of the music business, and the trans-national nature of the best-selling sounds, it remained true that the most successful musicians were American or British. Artists from France and Germany could break through their stranglehold briefly; musicians from other cultures were often condemned to an audience limited to their own countries.

In the late 1980s popular music could still be the arena where fundamental issues in mass culture and society were worked out. This is clearly seen in the changing "female iconography" of performers such as Madonna. For all its immediacy and contemporaneity, this reinterpretation was also historically articulate. Madonna's use of male backing groups, for example, had to be seen against the history of girl groups in pop music, while her turning of the stereotyped images of women to devastating advantage evoked the torch singers of the twenties and thirties.

Past and present interacted, too, in one of the most remarkable figures of the eighties, Michael Jackson. Jackson drew on black dance rhythms of the street, on stylistic elements in soul and disco, and the use of video (not forgetting his ownership of the rights of many Beatles songs), all this pointing to a mastery of contemporary materials and a successful attempt to reach – and profit from – as wide an audience as possible. In the same vein, the alterations to his image in 1987 – lightening of the skin, plastic surgery on the nose – were an insurance policy for maintaining the breadth of his appeal in a transnational, trans-racial business. But other interpretations are possible, when historical factors are considered. One, more negative, suggests that skin lightening has disquieting echoes of hair straightening preparations by means of which many blacks in the twenties and thirties sought to ease their way in the white-controlled world. But a second interpretation, reaching still further back, is more positive. "Whiting-up" is a reversal of the "blacking-up" done by minstrels of the turn of the century. In the context of his profoundly black music, Jackson in whiteface (white veneer on black body) draws attention to increasing black control in the white man's game.

At the same time, Jackson's knowing use of images and style suggest that more recent history has had its impact, too. In his minute attention to dress and to body language, in his confusion of sexuality and childishness, there are clear reminders of the seventies. Seen in this light, what may make Michael Jackson so unusual, therefore, is the interplay of the ecstatic and the extrinsic. Whether that encounter will be as productive as earlier ones in the popular music story remains to be seen.

▲ From the early 1970s David Bowie continually changed his image, consciously challenging his audience's confidence in established stylistic boundaries. His music changed direction several times in the later 1970s and 1980s, allowing him to keep at one remove from his fans.

◄▼ The less dispassionate styles of Prince (opposite) and Michael Jackson, by comparison, seem to signify greater self-identification, but control is always there. So too is ambiguity. Even in the blatantly erotic performances of Prince, the puzzling combination of lust and piety leaves audiences both involved and removed. For Michael Jackson's even larger following there is a double enigma: of "funky" physicality and innocence; and of a pale face singing black music.

Datafile

The 1970s and 1980s saw the final creation of a "world style", with international companies marketing identical clothes and goods in identical stores throughout the world. The result was for design to move upmarket, to look for new ways of offering added value by adding "style" to goods, whether by putting the designer's label on the outside of clothes, or by making the element of style ostentatiously visible.

▼ In the 1970s and 1980s the United States finally lost its pre-eminence in automobile manufacture to Japan. The motor trade throughout the world adapted to rising oil prices and fears of oil shortages by building smaller, cheaper and more fuel-efficient cars.

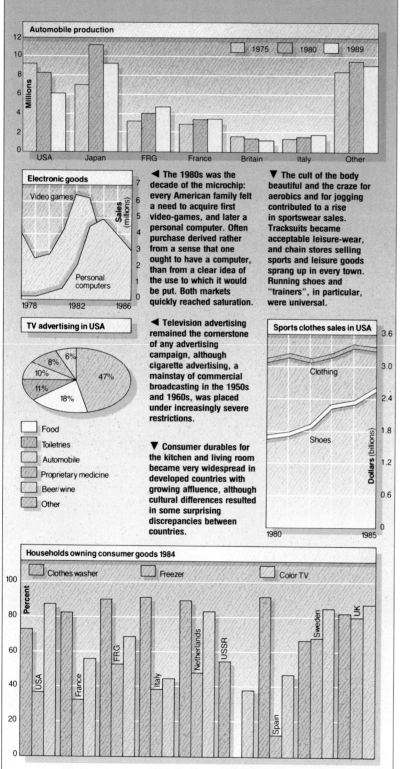

Automobile production

1975   1980   1989

USA   Japan   FRG   France   Britain   Italy   Other

Electronic goods

Video games

Personal computers

1978   1982   1986

◀ The 1980s was the decade of the microchip: every American family felt a need to acquire first video-games, and later a personal computer. Often purchase derived rather from a sense that one ought to have a computer, than from a clear idea of the use to which it would be put. Both markets quickly reached saturation.

▼ The cult of the body beautiful and the craze for aerobics and for jogging contributed to a rise in sportswear sales. Tracksuits became acceptable leisure-wear, and chain stores selling sports and leisure goods sprang up in every town. Running shoes and "trainers", in particular, were universal.

TV advertising in USA

47%   6%   8%   10%   11%   18%

- Food
- Toiletries
- Automobile
- Proprietary medicine
- Beer/wine
- Other

◀ Television advertising remained the cornerstone of any advertising campaign, although cigarette advertising, a mainstay of commercial broadcasting in the 1950s and 1960s, was placed under increasingly severe restrictions.

▼ Consumer durables for the kitchen and living room became very widespread in developed countries with growing affluence, although cultural differences resulted in some surprising discrepancies between countries.

Sports clothes sales in USA

Clothing

Shoes

1980   1985

Households owning consumer goods 1984

Clothes washer   Freezer   Color TV

USA   France   FRG   Italy   Netherlands   USSR   Spain   Sweden   UK

In the 1950s and even the 1960s high fashion, for all its caprice and change, had given the impression of a world of stability and consensus. As the West became increasingly crisis-ridden in the 1970s, first politically and then economically, this was reflected in the turbulence and confusion of fashion. Now, fashion originated on the streets, in art colleges and on student campuses.

A confusion of styles

It became a fashion cliché to say that *haute couture* was dead, that a pluralism of styles meant that everyone could wear "their own thing". In fact it was more complicated than that. There were very definite looks, and equally definite ways not to look. Fashion manufacturers and designers on the one hand, and consumers on the other, were becoming more sophisticated and more aware of the fragmentation of society into more subtly defined social groupings; the old identifications of class and generation gave way to definitions that no longer indicated just status, but also the sort of person you thought you were.

Artists and bohemians of the 19th century had originated the habit of dressing *against* the dominant mode, but by the 1970s the practice was so common that the notion of a dominant mode itself seemed to lose all meaning. Even "classic" styles – the Burberry raincoats, tweeds, tartans and cashmere cardigans of the British upper class – could be rejuvenated by the self-parody of Sloane or, in the United States, Preppie fashions. Hippy fashions, "clone" fashions (the new macho look for gay men), punks, new romantics, "Dallasty" dressing, Laura Ashley (a very middle-class style) and even feminist fashions all challenged the dominance of Paris. With the return, however, of a more open and flaunting smartness in the second half of the 1980s, the predictions of the death of Paris appeared to be premature, though contemporary designer dressing seems a marker primarily of money rather than class or status.

The fashion industry was also changing to meet these changed circumstances. At one end, mass-produced fashion was increasingly monopolized by a few huge firms who spread their production processes across many countries, exporting labor costs in particular to the Third World. At the other end, sweatshops began once more to proliferate in London, New York and other Western fashion centers. The old "middle-class couture" firms of the mid-century tended to be squeezed out, but there was room for new designers who created advanced looks and manufactured in relatively small quantities. At the consumer end, despite the proliferation of styles, the market was increasingly dominated by a few very large multiple chain stores.

THE NEW NARCISSISM

**Styles and lifestyles
Punk and post-punk
The designer culture
Popularizing high
design**

Men's fashions were increasingly drawn into the carousel of changing styles; the new narcissism expressed itself both in the bizarre designs of Jean-Paul Gaultier, who claimed that his Parisian styles were inspired by the King's Road, Chelsea, and in the smartening up of men's high-street shops, where designer sweaters, baggy trousers and Lacoste and Ralph Lauren style shirts were now to be seen.

The creation of lifestyles
Bombarded with mass-media images, both men and women with aspirations to style have been increasingly encouraged to perceive fashion as a performance and a game. In the 1950s the fashion magazines constantly advised women to "know your type and stick to it", whereas today their advice is more likely to be on how to create a whole variety of "looks". Fashion as performance, masquerade and play ties in with a greater eclecticism in fashion; it also fits with the continuing

▼ The eighties saw the shopping malls of the United States spread around the world where "consumer choice" turns out to mean branches of the same chain stores in whichever shopping precinct you happen to be.

thirst for "retro-chic". This recycling of fashions from the recent past has become a particularly significant element in mass-media representations. The global successes of television series such as *Brideshead Revisited* and *The Jewel in the Crown* relied in part on the meticulous reproduction of the fashions of the 1920s and 1930s respectively. What fashion took from these productions was an often romantic, indeed sentimental imagery of modes and manners which were in reality rigidly class-bound, imperialist and racist. By vaguely aping the styles of a decadent aristocracy, the British were able to justify their national past while transforming themselves into the heroes and heroines their grandparents might conceivably have been.

The recreation of such fashions gives the consumer a more distanced and ironic attitude to fashion. The consumption of fashion still relates to the identity of the wearer, but also increasingly to chosen "lifestyles". We no longer announce our

membership of a class or status group with our clothes; rather, it is common to invent a "lifestyle", while "personality" and "identity" are less stable than used to be believed.

The slow evolution of fashion lines is therefore to some extent displaced by fads that can be easily discarded, and some of these fads originate in the costumes of public figures: stars, royalty and television characters. The French designer Claude Montana thought up the fashion for wide shoulders bulked out with heavy shoulder pads, but it was American soap opera and Britain's Princess Diana that popularized it. On the other hand, the original Boy George look – Hasidic hat and curls, vivid makeup, and a kind of tent-like robe over baggy trousers – was the pop star's very own street style, widely copied by young *female* fans. The same was true of the 1985 Madonna look of sleaze, tousled locks tied up with rags, and heavy "fifties" lipstick.

The varying reception of these various fashions reinforced generation gaps at the same time as it narrowed some gender ones, just as the youth fashions of the 1950s and 1960s did. But 1960s fashions aimed to make *everyone* look youthful, and how far to raise your hem was a source of intense discussion among women over 30 years old at that time. Few people over 20 wanted to look like Boy George or Madonna.

Although students of the eighties wore black in the manner of the Parisian existentialists of the late forties, it was without their politics, and while they revitalized the dress and music of fifties' beatniks, it was often minus the social protest of the earlier time. Style came to replace content. Was it the case, then, that in the end the use of clothes to express dissidence merely, as British critic and jazz musician George Melly once suggested, turned "revolt into style"?

Revolt or style?

One counter-cultural fashion at least retained its power to shock for a decade: punk. A peculiarly British phenomenon, punk was born in the hot summer of 1976. It was an onslaught on all received notions of beauty, taste and decency, a fashion of *objets trouvés* and "made ups", usually the refuse of daily life – safety pins, plastic dustbin liners, lavatory chains, torn jeans, ocelot fur fabric, PVC and sex-shop satin – to create a look that exploded into the washed-out aftermath of the hippy scene, ousting kaftans, smocks, bell-bottom trousers, curls and natural faces in favor of shaved heads, rag-wrapped limbs and faces scarified with fright make-up of black lips and reddened eyes. One unusual feature of this "ugly" and shocking look was that, at the same time that it permeated mainstream fashion – every high-street hairdresser in the eighties could turn out young women and men with spiked hair and shaved necks – it has also remained a hard-line counter-cultural fashion, used by sections of the young to express their profound alienation from contemporary society. At the same time, in its esthetic connections with surrealism and the avant garde it operated to question what was meant by "beauty" or "ugliness", and brought the practice of art into the performance of everyday life.

Although punk influenced mainstream fashion, by the late 1980s that influence was waning, overtaken by the materialist ethos of the decade. Counter-cultural groups, often using forms of dress to express views of the world, have frequently been fashion innovators. But in a more general way 20th-century fashions have to a large extent abandoned the hierarchical meanings they once carried. Fashion was once attacked as the living symbol of wealth and privilege. Now it is more often feared as emblematic of a mass consciousness, of conformity, and a metropolitan uniformity without uniforms.

The designer culture

Once the whole of Western society had begun to participate in consumer culture, lifestyle became not only a phenomenon that affected subcultures but a commodity available to all. A range of manufactured lifestyles, each advertising its unique qualities, dominated the market-place and dictated consumption choices in the 1970s and 1980s. The boutique idea provided a basis on which countless retail set-ups were subsequently established. In Britain the success of the Laura Ashley and Next retail chains consolidated the role that the promotion of a complete lifestyle – clothing, furniture and interior decoration – played in selling goods to a particular group of customers. Whether nostalgic or modern, each consumer style functioned on the level of its visual and symbolic identity. In the second half of the 1970s one option emerged which emphasized the role of the designer in creating style. The "designer-jeans" phenomenon, launched in the United States as a marketing ploy to help individualize and put added value into otherwise anonymous, mass-produced artefacts, quickly spread. Hairdressers became hair-designers, and designer-shops appeared selling ranges of "designed" products, from paper-clip holders to chairs. The goods were united less by their function than by the claim to individuality in the esthetic sensibility which had created them and

▲ The pop star Madonna's image of 1985–86 deliberately made cultural bricolage and style sleaze into an ambiguous image of a femininity which vaguely suggested defiance and rebellion.

▶ Punk took anti-fashion dressing just about as far as it could go – only to be gobbled up by mainstream fashion, where it emerged in the spike hairstyles, unisex earrings and omnipresent black of the mid-1980s. Punk was the ultimate urban style – the violence and decline of the inner city reinterpreted in anarchistic terms on the human body.

▼ Madonna attracted imitators among pre-teen girls. Style and image are reaching younger age groups; and the marketers of the Madonna image welcome this, seeing in the nine- and ten-year-olds an easily manipulated market.

◀▲ Two couture influences dominated the 1980s: the Italian and the Japanese. In the early 1980s Japanese *haute couture* wrapped women in body-disguising shrouds in colors of black, mud and porridge. Issey Miyake, a truly innovative designer, modified these into garments which are still fluid and have immediate appeal and sensuousness (left). The Italians created a business-woman's mode which re-appropriated a certain masculinity and rendered it bold and alluring. The origins of the big shoulder pads of the mid-1980s was also to be traced to the American soap operas *Dallas* and *Dynasty* (above) but the Italians Armani and Versace brought the power-dressing look to *haute couture*.

▲ Swatch watches are just one example of the extension of style and design into more and more accessories; or the extension of gadgets and machines into the total outfit of the individual. The Filofax, the Walkman, the watch, the personal calculator – are they part of one's outfit or part of one's interior decor; more like a telephone or more like a handbag? Either way their style, shape and color form part of the total look which marks the wearer out as designer style, yuppie, high street or avant-garde.

which would, by implication, consume them.

Conran's Habitat principle lost its appeal to the "knowing minority" by moving downmarket. Something else was needed to re-inject added value into those products which courted an elite, taste-conscious market. The answer lay not only in selling "good taste" but in creating a whole design culture to surround and guarantee it. The use of the designer label served this function, isolating those objects to which it was attached from the mass of undifferentiated artefacts.

The design esthetic of the 1980s

The designer-shops of the early 1980s, in New York, Milan, Paris, Tokyo, Copenhagen, London, sold the same artefacts that had won prizes for good design in the 1950s. The same esthetic, characterized by geometric simplicity and monochromes, was present. Good taste required a return to the safe, well-trodden path of international Modernism. A cult-object movement developed in the 1980s. It suggested that only a small group of cognoscenti had enough knowledge and refined taste to identify these special objects. "Classic" objects from the near past such as the Zippo lighter, Arne Jacobsen's ash-trays and Alvar Aalto glass were re-appropriated and set alongside "new classics" such as Richard Sapper's Tizio light, and simple black alarm clocks and radios from the Braun company, which set out to emulate their qualities of timelessness and functional good taste.

Many manufacturers participated in the growing international fashion for designer goods. Richard Sapper's kettle designed for Italian metalwork manufacturer Alessi immediately became a cult object *par excellence*. Italy had been the first country in the postwar years to identify its upmarket products – mostly furniture, plastic products and electronic goods – with designers' names and as a result, men such as Archille Castiglioni, Vico Magistretti, Mario Bellini, Ettore Sottsass and Marco Zanuso became well known figures in the design world.

Even automobile design, until then the most anonymous of areas, created its own designer heroes in the 1970s. The Italian Giorgio Giugiaro became well-known internationally as the designer of the Volkswagen Golf and Fiat Panda. Italy experienced a second wave of design-related success in the 1980s, associated this time with an extension of the alternative ideas it had pioneered in the late 1960s.

The Italians had been the first to understand the limitations of the Modernist design esthetic, but by the late 1970s the rest of the design world had realized that the concept of "ultimate form" was obsolete. Now the radical designers of the 1960s emerged again to question conventional design values.

The Italian Post-Modern movement centered on the work of a small number of designers associated with two experimental groups – Studio Alchymia and Memphis. From 1979 they held regular exhibitions to coincide with the Milan Furniture Fair, borrowing the concept of the annual show from fashion designers, with whose philosophy they sought to identify themselves.

▼ The association between pop stars and fashion continued beyond the rebellious individuality of Madonna: here British pop group Madness are dressed in Mod revival style – though with 1980s coloring – by Jasper Conran.

Furniture and interior design were seen to be linked more with the concept of image than with ideal forms, and to be more part of the general process of mass communication and mass culture than ever before. This attempt to align design with mass culture became the hallmark of the New Design. Ironically, however, the experimental nature of the new movement meant that work was generally limited to the prototype stage and therefore became, in real terms, somewhat exclusive and expensive. This failure to achieve in practical terms what was envisaged in theory had often previously foiled attempts to inject a level of popular culture into the designed artefact.

The work of Ettore Sottsass, which had been so influential in the earlier period, continued to inspire much of the radical Italian design of the 1980s. His pieces emphasized the use of surface pattern, were banal in nature and appropriated from what he called "non-culture": the mosaic on the floor of suburban bars and the spongy pattern on the covers of government account books.

Alessandro Mendini, who also provided items for the Studio Alchymia collections, was preoccupied with the concept of "kitsch" produced by the mass dissemination of images in the contemporary environment. He used fine-art imagery – from Kandinsky and Seurat, for example – to stress the fact that even high culture, once duplicated, became part of the world of the banal. While Sottsass remained optimistic about the possibility of designs making significant cultural

▲ With its steel girders and glass top, the "Mainframe" desk, manufactured by Bonomi Design Limited, epitomized the "High-Tech" movement of the 1980s.

◀▲ The thinking behind Ettore Sottsass' bookcase – Carlton, which was designed for the first Memphis exhibition held in Milan in 1981, contrasted dramatically with Richard Sapper's whistling kettle, manufactured by Alessi in 1984. While the former represented a direct threat to the essentially "chic" values of the Italian design establishment, the latter confirmed its ideals by becoming a "cult" object.

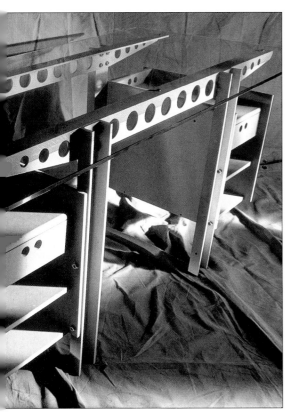

nology rather than innovative design for its own sake. Japan opted for the manufacture of small consumer machines because of the ease with which such goods could be exported in large numbers. Although in the area of technological goods it did not name its designers, the creators of Japanese fashion design, among them Issey Miyake and Yohji Yamamoto, became well-known names in the 1980s, influencing the minimal nature of fashion at this time.

As in the 1960s, fashion in the 1980s was still at the forefront of design, influencing other goods which formed part of the same lifestyle. While in the 1970s design culture had succeeded in providing lifestyle accompaniments for an elite, international set, by the following decade it was becoming democratized, mainly through the efforts of the mass media which set out to spread their sphere of influence across a much wider social spectrum. Product advertising, Sunday supplements, magazines and High Street retail outlets began to use the words "design" and "designer" to provide added value for a wide range of goods. Along with good health and male narcissism – two inventions of the advertising industry in the 1970s and 1980s – design became a popular catchword, guaranteeing added value for the consumer and increased sales and profits for the manufacturer.

▼ The main contribution of Japan to international design culture was that of a "high-tech" esthetic, visible in the sophisticated audio equipment which is sold to the whole world. Rather than encouraging a "user-friendly" approach to these new, complex machines, it opted for a "value-for-money" philosophy which suggested that the most complicated-looking equipment offered the most advanced technology at an affordable price.

statements, Mendini's more pessimistic work communicated the impossibility of combating fundamental social and economic laws by means of design.

In 1981 Sottsass launched his own design collection called "Memphis". Less esoteric than Alchymia, but still covered in brightly patterned plastic laminates, Memphis furniture soon became well-known images, disseminated by the mass media and used in countless advertising campaigns. Images which had their origins in the mass media were recirculated. While, superficially, Memphis initiated an international style revolution which penetrated fashionable quarters worldwide, on a deeper level it stood for the final demise of the European Modern Movement as the arbiter of taste and good design.

The free-for-all encouraged by the Memphis experiment became one of the characteristics of the 1980s and the problem of establishing criteria for evaluating design became increasingly difficult: "Appropriate" replaced "good" and the consumer moved to the center of the picture, displacing the earlier emphasis upon production and technology as the major determinant of good design. The link between design and ethics was broken and the possibility emerged of design embracing popular values.

By the 1980s, design culture had become part of international trading. Japan, which had hitherto sold its high-tech products on the basis of their technical reliability and low price, joined the bandwagon producing goods, such as the Sony Walkman, the Olympus camera and the Sharp hand-held calculator, which quickly became new design classics. They offered sophisticated technology at a reasonable price and epitomized the Japanese interest in encouraging advanced tech-

◀ In the 1970s and 1980s, the trend towards technological consumer items, designed for their functionality and anonymity, was expressed in high-value goods such as hi-fi and cameras. There was little to distinguish the products of rival firms.

The conflict between the power of the state and the rights of its citizens seemed to be turning the way of the people. As Communist rule faded in Eastern Europe, the Baltic countries moved toward independence. Soviet president Gorbachev seemed unlikely to stop them, though they set an unwelcome precedent inevitably followed by other states of the USSR. The brutal dictatorship of Pinochet in Chile also came to an end, and the movement in favor of democracy was evident in countries as remote as Burma (though the results of the election were soon suppressed), while in South Africa the long-awaited release of Nelson Mandela opened the way for constructive dialogue between the white government and its chief opponent, the ANC. Not all dictators were feeling the winds of change, however. Saddam Hussein of Iraq, having recently concluded a long, unjustified, savage and unsuccessful war against one neighbor (Iran), tried his luck again by invading a less formidable one, Kuwait, upon which Iraq had long-standing territorial claims. Saddam failed to realize that the Cold War was over, and the countries of the United Nations were almost all ranged against him.

▲ Nelson Mandela, symbol of hope and progress for South African blacks and for the oppressed worldwide, is released from jail. He was sentenced to life imprisonment in 1964 as organizer of the banned African National Congress.

● **1 Jan**: Cuba rejoins the UN Security Council after a 30-year break.

● **3 Jan**: Protesters riot in the Soviet republic of Azerbaijan, and KGB units are sent to restore order.

● **22 Jan**: Landslide vote at the congress of the Communist party of Yugoslavia to abandon the one-party system.

● **Jan**: Soviet president Mikhail Gorbachev visits the Lithuanian capital Vilnius to try to persuade the nationalist leaders of the rebellious republic to drop their plans for independence. (›24 Feb)

● **1 Feb**: Communist leaders in Bulgaria resign to make way for a broad-based coalition.

● **2 Feb**: President F.W. de Klerk lifts the 30-year ban on the ANC and the South African Communist party.

● **24 Feb**: The first genuine multiparty elections since 1917 are held in the USSR, for the new Lithuanian parliament. (›11 Mar)

● **26 Feb**: President Daniel Ortega of Nicaragua is defeated in the first truly free poll since his Sandinista movement took power in 1979.

● **26 Feb**: President Vaclav Havel announces that all Soviet troops will be withdrawn from Czechoslovakia by July 1991.

● **Feb**: In fighting in Beirut between rival Christian forces, some 200 are killed, mostly children.

● **10 Mar**: The military ruler of Haiti, Prosper Avril, is ousted from power.

● **11 Mar**: Augusto Pinochet, President of Chile, hands over power to Patricio Aylwin, ending his dictatorship.

● **11 Mar**: Lithuania declares independence, and Vytautas Landsbergis is elected as leader.

● **18 Mar**: East Germany holds its first genuinely democratic election. Right wing parties win a clear victory.

● **25 Mar**: Estonia's Communist party votes to break with the Soviet Communist party over a period of six months.

● **8 Apr**: King Birendra of Nepal agrees to demands to end Nepal's feudal-style monarchy and lift the 30-year ban on political parties.

● **9 Apr**: Troops enter Natal to end weeks of black factional fighting that has left around 400 dead (SA).

● **30 Apr**: Beijing lifts martial law in Tibet, 14 months after sending in troops to crush anti-Chinese demonstrations.

● **4 May**: The Latvian parliament votes for independence from the USSR.

● **28 May**: The National League for Democracy wins the first multiparty elections in Burma for 30 years.

● **Jun**: President Iliescu appeals to the miners to help deal with students' antigovernment demonstrations, provoking violence on the streets of Bucharest (Rom).

● **6 Jul**: The 16 NATO members agree to redefine their military strategy, and clear the way for a settlement with the USSR over a united Germany's defense role and closer European cooperation.

● **7 Jul**: Rioting breaks out in Nairobi after a rally to demand multiparty democracy (Ken).

● **27 Jul**: Arthur Robinson, prime minster of Trinidad, members of his cabinet, and 40 others are seized by Muslim extremists in a coup. The rebels surrender unconditionally on 1 Aug.

● **2 Aug**: Iraq invades Kuwait and on 8 Aug annexation is announced.

● **7 Aug**: Prime minister Benazir Bhutto is sacked by president Gulan Ishaq Khan, who accuses her government of "undermining the workings of the constitution" (Pak).

● **23 Aug**: The Republic of Armenia declares its independence from the USSR.

● **9 Sep**: Samuel Doe, President of Liberia, is beaten to death by rebel troops.

● **24 Sep**: The USSR parliament votes to give Gorbachev power to rule by decree, giving him authority to handle every aspect of reform. (›19 Oct)

● **3 Oct**: German reunification. The Volkskammer and Bundestag ratify the treaty of 20 Sep. (›4 Dec)

● **8 Oct**: Israeli border police shoot dead 21 Arabs during rioting around the Western Wall and the Dome of the Rock, Jerusalem. Iraqi president Saddam Hussein attempts to use the shooting to break the fragile Arab/Western alliance.

● **19 Oct**: The Supreme Soviet endorses the introduction of the market economy and adopts Gorbachev's plan to introduce it over two years.

● **17 Nov**: USSR parliament agrees to change the constitution in an attempt to prevent collapse. Gorbachev wins increased powers, the republics are to have more say in central government, but so too are the police, KGB, and army.

● **19 Nov**: The Cold War officially ends when 22 heads of state sign the Treaty on Conventional Armed Forces in Europe (CFE Treaty), which drastically reduces the amount of conventional weapons held by NATO and Warsaw Pact countries.

● **22 Nov**: British prime minister Thatcher announces that she will not fight on for the Tory party leadership. On 27 November, John Major defeats Michael Heseltine and Douglas Hurd to become party leader and prime minister.

● **4 Dec**: Helmut Kohl's Christian Democrats win the first nationwide elections in Germany since 1933.

● **9 Dec**: Lech Walesa wins a landslide victory in the Polish presidential elections.

● **Dec**: Anti-Communist violence grows in Albania.

SOCIETY

- **4 Jan:** At least 225 are killed and 400 injured in a train crash in south Pakistan.
- **19 Jan:** Marion Barry, the black mayor of Washington, is secretly filmed smoking "crack" and faces a possible prison sentence.
- **28 Jan:** Around 150 are feared drowned in Bangladesh when an overcrowded river ferry collides with another vessel and sinks.
- **Jan:** In Sudan, at least 600 are reported killed in clashes between Muslim tribesmen and non-Muslim southerners.
- **Jan:** Hurricane-force winds in UK kill at least 46, and some 3 million trees are lost.
- **1 Feb:** Troops and tanks are sent in to Kosovo to quell ethnic violence (Yug).
- **4 Feb:** New Zealand cricketer Richard Hadlee becomes the first to take 400 Test wickets.
- **11 Feb:** Nelson Mandela is released from Victor Verster prison near Cape Town (SA).
- **14 Feb:** The Perrier company withdraws its entire stock of 160 million bottles of mineral water from the world market after traces of benzine are found in the water (Fr).
- **14 Feb:** An Indian Airlines Airbus bursts into flames as it comes in to land at Bangalore, killing 92.
- **23 Feb:** UK ambulance union leaders reach an agreement with the management to end the long-running dispute.
- **6 Mar:** The USSR parliament passes a law sanctioning the ownership of private property.
- **Mar:** Violent demonstrations take place across England and Wales as councils set their poll tax rates.
- **1 Apr:** A riot erupts in Strangeways prison, and prisoners take control of buildings. The unrest spreads to other prisons in UK. The siege finally ends on 25 Apr.
- **3 Apr:** At least 32 are killed in the Punjab by a bomb believed to have been planted by Sikh separatists.
- **17 Apr:** Moscow imposes an economic blockade on Lithuania.
- **Apr:** Floods swamp vast areas of Queensland, New South Wales and Victoria (Aus).
- **9 May:** Desecration of Jewish graves in Carpentras, S France
- **10 May:** 50,000 students battle with police on university campuses throughout South Korea, protesting against the inauguration of president Roh Tae Woo's "dictatorial and undemocratic" Liberal Democratic party.
- **14 May:** Hundreds protest in Manila against the presence of US military bases. 55 are injured in clashes with police.

- **30 May:** France announces a ban on all imports of beef and cattle from the UK, joining USSR, Austria and West Germany, due to fears of the cattle disease BSE.
- **May:** 34 countries sign a declaration at the UN Environmental Conference at Bergen, Norway, agreeing to prevent and attack the causes of "environmental degradation".
- **May:** Ethnic violence between Mohajirs and Sindhis in south Pakistan claims over 200 lives.
- **22 June:** Earthquake in Northwest Iran kills 40,000 and injures at least 100,000.
- **1 July:** Germany reaches economic and monetary union.
- **7 Jul:** Martina Navratilova (USA) wins a record 9th Wimbledon singles tennis title.
- **27 Jul:** OPEC agrees to raise the official price of oil for the first time in 10 years. The deal is made to avert the threat of military action in the Gulf from Saddam Hussein, who wants to rescue Iraq's economy by boosting the price of oil, and who has forced the issue in recent weeks in a row with Kuwait, who openly flouts OPEC production quotas.
- **24 Aug:** A state of emergency is imposed on 27 townships in South Africa as the death toll from two weeks of violence reaches 500.
- **8 Oct:** UK formally joins the ERM.
- **Oct:** The Indian government faces opposition to its plans to improve the lot of the lower castes. Upper-caste Hindus take part in violent demonstrations, and dozens of students burn themselves to death.
- **29 Nov:** Germany begins to airlift food supplies to Moscow as USSR faces the threat of famine and rationing. One of the side effects of *perestroika* has been the collapse of the state agriculture and distribution system, and the problem has been made worse by hoarding and a flourishing black market.
- **1 Dec:** French and British workers shake hands, having dug through to each other in the Channel Tunnel.
- **7 Dec:** Four years of negotiations between GATT countries collapse, heightening fears of an international trade war. The deadlock arose over farm subsidies, and a final breakdown is only averted by setting a new deadline.
- Australia faces the worst recession since World War II. Bankruptcy is rife, and stock exchange trading is slow.
- The Nobel Peace Prize is won by Mikhail Gorbachev (USSR).
- International relief effort is set up to aid Romania, after reports of the catastrophic health situation there. The country has the highest death rate among the under fives in Europe, and the highest maternal mortality rate.
- Nintendo video games become a craze.

CULTURE

- **14 May:** Japanese Ryoei Saito pays US$83 million for Van Gogh's *Portrait of Dr Gachet*, making it the world's most expensive painting.
- A.S. Byatt's novel *Possession*, wins the Booker Prize (UK).
- Octavio Paz, Mexican essayist and poet, wins the Nobel Prize for Literature.
- The "Three Tenors' World Cup Concert" in Rome, with Luciano Pavarotti, Placido Domingo and José Carreras, is seen on TV all over the world.
- Release of *Shirley Valentine*, starring Pauline Collins (USA).
- Release of *Dick Tracy*, starring and directed by Warren Beatty (USA).
- *Ghost*, starring Patrick Swayze and Demi Moore (USA).
- *Pretty Woman*, starring Richard Gere and Julia Roberts, is released (USA).
- Bernardo Bertolucci: *The Sheltering Sky* (UK).
- The cartoon characters Teenage Mutant Hero Turtles become a craze.
- Archeologists discover an additional 644 miles of the Great Wall of China in Liaoning province up to the Korean border.
- Ceiling of the Sistine Chapel unveiled after 10 years' controversial restoration work (Vat).
- Cincinnati's Contemporary Arts Center acquitted of obscenity charges after their exhibition of photographs by the controversial homosexual photographer Robert Mapplethorpe (USA).
- Derek Walcott (St. Lucia) publishes his long poem *Omeros*.
- Release of the film *Cyrano de Bergerac* starring Gérard Depardieu (Fr).
- Release of the film *Dances with Wolves* starring Kevin Costner (USA).

SCIENCE

- **30 Jan:** Guy's Hospital (UK) performs the world's first successful heart surgery on a baby in its mother's womb.
- **Apr:** The Hubble space telescope launched from the shuttle *Discovery*.
- **Oct:** Launch of spacecraft *Ulysses* on a mission to oberve the poles of the Sun in 1994 and 1995. The craft is built jointly by ESA and Nasa.
- **20 Dec:** Pierre Chambon and colleagues report the discovery of the gene which may be crucial in the spread of breast cancer (Fr).
- Nobel Prize for Physics is won by Jerome Friedman, Henry Kendall (USA) and Richard Taylor, for their pioneering work in the discovery of the structure of protons and neutrons.
- Nobel Prize for Chemistry is won by Elias James Corey (USA) for finding new ways of producing and synthesising chemical compounds.
- WHO reports the development of an effective male contraceptive which is reversible and gives minimal side effects.
- US astronomers discover a new moon of Saturn, the smallest of the 18, and the first to be found orbiting within the rings.
- Canadian geologists find tiny rings and discs in sandstone 600 million years old, making them the oldest fossils of multicellular animals.
- A Japanese laboratory succeeds in producing a plastic which exhibits magnetic properties at low temperatures. It can be pressed into thin films to make new types of magnetic sensors.
- Scientists in the USSR produce diamond powder from carbon soot using only a conventional laser.
- Studies in the USA on the survivors of Nagasaki and Hiroshima show the risks from exposure to low levels of radiation is 3 to 4 times higher than previously thought.
- Fred Gage and colleagues inject modified cells from rat skin into the brains of rats suffering the equivalent of the human condition Parkinson's disease, and find brain function is partially restored (USA).
- Astronomers in Canada report that the Pole Star is changing from a star which pulsates into one which is stable, a process which will take about 10 years. The star has been pulsating for 40,000 years.
- Pellets of fat and fishmeal with live viruses inside are distributed in the European countryside. The viruses immunise foxes against rabies and the process is helping to eradicate the disease and prevent it spreading to domestic animals.
- Canadian scientists discover that killer whales "speak" a number of different "dialects" and "languages".

Saddam Hussein's refusal to obey a UN resolution requiring the evacuation of occupied Kuwait brought about another war conducted by the USA, actively supported by a number of other countries, and regarded with benevolent neutrality by most of the remainder. In a short, hi-tech campaign, the Iraqis were swiftly driven from Kuwait; but the USA, fearful of arousing the hostility of the Arab world, forebore to carry the campaign to its logical conclusion – the overthrow of Saddam. The result was civil war in Iraq, death and destruction for the Kurds in the north and the Shi'ites in the south, and the continuance of Saddam's regime. The total collapse of the Communist system in Europe and the disintegration of the USSR, the most momentous political development since 1945 – fueled by the refusal of the Russian Federation to accept an attempted coup – was welcomed by the majority of the people. It did cause some international concern, since the world would be left with only one superpower, the USA. It seemed probable too that some of the individual republics would experience problems like those of another fracturing federation, Yugoslavia, approaching the brink of full-scale civil war.

▲ Oilwells blaze on the Kuwait–Iraqi border during the Gulf War. The deliberate destruction of wellheads led to widespread fears for the environmental consequences even after the cessation of hostilities permitted experts to bring them under control.

● **4 Jan:** President Siad Barre of Somalia announces he is ready for peace talks with rebels and opposition groups and will accept the outcome of negotiations. However, fighting continues. (›27 Jan)

● **16 Jan:** War breaks out in the Gulf when US-led allied forces launch an air strike on Baghdad. The UN deadline for withdrawal from Kuwait had expired at 5 pm GMT.

● **18 Jan:** Iraq fires Scud missiles on Israeli cities in an attempt to force Israel to enter the war, and therefore split the allies.

● **20 Jan:** Iraq fires 10 Scud missiles at Riyadh and Dhahran, in Saudi Arabia. US spokesmen say that one landed harmlessly and the rest were intercepted by Patriot missiles.

● **24 Jan:** The allies liberate the first piece of Kuwait, the island of Qaruh, after a 5-hour battle.

● **27 Jan:** Somali president Barre flees after rebels overrun his palace.

● **Jan:** Yugoslav government accuses Serbia of undermining the monetary system and jeopardizing the federal program of economic reforms when it emerges that the republic illegally printed currency to prop up its bankrupt economy.

● **1 Feb:** In a speech at the opening of parliament, president de Klerk announces that the Land Acts of 1913 and 1936 and the Group Areas Act of 1966, reserving most of the land for whites and segregating residential areas, will be abolished during the current parliamentary session (SA).

● **3 Feb:** The Italian Communist party disbands itself, abandons Marxism, and is renamed the Democratic Party of the Left.

● **5 Feb:** Sudan decrees a federal system in an attempt to end seven years of civil war.

● **10 Feb:** Referendum in Lithuania votes in favour of independence from Moscow.

● **20 Feb:** President Ramiz Alia takes over "all powers" in Albania, to bring about reform in the country. A student strike in Tiranë had threatened to become a nationwide protest. (›27 Apr)

● **20 Feb:** Slovenia votes to give local laws precedence over federal legislation, the first formal step toward independence. Croatia follows suit on 21 Feb.

● **23 Feb:** Military leaders seize power from the elected government in Thailand, with the support of King Bhumibol.

● **28 Feb:** Bangladesh is thrown into new political uncertainty after the first democratic election in its history leaves no party with an outright majority.

● **28 Feb:** US president George Bush announces that the war to liberate Kuwait has been won and that fighting is to stop at 5 am.

● **4 Mar:** The port of Basra in south Iraq falls to forces opposed to Saddam Hussein and fighting spreads to other cities. Kurdish rebels also begin fighting in the north of the country.

● **17 Mar:** The first ever referendum in the USSR is held, on whether the USSR should be preserved as a federation of equal sovereign republics. The result is a narrow majority in favor.

● **29 Mar:** Giulio Andreotti resigns as Italy's prime minister, ending the 49th postwar government. He is forced to resign by demands from the Socialist party and president Cossiga.

● **Mar:** European states, USA and Canada urge nonessential embassy staff and families to leave Ethiopia after victories by northern rebels in their offensive launched on 23 Feb.

● **9 Apr:** Georgia proclaims formal independence from Moscow. On the following day, USSR troops move in to reassert control in the racially troubled South Ossetia region, causing the nationalist authorities to proclaim a general strike in protest.

● **17 Apr:** US forces move into northern Iraq to start setting up safe havens for Kurdish refugees.

● **27 Apr:** The first US government aircraft since 1979 lands in Iran, with blankets for Kurdish refugees.

● **Apr:** For the first time since the end of the Vietnam war, the USA gives a symbolic amount of aid to Hanoi. The move is prompted by Hanoi's cooperation in accounting for 2,276 US soldiers still missing from the war and in ending the Cambodian civil war.

● **Apr:** Rebel Kurds regroup for an attack on key cities, now that they are no longer hampered by their families, which are in refugee camps on the Iranian and Turkish borders.

● **Apr:** The ANC rules out any form of legislative veto for minority groups in a post-apartheid society, saying it would frustrate majority rule by universal suffrage (SA).

● **16 May:** General strike begins in Albania, bringing down the Communist government after 20 days.

● **21 May:** Rajiv Gandhi, former prime minister of India, is killed in a bomb attack.

● **3 Jun:** President Gorbachev and regional leaders decide to drop "socialist" from the country's name and call it the Union of Soviet Sovereign Republics, though official news agency Tass is told that the decision does not mean a rejection of socialist ideals.

● **17 Jun:** The longest general election in India comes to an end, resulting in another hung parliament. P.V. Narasimha Roa becomes the new prime minister.

● **20 Jun:** The German parliament votes to move the country's seat of government from Bonn to Berlin.

SOCIETY CULTURE SCIENCE

- **24 Jun:** Unconditional and unlimited ceasefire comes into operation in Cambodia, ending the 12-year conflict.

- **27 Jun:** Open warfare breaks out in Slovenia as Yugoslav tanks move in to bring the rebel republic to heel. On 30 Jun, the Yugoslav army agrees to withdraw and a fragile peace ensues.

- **1 Jul:** Leaders of the six Warsaw Pact countries meet in Prague and sign a protocol terminating the alliance.

- **7 Jul:** Federal troops intervene in eastern Croatia to break up a day-long gun battle between Serbs and Croats.

- **16 Jul:** President Bush, at the G7 summit in London, wins unanimous support for renewed use of military force if Iraq continues to defy the resolution demanding the destruction of all Iraqi nuclear weapons.

- **29 Jul:** US and USSR negotiators initial the most complicated arms control agreement ever, after nine years of talks.

- **Jul:** Reports are received that a ceasefire agreement has been reached between the Lebanese government and the PLO.

- **18 Aug:** President Gorbachev is imprisoned at his holiday villa by hardline Communist conspirators carrying out a coup. The coup crumbles on 21 Aug, and its leaders flee Moscow, as Boris Yeltsin, president of Russia, rallies the population. Gorbachev is restored as president.

- **25 Aug:** Gorbachev resigns as leader of the Communist party in the USSR, and the party prepares to dissolve, ending seven decades of Communist supremacy.

- **30 Oct:** Talks begin in Madrid between Israel, Syria, Jordan and Palestinian delegates.

6 Nov: Last oilwell fire ignited by retreating Iraqis during the Gulf War is extinguished in Kuwait.

8 Nov: EC imposes an economic embargo on Yugoslavia in an attempt to halt the civil war between Croatia and Serbia.

21 Nov: Boutros Boutros Ghali, deputy prime minister of Egypt, is chosen to succeed Javier Pérez de Cuéllar as secretary-general of the United Nations.

8 Dec: Russia, Ukraine and Belorussia create the Commonwealth of Independent States (CIS) to replace the USSR.

11 Dec: Maastricht Treaty is signed by the 12 member-states of the EC, giving increased power to the EC Commission in Brussels, and paving the way for a single European currency by 1999.

19 Dec: Australian prime minister Bob Hawkes is ousted and replaced with former treasury minister Paul Keating.

25 Dec: Mikhail Gorbachev resigns as president of the Soviet Union after the latter ceases to exist.

- **1 Mar:** US expert "Red" Adair is called in to tackle blazes on all Kuwait's 950 producing oilwells, which have been set alight by Iraqi troops or allied bombing.

- **27 Mar:** The IOC readmits South Africa to the Olympics after a 30-year absence.

- **4 Apr:** The USSR parliament is told that the country faces imminent financial collapse as its 15 republics have either neglected to pay or frozen their agreed contributions to the central budget.

- **22 Apr:** The first UN relief supplies for Kurdish refugees reach Iraq. 20,000 per day are said to be returning to Iraq.

- **30 Apr:** Israel prepares to rescue around 20,000 Ethiopian Jews trapped in Addis Ababa before it falls to rebel forces, in one of the largest airlifts in history.

- **Apr:** The EC lifts most of the remaining sanctions on South Africa.

- **Apr:** A cholera outbreak in South America reaches epidemic proportions.

- **12 Jun:** Mount Pinatubo erupts, threatening to obliterate the US 13th Air Force at Clark Air Base (Phil).

- **Jun:** Referendum in Leningrad votes to change its name back to St Petersburg.

- **1 Jul:** Sweden applies formally for membership of the EC, after months of speculation over whether it would affect its policy of neutrality.

- **17 Jul:** G7 leaders promise USSR a special association with the IMF and World Bank, which would offer help and advice, as well as technical help from the OECD, though there are no offers of financial aid.

- **18 Jul:** Massive flooding affects half of China after torrential rains in the north and west – the worst since the 1930s.

- **8 Aug:** John McCarthy, UK hostage in Beirut for 1,943 days, is released.

- **5 Nov:** Death of British tycoon Robert Maxwell, drowned off the Canary Islands.

7 Nov: "Magic" Johnson, US basketball star, reveals he carries the AIDS virus.

- It is revealed that the trade in babies in Peru has risen dramatically since austerity measures aimed at controlling the economy plunged millions into abject poverty. Childless Western couples offer $10,000–$17,000 for a baby.

- Collapse of the Bank of Credit and Commerce International on the discovery of massive fraud, panics investors worldwide.

- Nobel Prize for Peace is awarded to human rights campaigner Aung San Suu Kyi (Burma)

- **21 Feb:** Death of ballerina Margot Fonteyn, aged 71 (UK).

- **3 Apr:** Death of writer Graham Greene, aged 86 (UK).

- Franco Zeffirelli's film of *Hamlet* starring Mel Gibson, Alan Bates and Glenn Close is released (USA).

- Jonathan Pryce and Lea Salonga, stars of the Broadway production *Miss Saigon* win Tony awards for the best musical acting.

- Pulitzer Prizes are won by Neil Simon for his play *Lost in Yonkers* and by John Updike for his novel *Rabbit at Rest* (USA).

- Egyptian experts announce the discovery of a previously unknown Pharaonic city hidden beneath a village on the outskirts of Cairo.

- Trevor Lloyd Davies, a physician, and his wife Margaret, a theologian, put forward the hypothesis that Jesus did not die on the cross, but that he lost consciousness because of diminished blood supply to the brain, was taken to have died, and was later resuscitated (UK).

- Nobel Prize for Literature awarded to Nadine Gordimer (South Africa)

- The film of *JFK*, by Oliver Stone, is released (USA).

- The film of *The Silence of the Lambs* stars Anthony Hopkins and Jodie Foster.

- Dramatic fall in the value of art sales.

- The bicentenary of the death of Wolfgang Amadeus Mozart is celebrated throughout the music world.

- Experts from the International Atomic Energy Agency warn of the risks of a nuclear disaster in Bulgaria at the plant at Kozlodoy.

- UK researchers find a way of assessing how long people with HIV are likely to remain healthy before developing AIDS. The lower the levels of a certain type of white blood cell, the higher the risk.

- UK scientist Peter Jones works out how snowflakes form by discovering why some fall as stars and other as tiny plates of ice.

- The study of tiny beads of glass in Haiti by US scientists gives the clearest evidence yet that dinosaurs were extinguished by a cataclysmic event 65 million years ago.

- Japanese and US astronomers discover an erupting quasar, 2 billion light years away, which emitted as much energy in three minutes in 1989 as the sun does in 1 million years.

- Scientists develop heart operations that could make transplants largely unnecessary. The techniques involve rebuilding damaged areas of heart with muscles taken from the patient's body.

- Scientists produce an inhalent form of calcitonin, a drug that helps prevent the bone-loss disease osteoporosis. (UK)

- US scientists use genetic engineering to breed pigs that have hemoglobin in their blood, making an important step forward in the search for a substitute for human blood.

- Texas Instruments and South California Edison announce a new low-cost process for producing solar cells.

- US scientists suggest a high-fiber diet could help protect some women against breast cancer.

- Researchers extract a chemical from the leaves of the European Yew which has produced results in the treatment of ovarian cancer.

- US and European researchers announce that they have isolated the gene responsible for fragile-X syndrome, the most common cause of mental handicap.

- UK researchers discover a link between some cot death cases and a variety of microorganisms and fungi found in mattresses; babies lying face down are therefore able to inhale them.

- Irun Cohen and colleagues at the Weizmann Institute, Israel, report that they have found a naturally occurring peptide which cures diabetes in mice.

- AIDS has now attacked more than 170,000 Americans since 1981 and another 6,000 develop the disease every month. By the year 2000, 40 million people worldwide may be infected with HIV, according to WHO.

- Magellan probe maps the surface of Venus.

EPILOGUE

The breakup of the Soviet Union was a historic turning point. It was not, however, the end of history, though it was announced as such by the American historian Francis Fukayama (*The End of History and the New Man*, 1992). The fact that such a thought could be taken at all seriously proved once again how frivolous intellectual fashions can be. Yet the illusion persisted: now that there was no longer a tangible threat, now that the fear of a possible atomic holocaust from either of the superpowers had been removed, people felt they could breathe more easily.

In 1990 the Cold War came to an end. This undeclared conflict had influenced almost all events all over the globe, but its impact should not be overstated. It had lasted less than half a century, and it only influenced events, and was never totally responsible for them. After 1990, new conflicts started up and old ones re-emerged. Who would have believed that the disappearance of Soviet hegemony would occur without people being united more peaceably in friendship and democracy? That the reality would be so different, so bloody, so dismal was hardly to be anticipated. Certainly it was not foreseen before the events had actually taken place.

The history that seemed to explain and forge current events was traditionally thought to have begun in 1945, with the years since 1933 as a prelude to them. What came before was undoubtedly interesting, but hardly had a bearing on domestic or international affairs, let alone world politics. Yet, with the breakup of the Soviet power bloc, the relevance of the treaties struck after World War I to the modern conflicts in middle and eastern Europe was starkly evident. Even this was not enough to unravel the causes of conflict: the dividing lines between the warring parties in the former Yugoslavia involved much more ancient disputes – between Rome and Constantinople, between Christendom and Islam.

Yet economic crisis was not limited to eastern Europe, or even to Europe at all. Where material needs are so pressing, why should we look to history to explain conflict? There are various answers. The power of the economy is much greater today, when there is a single world economy, than in earlier

times when, however global a country's interests, its economy was insulated to a degree from events in other economies. Today, the greatest economic power is not a bank, or an industry, or a state: it is the market itself, though this has no face and no will of its own. In Washington, as in Bonn, in Tokyo as in Paris, the market matters every day, and its shifts influence government policies as well as those of largescale enterprises.

The economy determines events, but does not account fully for them. This had been evident for a long time. It was not the economy itself that forced Hitler to make war, but his false conception of the economy. Germany did not in fact need "living-room in the east", but Hitler thought that it did. It was the ideas in his head, more than the economic reality, that drove millions of people to their deaths. Similarly, today there would still be a state of Czechoslovakia if the majority of Slovaks in 1992 had shown more interest in economic questions. Instead they looked to the nation-state as a more important and urgent matter, despite the danger of impoverishment resulting from their separation from Prague. The problems of economic and social instability in the states of former East Germany now incorporated into the Federal Republic would have been far less if the Federal government of 1990 had placed less faith in the ability of the untrameled free market to bring about economic recovery.

With hindsight it is a wonder that Soviet power dissolved without immediate bloodshed. The popular revolution against those leaders who claimed to embody revolution took place without violence, in Moscow and Leningrad (St Petersburg), as in Dresden and Leipzig. Only in Bucharest did conflict ensue, with no clear victory for pluralist democracy.

Hardly had the world got over its surprise at this tense but peaceful revolution when violence spilled over elsewhere in the world, with the invasion of Kuwait by Iraq. For the first time since the early 1950s the United Nations intervened militarily to resist aggression. In 1950 this had been possible because the Soviet representative to the UN was absent for the vote; this time the collapsed Soviet Union, like Communist China, needed economic assistance from the West and was unwilling to distance itself from Western policies.

Victory for the United Nations was assured by its military might: virtually all the death and destruction wrought by the war of January–February 1991 was suffered by the Iraqis. Despite this the meaning of the conflict remained unclear. Saddam Hussein, the defeated ruler of Iraq, remained in power, and the men who pillaged Kuwait went unpunished. Though Kuwait's sovereignty was restored, democratic rule was still not introduced, so the struggle cannot be said to have been for the free citizens of a free nation. During the war, no-one in the world community came to the aid of the freedoms of the oppressed Kurdish minority of northern Iraq; as soon as the war had ended the attention of the allies moved away from the region. Then, in a reversal of policy, there was a move to protect the Kurds in Turkey, a nation supporting the alliance against Iraq. It is true that military intervention was justified, but a clear policy was lacking.

With the questions of principle so hard to define, the motivation of the powers controlling the war were ambiguous. Had Kuwait not been a crucial supplier of crude oil to the

West, the United States would probably never have taken up arms against Iraq. Had Britain and France not wanted to preserve their positions as permanent members of the UN Security Council, they too would probably have taken a less hard line. Even more important was the disquiet felt about the right, or duty, of the world to defend the victims of aggression.

The same unease has been felt in response to the carnage in the former Yugoslavia, and this time it was not possible clearly to invoke international law to overcome the aggressors: though new states had been formed and recognized, the violence and ensuing criminal acts had many of the hallmarks of a bloody civil war. What was the right course of action? What should we choose to do? Would it be right for us to intervene militarily? And who were "we"? – the United Nations, individual states acting alone, the United States, France, Britain – or the European Community?

The blue helmets of the United Nations peacekeeping forces, already known in conflicts in various parts of the world, could at least try to stop further bloodshed by their presence, but they had no orders to fight back against aggression. In 1992–93 they became increasingly involved in the struggle to bring humanitarian aid to the victims of war, a task that alleviated suffering yet appeared to legitimize the aggression. For, if the UN troops evacuated the women and children from a be-leaguered Bosnian town, by implication they were also hand-ing over the men to be massacred, and consequently they

seemed to become accomplices in the terrible and criminal policy of ethnic cleansing practiced by the Serbs.

Did the war in Croatia and Bosnia give the lie to the rhetoric of "one Europe"? The only simple answer to this question can be found in the eclectic arguments of many of those who op-posed moves towards greater unification of Europe, in par-ticular of those who were the staunchest opponents of the Maastricht treaty in France. On the one hand they complained of the European Community's weak foreign policy; on the other they argued that the Community should not be permit-ted to exercise authority over its member states. The Com-munity could only have intervened militarily if a general military force was deployed; yet no such force was even plann-ed for the foreseeable future.

An important step in this direction was taken at the Ger-man–French summit in La Rochelle, which proclaimed that one of the duties of the projected German–French Corps within a united Europe was the reestablishment of peace in Europe. This implied an obligation to intervene in existing conflicts. Yet this formula was barely mentioned in either country. Not in Germany, whose troops were already engaged in UN peace-keeping activities elsewhere in the world, but whose Nazi past

▲ A bullet-scarred crucifix with the Croatian flag, 1991.

◄ Bosnians in a Serb internment camp, 1992.

153

forbade the use of those troops in middle or eastern Europe, an issue that retained its significance for many and meant that Germany was forced to refrain from retaliation and take on a purely observational role.

France and Britain had accused Germany of hypocrisy, or at least inconsistency, in forcing its European partners to recognize Croatia as an independent state yet being unwilling to face the consequences of this decision by helping defend it against Serb aggression. But President Mitterrand of France himself was unwilling to let France intervene in former Yugoslavia. He was vigorously condemned for this, but perhaps unfairly. In truth all the European government heads faced a truly tragic quandary, since whatever course of action they followed would lead to terrible results. A decision not to intervene would mean that mass murder, oppression, starvation and forcible expulsion would be allowed to continue; the charge of complicity, which with hindsight was laid against Pope Pius XII and F.D. Roosevelt for their actions in the 1940s in the face of the Holocaust, would be invoked once more. Yet how many thousands, or hundreds of thousands, of French or British soldiers would be needed to protect every town and village; would the electorate accept the inevitable losses?

The bloody tragedies of the former Yugoslavia, and of parts of the former Soviet Union (not to mention other countries

such as Somalia) might have dispersed any despair over events in Western Europe. The joy that had been so evident in 1989 and 1990 seemd to vanish completely, but was the disappointment a hypocritical one, itself a factor in causing the new mood of self-pity? For 40 years millions of West Germans had assumed that they felt a deep sympathy for those in the East, with their lack of material and political freedoms. Now that the Wall was down, this sympathy could be transformed into genuine solidarity: but the task turned out to be much more difficult than merely condemning the division of the country.

There were significant achievements. Under Article 23 of the Constitution, the former German Democractic Republic became part of the Federal Republic of Germany, with a democratic foundation to its basic laws. In 1990 Article 23 was abolished since reunification was complete and the eastern border with Poland was recognized. In 1992, Article 23 was reestablished, to permit Germany to transfer rights to the European Union. For France, Britain and The Netherlands, the reunification of Germany meant that the move towards a deeper unification of the European Community itself was facilitated: there was no longer the schizophrenia of entering the Community while the East was even more divided from it.

Reunification does mean that the Community will have to assume greater responsibility for the entire social and economic development of the countries of the old Soviet empire. The Community itself has recognized this: in December 1992 a summit conference of the 12 member-states in Edinburgh declared that these countries, in the same way as Portugal and Ireland, should be development territories within the EC and as such should receive special aid. However such aid can only be a drop in the ocean of what is needed for reconstruction, as was seen during the first two years of the reunited Germany.

There are many reasons why the unification of Germany was still not complete, economically, socially or spiritually, four years after the fall of the Berlin Wall. There were mistakes and omissions. Confidence in the power of the market to heal faults was too great. In the West there was arrogance and an imposition of will; in the East, unrealistic expectations that living standards could be brought into line with the West. From 1990–91, the worldwide recession slowed the pace of reconstruction, and German fears for the future merged with general fears throughout Western Europe of a slowdown of growth.

Sadly such fears are as widespread as fundamental aspirations. One fear became more urgent than any other, namely the fear of Germany's new-found power. For many citizens of the Community, the joy at the collapse of the undemocratic GDR was overshadowed by the potential power of the united Germany. This fear was dispelled, only to be replaced by its opposite: a weak Germany in a Europe increasingly dependent on German economic might. France was Germany's largest customer and supplier; Hungary and Poland equally needed a thriving German economy. The answer to the question whether Germany should still be feared is still the same as that given by Frenchmen striving to develop a working partnership with Germany since the war, "Germany should never be feared. But we must care for its future, and have solidarity with those Germans who share your worries, and equally worry about the future of France."

The rise in both countries of the extreme rightwing, hostile to foreigners, emphasizes the truth of this. In the French parliamentary elections of March 1993 over 12 percent of the vote went to the National Front of Jean-Marie Le Pen. On the question of immigration the policies of France and Germany differed significantly. People who speak no German but whose grandparents, though living on the Volga, speak German, automatically become German citizens if they move to Germany, yet a child of Turkish parents born in Frankfurt, who speaks only German and has never visited Turkey, is a Turk. In France, by contrast, there are very few young people of foreign nationality, even though there are thousands of young French Muslims of African descent.

In most of the wealthy countries of Europe the question of immigration became a central political and social issue, as the flow of people from the Third World could be blocked, but not

◀ The world community celebrated at Expo 92 in Seville.

155

Tokyo and New York there is encouragement for the notion of a unified partner in Europe.

Liberal democracy is certainly under threat in many areas, but few would have believed, a few years ago, that there would already be freedom of choice and expression in Moscow, Prague and Budapest. South Africa still endures misery and tyranny, but the pace of change has begun to quicken, and things would be far, far worse if it had not.

In culture, too, it is possible to be too pessimistic. It is true that television rarely offers more than cheap entertainment. But the costs of other forms of culture have risen. And though the frenzied enthusiasm of young people in Germany, France and the United States for rock stars such as Bruce Springsteen may be deplored by cultural conservatives, the continued popularity of choral singing, and the new enthusiasm for Mozart and Schubert at all levels of society and not just among the cultural elite, are pointers away from cultural despair.

There are two crucial positive features. One involves political ideology. The most vehement of the hardliners have been ousted. This does not mean there are no longer any clearly-held ideas: on the contrary, people generally believe in the necessity of giving room to the free market; people believe that the law and the state should strive for social justice, for protection of the weak and for the redistribution of private wealth. Marxism may be dead, but so is the doctrinaire monetarism that prevailed in the 1980s.

The underlying beliefs have simply been standardized. As Marxism has declined in the West, so we have lost those people who claimed that basic rights and freedoms were an illusion and that the power structure of society had to be changed before people could recognize and claim true freedom. On the other side, the churches, too, have changed, especially the Catholic Church. When Pope John Paul II says that freedom, equality and fraternity – the slogan of the French revolutionaries of 1789 – are also relevant as Christian values, he is expressing a congruity of belief between Christians and atheist humanists, of a type that would have been anathema to the popes of the 19th century.

There is still an enormous misunderstanding about concepts of freedom, equality (generally today called rights), and fraternity (today known as solidarity). Fraternity means putting aside one's own freedom for the freedom of others. It was with this concept that the Chinese students sacrificed their lives in Tiananmen Square, as well as many others, young and old, all over the world. In the West freedom cannot be taken for granted, or approached in a self-indulgent manner.

We stand at the end of a century that, in retrospect, looks particularly tragic. This judgment is justified, considering the two World Wars, the horrors of Auschwitz, and the misery so prevalent in the world today. But the positive achievements are strong and widespread. One of these, ironically, is that through the media we are more aware of the negative than were our ancestors a century ago. Today, awful misery and exploitation of children through the Third World is prevalent. But when similar misery and exploitation occurred in coalmining regions of France, Germany or Britain a hundred years ago, how many of the rich were aware of it, even those working in the same industry?

Is perception progress? Certainly so: it is easy to remember only what is most deplorable about what we see. But perception of evil must be accompanied by a firm will to change things for the better, in the name of the basic values discussed above. It is not merely to be provocative that we insist that people at the end of the century are more driven by ethical considerations than those at its beginning.

stemmed. The resurgence of a militant form of Islam has directly influenced the debates about the nature of a "multicultural society". While nationalism and a hate-ridden opposition to outsiders have influenced the ability of neighboring cultures to live together, the concept of an integrated society has grown stronger; one in which differences between people can enrich that society, though only if the basic values and groundrules of a free democratic system are respected.

Other fears will decline when unemployment falls and the fear for one's job (actual or prospective) ceases to be an overwhelming one. Nevertheless, three fears remain, which will probably endure to the turn of the century. The first is the fear of a nuclear catastrophe. A reactor accident is particularly possible in eastern Europe and to a lesser extent in France, while the breakup of the Soviet Union has led to a dangerous spread of nuclear weaponry. The fear of environmental disaster – from global warming, or the destruction of the rain forests, perhaps – is similarly justifiable if we forget the basic lesson of ecology that the human race is merely one species among many on Mother Earth. The final fear is of ever-faster spread of deadly disease. The culmination of all these fears is that social and private lives intertwine as never before. The case of AIDS touches even our most private aspect of life, our sexuality.

Is it right to approach the new millennium with an all-pervading pessimism and anxieties about impending tragedy? Only if the worst fears are realized in every field. Economically, it is true that the gap between rich and poor countries has grown, rather than narrowed, in recent years. However the distinctions between the Third World and the First are no longer clearcut: Singapore, South Korea and Taiwan have shown that it is possible to escape the inevitability of Third World poverty. Europe, as a whole, is far more prosperous, and has better political prospects than in the 1970s. Although the United Nations has not completed its task of readjustment to the post-Cold War era, enormous strides have been taken in this direction with the simple fact that UN involvement is expected in disputes, rather than feared and opposed. The same can be said for the European Community: whereas many of its members fear that its institutions will become too centralized, there is a general wish for the Community itself to become even stronger, until people in eastern Europe will see joining it as the only way out of the horrors of rabid nationalism. In

▲ The UN helping hand reaching to Bosnian refugees.

▶ Hope and hunger in Somalia, 1992.

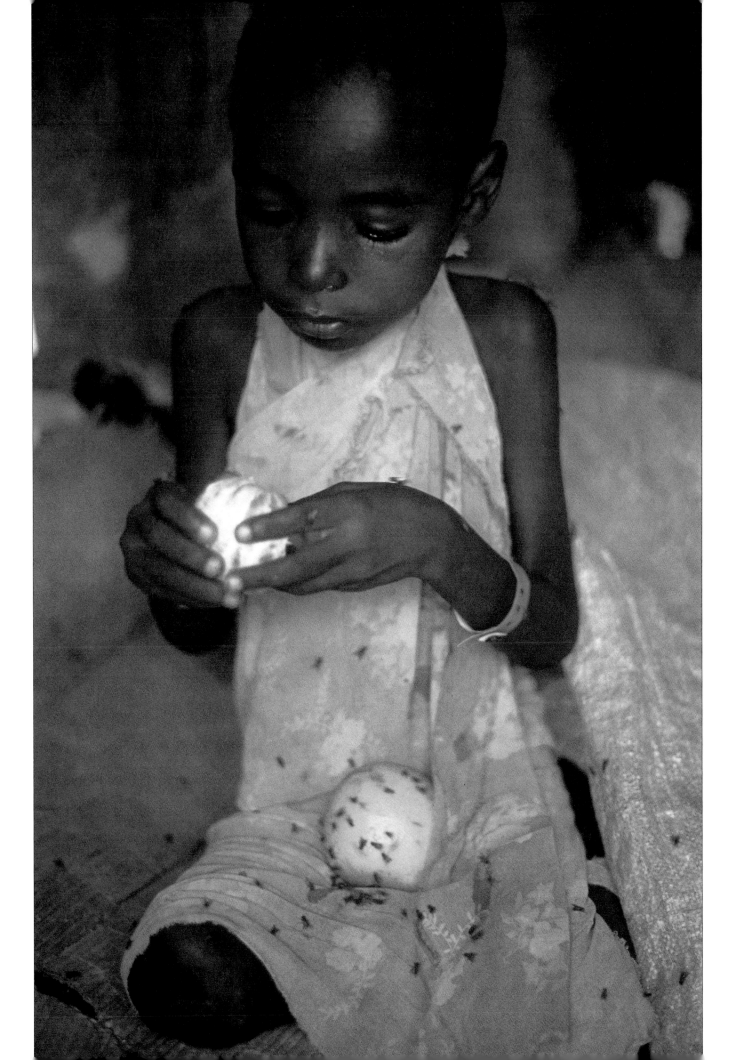

BIOGRAPHIES

Allen, Woody 1935–
US film actor, director, screenwriter, playwright
and jazz clarinetist. His cynical, self-deprecating
style colored 1970s American humor. *What's New
Pussycat?* (1965) was his first screen credit
(writer/actor), followed by other parodies,
including *Love and Death* (1975). Greater success
came with *Annie Hall* (1977) and *Manhattan* (1979),
and in the eighties his subject matter broadened,
in films such as *Midsummer Night's Sex Comedy*
(1982), *Stardust Memories* (1980) and *Hannah and
Her Sisters* (1986). In 1992 he endured a highly
publicized divorce from Mia Farrow.

Amin (Dada), Idi 1925–
Ugandan dictator. An army officer Amin led a
coup against Milton Obote in 1971, installed
himself as president and military leader, and
dissolved parliament. In 1972, he expelled all
Asians from Uganda. He reversed the pro-Israeli
policy in favor of the Palestinians and Libya, and
was accused of involvement in the hijacking of an
airliner carrying Israelis in 1976. Border disputes
strained relations with Tanzania and Kenya. It is
alleged that he persecuted tribes other than his
own, and that 100,000–300,000 people were
tortured and killed during his presidency. In 1978
he attacked Tanzania, and Tanzanian troops and
exiles invaded Uganda. Amin escaped abroad.

Arafat, Yasir 1929–
Chairman of the Palestine Liberation
Organization. In 1956, Arafat cofounded the
resistance group al-Fatah ("the victory"), later
becoming its leader. In 1969 al-Fatah gained
control of the recently established Palestine
Liberation Organization, with Arafat as its
chairman. In 1973, as head of the PLO's political
department, he decreased the emphasis on military
action. He gained widespread recognition for the
PLO, and in 1974 addressed the United Nations
General Assembly. He temporarily lost overall
control of the PLO in 1982 when Israel invaded
Lebanon. In the late 1980s he condemned
terrorism, and, after the declaration of a Palestinian
state, seemed to recognize the state of Israel.

Assad, Hafiz al- 1928–
Syrian president. In 1946 Assad joined the
socialist, Arab nationalist Ba'ath party. In 1955 he
graduated as a pilot and went to the Soviet Union
to train in night flying. After the 1963 Ba'ath coup
he was made a general and air force commander.
Despite Syria's decisive defeat in the 1967
Arab–Israeli war while he was defense minister, in
1970 Assad became president after a bloodless
coup. His position was ratified by election in 1971,
and re-election in 1978. While hostile to the Iraqi
Ba'ath regime, he forged links with other Arab
states and cultivated the Soviet Union without
breaking with the USA. In conflict with Israel over

Lebanon, claimed by Assad for Syria, he
denounced the 1980 Egypt–Israel peace treaty and
signed a 20-year friendship treaty with the Soviet
Union. In 1982 he closed Syria's border with Iraq
and cut off an Iraqi pipeline through Syria, taking
Iran's side in the Iran–Iraq war. His regime was
draconian; in 1982 he killed some 100,000 rebels. In
the crisis precipitated by Iraq's invasion of Kuwait
in 1990, Assad joined the UN allies.

Baker, James 1930–
US politician. Baker, a Princeton graduate, joined
the Marines as a lieutenant (1952–54). In 1957 he
graduated in law, and practiced law until his wife's
death in 1970, when he first became politicized, as
a Republican; he supported George Bush in his
run for the senate. In 1975 he joined the
department of commerce as an under secretary,
and supported Gerald Ford's presidential
campaign before returning to legal work. In 1978
he stood unsuccessfully for the office of Texas state
attorney general; his result was nonetheless
outstanding for a Republican in Texas. In late 1985
he presented at an IMF conference a plan for debt
assistance for the "developing world". Baker,
Meese and Deaver, were known as the "Big
Three", the powers behind the throne of the
Reagan administration. He was particularly valued
for his brilliant political campaign strategy.

Baryshnikov, Mikhail 1948–
Soviet US ballet dancer. After studying with
Alexander Pushkin, in 1966 Baryshnikov joined the
Kirov ballet company as a soloist, rising quickly to
be *premier danseur noble*; he won several awards.
He defected in 1974 to the USA where he was the
star of the American Ballet Theater until 1978,
when he joined Balanchine's New York City Ballet;
but Balanchine's style did not suit him, focusing as
it did on the ballerinas and making technical
demands beyond the scope of the Soviet
repertoire. In 1980 he returned to ABT, soon
becoming its artistic director. A virtuoso superstar
in the tradition of Nureyev and Nijinsky,
Baryshnikov was especially known for his sultry
presence and his soaring apparently effortless
leaps. He appeared in movies and made countless
TV appearances.

Baselitz (Kern), George 1938–
German painter and wood-sculptor. Expelled from
his art course at the East Berlin Academy, for
"socio-political immaturity", Baselitz completed
his studies at the West Berlin Academy after the
family moved to the West. He exhibited in 1961
and 1962, and co-authored, with E.Schönebeck, the
Pandemonium Manifesto and poster. In 1963,
police removed sexually explicit paintings from his
first solo exhibition; in 1965, after a lawsuit, they
were returned to Baselitz, who continued to
exhibit. He rooted his work formally in the

classical tradition, while challenging it in content
and detail, as in *The Rebel* (1965). From 1967 he
exhibited abroad. In 1969, with *The Forest on its
Head*, he began to paint upside down, challenging
the facility of both painter and perceiver, and
producing a surprising realism. From 1978 he was
a professor at Karlsrühe Academy. In 1980 he
began to produce painted wooden carvings, and
created a stir when, for the German Pavilion at the
1980 Venice Biennale, he produced a single carved
figure. In 1983 he took a professorship at the West
Berlin Art College. He exhibited all over the USA
and Western Europe.

Basquiat, Jean-Michel 1960–88
US graffiti artist. Half Haitian, half Puerto Rican,
he began to paint graffiti as a recalcitrant
schoolboy; in this genre, his work was
distinguished by an above-average educational
level, some interest in classical art, and excellent
graphic ability. Public recognition came soon, with
exhibitions in New York in 1981, 1982, and 1983,
and in West Germany in 1983. He became very
wealthy, selling his paintings, of cars or guns or
Richard Nixon, for high prices soon after their
production. Warhol was a patron and a
collaborator. Basquiat became drug-addicted and
died of an overdose.

Bausch, Pina 1940–
German choreographer. An excellent dancer in
childhood, Bausch trained in classical and modern
dance at Essen, under the Expressionist Kurt Jooss
and from 1959 to 1961 under Anthony Tudor at the
Juilliard School, New York. She then joined the
Metropolitan Opera Ballet Company, and in 1962
returned to Germany, as a soloist in Jooss's
company. She began choreographing in 1968: the
strong formalism and emotional intensity of her
work brought recognition. She became the
company's artistic director, and *In the Wind of Time*
(1969) won a prize in Cologne. After a brilliant
staging of the dances in *Tannhäuser* (1972), she was
made director of the Wuppertal Opera Ballet. She
explored sexuality, in the physically violent
Bluebeard (1977) and *Kontakthof* (1978), worked out
with the dancers. In 1980, her companion and
collaborator, designer Rolf Borsik, died – after this
the range of her dances altered, from the dynamics
of close human relationships, to the global fear of
disaster, as in *Dance Evening: Cremations* (1984).
She does not claim that her work is dance but
"expressing feelings".

Bednorz, Johannes Georg 1950–
Swiss physicist, coinventor of an important new
category of superconductors. He graduated in
physics from the University of Münster in 1976
and then joined the IBM Research Laboratory at
Rüschlikon, working under K.A. Müller. The main
subject of their research was superconductivity. In

Zulfikar and Benazir Bhutto

Harrison Birtwhistle

Bjorn Borg

the years after World War II superconductors found many practical applications, but all had the disadvantage of working only at very low temperatures. In 1986 Bednorz and Müller announced the discovery of a new kind of "high-temperature" superconductor effective at temperatures attainable with the aid of liquid nitrogen. Bednorz and Müller shared a Nobel prize in 1987.

Begin, Menachem W. 1913–92

Israeli prime minister. Born in Poland, in 1938 Begin headed the Zionist Betar youth movement, demanding a homeland on both banks of the Jordan. After the German invasion of 1939 Begin fled to Lithuania, and in 1940 the Russians deported him to Siberia. Upon his release in 1941 he joined the Free Polish Army, and in 1942 was sent to Palestine. He left the army in 1943 and became leader of the Irgun until 1948, when they disbanded, and he founded the Herut party, seeking Israeli sovereignty on both sides of the Jordan, no Palestinian state, and economic laissez-faire. In 1977, he came to power as head of the Likud coalition. He took a hard line on the return of territories occupied in 1967, and began the Israeli colonization of the West Bank. He did, however, withdraw from the Sinai peninsula as part of the peace treaty signed in 1979, with President Sadat of Egypt, for which they were jointly awarded the Nobel Peace Prize in 1978. In 1982, Israeli troops invaded the Lebanon and bombed Beirut in an attempt to destroy PLO bases. The PLO withdrew, and while under Israeli occupation, hundreds of Palestinian civilians in Beirut were massacred by Lebanese Christians. Begin resigned in 1983.

Bhutto, Benazir 1953–

Pakistani prime minister. Oxford and Harvard-educated daughter of Z. Ali Bhutto, Benazir spent seven years under house arrest, and two further years as PPP (People's party) leader in exile. In 1986 she returned after General Zia's downfall, and became prime minister in 1987. She returned Pakistan to the Commonwealth, but soon fell foul of her coalition partners, the pro-Zia president, and the voters, as a result of alleged corruption, her failure to deal satisfactorily with explosive situations in Sind and the Punjab, and her perceived policy of conciliation in foreign affairs, notably with India; her indulgence toward her husband's criminal indiscretions did not help. She was defeated in the 1990 elections, and subsequently charged with corruption.

Bhutto, Zulfikar Ali 1928–79

President and prime minister of Pakistan. As foreign minister (1963–65) Bhuto forged a closer link with China at the expense of the West. In 1966 he resigned in protest over the peace reached with

India after the Kashmir war, and in 1967 founded the Pakistani People's party. He spent two years in prison for accusing Ayub Khan of being a dictator. In elections held in 1970, after Ayub Khan had been deposed by Yahya Khan, the People's party won in West Pakistan, but lost in the East to the separatist Awami League, with whom Bhutto refused to form a coalition. In 1971 Bhutto succeeded Yahya Khan as president, following a civil war in which East Pakistan, assisted by India, became the independent state of Bangladesh. Bhutto nationalized major industries and taxed landed families. In 1973 he became prime minister under a new constitution transferring power to this post. He maintained martial law and strengthened Pakistan as an Islamic state. In the 1977 election his party won a large majority, but was accused of electoral fraud. That same year General Zia al Haq, the head of the army, seized power and arrested Bhutto for allegedly conspiring to murder a political opponent in 1974. He was found guilty, and executed in 1979, despite appeals for clemency from many heads of state.

Biko, (Bantu) Steven 1946–77

South African political leader and thinker. Biko studied medicine at Natal university (1966–72), and absorbed the writing of the Black Power movement, as well as Frantz Fanon and the enlightened socialist Julius Nyerere. He led the black consciousness movement in South Africa, perceiving that people whose whole life experience of themselves was as inferior could not take positions of power and equality; the inner balance had to be redressed. He was a rare example ; he radiated dignity, courage, commitment, humor and had the ability always to respond to the humanity of any other person, whatever the situation. He founded a national black students' organization and cofounded the Black People's Convention. He worked in community development and set up a trust fund to help political prisoners. Although he was frequently subject to banning orders, much of his writing and speech was published. He died in police custody – accidentally, according to a government statement later retracted in the face of photographic evidence and international pressure.

Birtwistle, Harrison 1934–

British composer. Birtwistle, a clarinetist, was a scholarship student at the Royal Manchester College of Music with Peter Maxwell Davies. He formed the New Music Manchester Group to play modern music, especially that of the neglected Second Viennese School. He played in an army band during his national service, and then studied clarinet under Reginald Kell at London's Royal Academy of Music. He gradually turned from professional clarinet-playing to full-time composition, and some teaching, first at a Dorset

school; then in 1966 he taught at Princeton. In 1967 he and Maxwell Davies founded the Pierrot Players, who became the Fires of London in 1970, when Birtwistle worked with the Matrix theater company. In 1973 he returned to the USA to teach at Swarthmore College, Pennsylvania, and then in 1975 was made musical director of London's new National Theatre. His work is ritualistic in form and manner, often dealing with death/rebirth myths. *Tragoedia* and *Ring a Dumb Carillon* (both 1965) established him as the most original of contemporary British composers. *The Triumph of Time* (1972) is a massive orchestral piece; and the opera *The Mask of Orpheus* (1986), a compelling production, takes "theater of cruelty" further than Artaud did, using repetition, and archetypal images to stir the depths of the psyche.

Borg, Bjorn 1956–

Swedish tennis player. The first man to win the Wimbledon singles title five times in succession (1976–80) since the 1900s, he began playing very young and turned professional in 1972. He won the Italian Open at 17, the French at 18, and by 1975 had broken the record for consecutive cup singles wins. His most powerful shots were his serve and the two-handed backhand. He won the French Open six times (1974–75 and 1978–81) and the World Championship three times (1978–80), retiring in 1983, to stage an unsuccessful comeback in early 1991.

Botha, Pieter W. 1916–

South African prime minister. He entered parliament in 1948 as a member of the National Party, serving in several ministerial posts before becoming prime minister in 1978. Nationalist activities in neighboring countries led to increasing black unrest in South Africa, and renewed demands for the abolition of apartheid. Botha strengthened the armed forces, which raided these countries regularly, and funded antigovernment groups within them. At home, he abolished some minor apartheid laws, granted nominal independence to black homelands, and reformed the constitution, allowing limited political rights to Asians and coloreds, though not to blacks. As a result of this, the right wing of the party broke away in 1982 to form the Conservative party. After a cabinet revolt Botha was forced to resign in 1989.

Botham, Ian 1955–

British cricketer. He made his debut for Somerset Country Cricket Club in 1974 and first played for England three years later. An all-rounder of exceptional power and ability, he almost single-handedly saved England from losing the Ashes in 1981. His ebullient character has often led him into trouble off the pitch. He became one of the leading wicket-takers in Test cricket.

▲ Jimmy Carter (center)

▲ Subrahmanyan Chandrasekhar

Boyer, Herbert Wayne 1936–

US biochemist. After graduating in the University of Pittsburgh he held various research posts until appointed professor of biochemistry in the University of California, Berkeley. By 1970 it was well established that the synthesis of protein is controlled by the helical, ladder-like DNA molecule. In theory, therefore, new powers of synthesis could be conferred on a cell if a DNA fraction derived from some other species could be, as it were, spliced into the normal DNA. In 1973 Boyer turned theory into practice by grafting into the DNA of *E. coli* some extrachromosomal DNA present in the form of plasmids.

Bush, George 1924–

41st US president. Bush graduated from Yale in 1948, after wartime naval service. He became wealthy through oil, and entered the house of Representatives (1967–71). In 1970 he became ambassador to the UN, and in 1974, head of the US liaison office in China. In 1976 he became director of the CIA, which was at an all-time low. He was a contender for the Republican presidential nomination against Ronald Reagan in 1980; when elected Reagan made Bush his vice-president. When Reagan stood down in 1988 Bush was elected president. His slightly vague public persona did not inspire confidence; neither did Dan Quayle, his ineffectual vice-president. But Bush acted decisively – and controversially – in sending troops into Panama in 1989 to capture the despotic President Noriega and bring him to trial in the USA on drugs charges, after a rigged and coercive election campaign and his annulment of the result. And in 1990 Bush took a leading role in the crisis sparked by Iraqi president Saddam Hussein's invasion of Kuwait; in the ensuing war, of 1991, the bulk of the UN-backed Allied forces were American, and again Bush was in the global spotlight. However, his domestic policies were insufficient to ensure his reelection in 1992.

Carter, James Earl ("Jimmy") 1924–

39th US president. Democratic governor of Georgia from 1971 to 1975, in 1976 Carter was elected president. He attempted wide-ranging internal reforms, which were largely blocked by Congress. In 1977, he agreed to cede control of the Panama Canal by the year 2000. In 1978, his mediation ended the official state of war existing between Egypt and Israel since 1938. In 1979, he broke off relations with Taiwan and opened full diplomatic relations with China, also signing the SALT II treaty with the Soviet Union, which the Senate refused to ratify. Also in this year, militant Iranian students occupied the US embassy in Tehran, holding 66 hostages. The Iranian government refused to negotiate for their release, and Carter suspended relations with Iran. In 1980, a military

operation to free the hostages failed. Meanwhile, Carter applied economic sanctions against the Soviet Union in response to its invasion of Afghanistan, whose communist regime was faltering, and called for a boycott of the 1980 Moscow Olympics. At home, inflation rose, and unemployment remained high, and in 1980 Carter lost the presidency to Ronald Reagan.

Ceauşescu, Nicolae 1918–89

Romanian political leader. Ceauşescu joined the Communist party in 1933, and sided with its nationalist wing. Imprisoned in 1936 and 1940 for antifascist activities, he was deputy minister of agriculture (1948–50) and deputy minister for the army (1950–54). He then joined the secretariat of the central committee, and in 1955, the Politburo. In 1957 he became deputy leader, and in 1965 succeeded Gheorghiu-Dej as general secretary. In 1967 he became head of state, and president in 1974. Domestically, he accelerated industrialization, maintained the orthodox Communist regime, and fostered a personality cult around himself. At the same time, he worked for economic independence from the Soviet Union. Abroad, he remained within the Warsaw Pact, but asserted Romanian sovereignty. He remained neutral in the Sino-Soviet conflict. He developed good relations with First and Third World countries but in the late 1980s his foreign policy was compromised, and his rule overshadowed by increasingly harsh and cruel legislation, the nepotism and high Stalinist character of his personal regime, at last brought to the eyes of the world, and the destruction of the once stable economy by irrational policies including exporting most of the food and fuel needed domestically and destroying rural society by demolishing villages. More and more influenced by his equally self-obsessed wife, he also passed legislation by which every woman was compelled to bear six children. In 1989 the people rebelled, the military joined them, and Ceauşescu and his wife were tried and executed.

Chandrasekhar, Subrahmanyan 1910–

Indian-US astrophysicist. He studied physics at the Presidency College, Madras, and then did research at Cambridge, UK (1931–37). In 1937 he was appointed professor of physics in the University of Chicago. His particular interest was in white dwarfs – stars in the last stage of development, which have collapsed inward under their own weight to form an exceedingly dense shell – roughly equal to the size of the Earth – sustained by the outward pressure of plasma within it. Only certain stars can undergo this change, those which conform to the so-called Chandrasekhar Limit, in having a mass no greater than 1.4 times that of the Sun. Chandrasekhar received a Nobel prize in 1983.

Coe, Sebastian 1956–

British distance runner. Coe originally studied economics, but was successful early as a runner when he won a bronze medal in the 1975 European 1500m junior championship. He had injury problems but still ran strongly in 1978; his career was crowned in 1979 by breaking three world records (the 800m, mile, and 1500m) in two months. In 1992 Coe was elected a Conservative member of parliament.

Collins, Joan 1933–

British actress. After studying at London's Royal Academy of Dramatic Art, and working as a model, she made her film debut in 1952, under contract to Rank Organization. A long and undistinguished film career followed, in what she described as "wallpaper parts", relieved by the occasional good role. She moved into the international sex symbol arena with *The Stud* (1978); and in 1982 her career took off, with the part of the bitchy Alexis in the massively popular glitzy American soap opera *Dynasty*. She was renowned for her unfading beauty, still exquisite in her fifties. She wrote a book about the slow recovery of her daughter, brain-damaged in a car accident, and campaigned for improvements in care for brain-damaged children.

Cruyff, Johan 1947–

Dutch soccer star. Cruyff joined his local football club in 1957; in 1965 came his first professional contract, with Junior Ajax, for $2.25m, a record transfer fee. Cruyff helped Ajax to six league titles, four national cups, and three European championships, and was Dutch Player of the Year from 1967 through 1969. In 1973 he transferred to Barcelona; under his captaincy the team won the national league championship in 1974 and were runners-up in 1976–77. In 1978 he went to the USA to play, but soon retired, finding the intrusive attention he received from the public intolerable. In 1979 he was named the North American Soccer League's Most Valuable Player. In 1981 he had surgery for a groin injury. Cruyff could play equally brilliantly in any position, and other players have remarked that they were tempted to stop playing and watch him. He held the whole game in his head, and would give instructions to other players. He won the European Player of the Year award five times.

De Klerk, F.W. 1936–

South African political leader. After graduating in law with distinction, de Klerk worked as a lawyer before entering parliament in 1972; Vorster made him a minister in 1976 and he continued in various ministerial posts until 1982 when as Botha's minister of internal affairs he was promoting a policy of racial power-sharing as the only route to peace and stability; he was made leader of the

▲ Joan Collins

▲ Deng Xiaoping

▲ Milton Friedman

ruling National Party, and, in 1989, became president. In 1990 he unbanned the African National Congress and released its deputy president Nelson Mandela from prison, and took steps to dismantle apartheid, removing the last major apartheid laws in 1991. However, some minor laws remained, which had not been the object of international outcry, and these were used by diehard rightwing councils, especially in rural areas, to maintain segregation.

Delors, Jacques 1925–
French politician and European community leader. Delors graduated in economics and took a managerial post in the Banque de France, (1948–62). He then took charge of the social department of the central economic planning committee until 1969, when he reverted to university lecturing. Elected in 1973 to the Banque de France general council, in 1974 he joined the Socialist party and, as adviser to Chaban-Delmas in the effort to establish a "new society", founded a think-tank to discover ways of redressing social inequities. In 1976 he was the Socialist party's national delegate for international economic relations. In 1979 he entered the European parliament and became chairman of its economic and monetary committee. Domestically, as finance minister (1981–84), he demanded a slowing-down of reform and oversaw a series of devaluations, and in 1982 a price and wage freeze. Initially he was criticized for excessive austerity; but by 1983–84 President Mitterrand began to share his point of view. As head of the EC from 1988 he pursued economic unity, which he saw as leading naturally to the integrated Europe he dreamed of. A Chevalier de la Légion d'Honneur, he has written three books about social change.

Deng Xiaoping 1904–
Chinese Communist leader. He began his career in government as vice-premier (1952). His most important role was in the Chinese Communist party (CCP) of which he became secretary general (1954) and a Politburo member (1955). Attacked during the Cultural Revolution in the 1960s, Deng was dismissed. He was reinstated in 1973 and made deputy premier. In 1975 he was appointed vice-Chairman of the CCP Central Committee, a member of its Politburo, and chief of staff. His push to modernize China alienated Mao and he was again removed from power in 1976, but had returned by July 1977. He opened up Sino-US relations, began attacks on his former opponents and aimed to destroy the cult of Mao and modernize China. He introduced self-management for peasant farmers and financial rewards for industrial efficiency, installed highly trained managers and technicians to run industry and the economy, and initially increased personal freedom. He followed an "open door" policy to foreign

technology and capital and bureaucratic reforms were carried out to facilitate modernization. Named chief deputy premier in 1980, Deng retired soon after but retained his political power. In 1989, his credibility as a reformer was severely damaged after prodemocracy demonstrations in China were crushed with savage force, leaving thousands dead, and alleged ringleaders rounded up and shot following summary show trials.

Domingo, Placido 1941–
Spanish tenor. Son of zarzuela players (an ethnic Spanish operetta form), and brought up in Mexico, he studied piano at the National Conservatory. After various jobs, including trying bullfighting, in 1961 he made his operatic debut. He then joined an opera company in Dallas, Texas. From 1962 to 1965 he was with the Hebrew National Opera in Tel Aviv. In 1965 came his opera debut in New York; in 1968 he sang there at the Metropolitan Opera House, and in 1969 at La Scala, Milan. Thousands of concerts and many recordings have followed. A man of striking looks, strong presence and great dramatic ability, he was rated, as was also Luciano Pavarotti, the world's greatest tenor of his time.

Eco, Umberto 1932–
Italian writer and semiotician. As a philosophy student at Turin he was drawn to the medieval philosophers. After gaining his doctorate in 1954 he worked for five years with the state TV network. He taught at Milan and Turin universities and from 1956 to 1964 lectured worldwide. He was nonfiction editor at a major publishing company (1959–66). As a writer he felt an affinity with James Joyce, and was a member of the avant-garde literary group "Gruppo 63". From 1971 he was professor at Bologna. Concerned with esthetics and semiotics, he has written extensively on these subjects, notably *The Absent Structure* (1968) and *Forms of Content* (1971). His medieval detective novel *The Name of the Rose* (1980) brought him immediately to a worldwide audience; a series of other successful novels followed, like *Foucault's Pendulum* (1990). They dealt with problems of language, paradox and time as did his nonfictional works; but they sold better.

Evert, Chris 1954–
US tennis player. By 1988 she had earned a record $60 million in prize money and sponsorship deals. A popular and respected player, her game was characterized by powerful volley shots. She came to prominence in 1970, when she beat Margaret Court, reaching the semi-finals of the US championships in 1971, then the youngest to do so. She won the US Open (1975–8, 1980 and 1982), the Wimbledon singles (1974,1976, and 1981) and the French Open (1974–5, 1979–80, 1983 and 1985). She retired in 1989.

Ford, Harrison 1942–
US movie actor. Bright, but not academic, Ford started acting at college and was soon signed up by Columbia. Cast in a succession of bit parts, he became disillusioned with life in the film world and started working as a carpenter. In 1973 he had a part in the very popular *American Graffiti*, but did not make his name until *Star Wars* (1977), the blockbusting science-fiction space epic, in which he played a leading heroic role. He also appeared in the equally successful follow-ups *The Empire Strikes Back* (1980) and *Return of the Jedi* (1983). Other good, if small, parts followed; and then *Raiders of the Lost Ark* (1981) made him a household name. A succession of sequels, and other starring roles, followed thick and fast. They included the serious and moving *The Witness* (1985); *Working Girl* (1988); and he was still playing his *Raiders* character, Indiana Jones, in 1990.

Foucault, Michel 1926–84
French structural philosopher. From 1960 to 1968 he taught at various universities in France and abroad. *Madness and Civilization* (1961) was the result of his examination of mental illness and its treatment. He also studied the penal system, and identified as crucial the "principle of exclusion" by which rules are generated often arbitrarily which lead to definitions like "sane/insane". Foucault was deeply concerned about social issues, and called his focus "the history of the present". From 1970 he was a professor of the history of systems of thought. Through his massive *History of Sexuality in the Post-Freudian World* (1976–84) he became known as a leading commentator on and analyst of sexual attitudes and behavior after Freud. Foucault dissolved the, actually arbitrary, boundaries between philosophy, science, history and sociology.

Friedman, Milton 1912–
US economist. Friedman worked at Chicago University and for the US Treasury before becoming professor of economics at Chicago (1948–79). In 1957, he challenged the accepted Keynesian economic approach with his paper, *A Theory of the Consumption Function*, working with lifetime rather than current income. This challenge continued with the publication of *Studies in the Quantity Theory of Money* (1956), advocating the control of the money supply to control the economy. This work radically altered the perspective of economics and marked the start of the now familiar dichotomy between Keynesian and monetarist approaches. Friedman's other major impact on economics came in 1968 when he declared his theories on "the natural rate of employment", that is, the lowest level of unemployment which the economy can stand without incurring progressive inflation. In 1976, he received the Nobel Prize for Economics.

Kenichi Fukui

Indira Gandhi

Germaine Greer

Fukui, Kenichi 1918–

Japanese chemist. He graduated as an engineer at Kyoto University in 1948: he was appointed professor of physical chemistry there in 1951. From the 1950s Fukui devoted himself to studying the mechanics of the way in which molecules interact, developing (1954) the hypothesis that the site of reaction is the highest electron orbital of one and the lowest electron orbital of the other. This results in a new combined orbital which he called a frontier orbital. Similar ideas were developed by the American chemist Roald Huffmann, with whom Fukui shared a Nobel prize in 1981.

Gandhi, Indira P. 1917–84

Indian prime minister. The daughter of Nehru, Mrs Gandhi became president of the Congress party in 1959. In 1966, she became prime minister, but the party split in 1969 over her nationalization of major banks and she lost her overall majority, regaining it in 1971. In the same year, West Pakistan lost the war against India and East Pakistan, which subsequently became the independent state of Bangladesh. Drought and international inflation led to a decline in law and order, and in 1975, the High Court ruled that Mrs Gandhi had breached election laws by misappropriating funds. She declared a state of emergency, and centralized power in herself, curtailed civil liberties and arrested political opponents. Defeated in the 1977 elections, in 1978 she founded the new Congress-I party, was elected to parliament, and later expelled. In 1980, Congress-I won a majority, and she became prime minister once again. Abroad, she worked on India's role among the developing nations, and remained on good terms with the Soviet Union, although she opposed the occupation of Afghanistan. At home, she introduced social and economic reform, but Indian minorities were demanding more independence, particularly Punjabi Sikhs, some of whom used violence. In 1984, the army attacked the Golden Temple of Amritsar, and nearly 500 Sikhs died. In the same year, Mrs Gandhi was killed by Sikh bodyguards.

Gaultier, Jean-Paul 1952–

French fashion designer. Gaultier made his first design sketches aged 14, and in 1969 submitted them to several designers; Pierre Cardin invited him to join his house for a year. Gaultier worked for other designers, including Patou, as well as at Cardin's manufacturing base in the Philippines, before setting up his own company in 1977. His first show, in 1976, was chaotic, but his witty, eccentric, young, showy clothes captured the public's imagination and he became one of the most popular ready-to-wear designers. He was inspired by London street clothes of the late 1970s; he mixed fabrics, cuts, and styles in a parody of fancy or fetishistic dress.

Glass, Philip 1937–

US composer. Glass played flute and piccolo as a child, and in 1956 he graduated in math and philosophy from the University of Chicago. In 1957 he went to the Juilliard School of music; in 1964 he went to Paris on a Fulbright scholarship. He studied under Nadia Boulanger, and in 1965 met Indian sitarist Ravi Shankar, whose music crucially influenced him; he studied eastern music and appreciated its principle of massing sound components. He returned in 1967, after a global hitchhiking trip, to New York to create "a new music". This was initially modular, using unison and focused on rhythmic intricacy. The Philip Glass Ensemble, set up in 1968, became a cult success. His major New York debut, *Music in Twelve Parts*, lasted six hours including a 90-minute break, and used chromatic intervals and dreamlike harmonies. His opera *Einstein on the Beach*, premièred in France in 1976, toured the world and sold out in New York. Equally successful were *Satyagraha* (1980) and *Akhnaton* (1984) with a partly ancient Egyptian libretto. The 1986 album *Songs from Liquid Days* was very popular.

Gorbachev, Mikhail Sergeyevich 1931–

Soviet leader. A member of the Communist party central committee from 1971, Gorbachev was made a full member of the Politburo in 1980, and became increasingly powerful, taking over as Party leader in 1985. He immediately undertook a campaign against corruption and economic mismanagement in the party bureaucracy. In 1986 he launched the drive for *glasnost* (openness). From 1987 the state encouraged private enterprise. Companies were now also allowed to go bankrupt. In the same year Gorbachev announced proposals for economic *perestroika* (reconstruction), which aimed to decrease the authority of central government and promote democracy. In 1989 he allowed independent candidates to stand for election. The industrial sector was modernized and encouraged to become self-financing. Abroad he withdrew the Red Army from Afghanistan, initiated the ending of the Cold War and signed the INF treaty with the United States, agreeing to dismantle some of the nuclear weapons stationed in Europe. He became president of the Soviet Union in 1988. The lack of success of his agricultural policies, the continuing weakness of the Soviet economy compared to those of other major powers, and the desperate shortage of consumer goods, made Gorbachev increasingly unpopular at home. In 1989 and 1990 he did not attempt to prevent the dissolution of the "Eastern bloc", as, following East Germany, country after country abandoned the single-party domination of Communism, and left the Soviet aegis. His domestic unpopularity increased with the use of military force to suppress unrest in Lithuania. As the Soviet Union shook with such attempts at

secession, strikes and a spiral into hunger and poverty, Gorbachev trod an uneasy path between the reactionary Communist old guard, and reformers like Boris Yeltsin, who demanded an acceleration of the pace of reform; his response was to accumulate formal power in his own hands. He lost much credibility in the coup attempt of 1991; on the dissolution of the Soviet Union he retired from active politics.

Greer, Germaine 1939–

Australian feminist. Greer took a first degree in Australia and then obtained a doctorate at the British University of Cambridge. She remained in Britain and lectured at the University of Warwick (1968–73). She shot to prominence with the publication of her first book, *The Female Eunuch*, in 1970, which sold millions of copies. Analyzing the prevalence to misogyny in society and culture, Greer attacked the misrepresentation and denial of female sexuality under patriarchy and portrayed marriage as a legalized form of slavery for women. In *Sex and Destiny* (1984) Greer diverged from current feminist theories about the family by advocating the return to large extended families.

Griffith Joyner, Florence 1959–

US athlete. She started racing, and beating boys, aged seven. At university she was diverted to running, and followed her coach Bob Kersee to University College, Los Angeles. In 1984 she won the Olympic 200m silver medal. She trained intensively for the 1988 Olympics, and broke the 100m record twice at the trials, once in 10.49 sec, a time previously thought impossible for a woman. She won gold medals for the 100m, 200m and 400m relay. "Flojo", as she was known, was dubbed "the world's fastest woman". She was also known for her six-inch nails, and the sensational clothes and make-up she ran in.

Gromyko, Andrei A. 1909–89

Soviet politician. A Communist party member from 1931, Gromyko was appointed to the People's Commissariat of Foreign Affairs in 1939, and became counselor at the Soviet embassy in Washington. In 1943 he was appointed Soviet ambassador to the United States. He attended the Tehran, Yalta and Potsdam conferences, and in 1946 sat on the UN Security Council, where he used his veto 25 times. Promoted to deputy foreign minister in 1946, he became chief Soviet representative in the UN General Assembly in 1949, and in 1952–53, was ambassador to the UK. He became a full member of the Communist party central committee in 1956 and foreign minister in 1957. In 1962 he took part in talks with President Kennedy to resolve the Cuban crisis, and in 1967 his diplomatic efforts paved the way for the nuclear nonproliferation treaty. He was a member of the Politburo by 1973. In 1985 he became

President (titular head of state), an office taken over by Gorbachev a short time later. Although a major figure in the Cold War, Gromyko was widely regarded as the principal engineer of Gorbachev's rise to power. Nevertheless, Gorbachev did not attend his funeral.

Haig, Alexander M. 1924–
US general. An army officer, Haig was appointed military aide to Henry Kissinger in 1969. He then went on to become the chief deputy of the National Security Council, and in 1973 Nixon made him the army's vice-chief of staff. Now a four-star general, Haig advocated a harder line in Vietnam, and also in 1973 he became chief of White House staff. He is believed to have helped persuade Nixon to resign, and to have effectively ruled the country toward the end of the administration. It has been alleged that he was involved in wiretapping, and in plans to overthrow Allende in Chile and bomb Cambodia. During 1974–79, he was supreme commander of the NATO forces in Europe, and from 1981 to 1982 served as secretary of state under Reagan.

Haring, Keith 1958–
US graffiti artist. Haring studied Abstract Expressionism in 1979–80, but found it trivial; he studied semiotics, made videos, and drew on huge rolls of paper on his studio floor, with the street doors open so that passersby could see his work. In late 1980 he began to draw on black paper rectangles he put up around subways, producing images like *Radiant Child* and *Barking Dog*. He became a superstar, his works commanding vast prices worldwide. He designed clothes for stars such as Madonna; he loved children and frequently worked for them. In 1986 he painted a mural, of a chain of people, on the Berlin wall, using the colors of the East and West German flags. He has claimed influences from primitive art and the work of Andy Warhol.

Havel, Vaclav 1936–
Czech playwright and president. Havel began to publish essays in 1954, and soon turned to writing plays. His first solo play, *The Garden Party* (première, 1963) was translated all over Europe, and he became Czechoslovakia's most popular playwright. *The Memorandum* (première, 1965), his best-known play, is "about all systems which destroy human personality" seeming to allude specifically to Stalinism and its aftermath. He consistently criticized the Communist regime. In 1968 he went to the USA for *The Memorandum*'s US première; then Soviet forces invaded Czechoslovakia, and he broadcast to "Western intellectuals", demanding human rights at home and abroad. He was interrogated, barred from writing, and his passport was confiscated; twice jailed, he had to do menial work. Two plays were

circulated secretly. His writing was now concerned with the breakdown of society (*The Mountain Hotel*). In 1975 he introduced the semiautobiographical character Vanek, a man uncorrupted by the exigencies of the system, whose simple questions catalyze the action around him. A founder member and signatory of Charter 77, he was again arrested; he continued his activities, and in 1979 was jailed for 4 ½ years. He won several prestigious awards, including (1986) the Erasmus Prize. In 1989 he was imprisoned for four months (after parole), and then arrested again, but released at the request of his doctors. Between then and 1990 the Communist regimes of most of the Eastern bloc collapsed, and Havel became president of a democratic and free Czechoslovakia. On the breakup of Czechoslovakia in 1993 he became president of the new Czech Republic.

Hawking, Stephen William 1942–
British theoretical physicist. After reading physics at Oxford he did postgraduate research at Cambridge, where he has remained. In 1979 he was appointed to the Lucasian professorship of mathematics. Despite a disease which has all but robbed him of speech and movement, he has directed his genius to elucidating the structure of black holes showing (1971) that these can issue not only from the collapse of stars but also – as mini-black holes – from the time of the original "big bang". He predicted that when found such mini-black holes will emit "Hawking radiation" at a fixed rate. He is now working on a quantum mechanical theory of gravity which will subsume the four basic forces.

Honecker, Erich 1912–
East German politician. Honecker joined the German Communist party in 1929, and in 1935 was imprisoned for anti-Nazi activities. Freed by the Russians in 1945, he joined the Communist party's central committee. Chairman of the Free German Youth movement (1946–55), he helped to found the Socialist Unity party (SED), whose central committee he joined in 1946, and in 1958 he became a member of the Politburo. He supervised the building of the Berlin Wall in 1961. Party secretary in 1971, he became head of state in 1976, pursuing the hardline policies of his predecessor Ulbricht, more responsive to Moscow but opposed to détente. He resigned in 1989. Despite moves to try him for the deaths incurred on the Berlin Wall, he suffered from terminal cancer and in 1992 was allowed to travel to South America.

Hubel, David Hunter, 1926–
Canadian-US neurophysiologist, noted for research on the physiology of vision. He graduated at McGill University, Montreal, first in mathematics and physics (1947) and then in medicine (1951). After various appointments in neurology he joined

the Harvard Medical School in 1959, where since 1982 he has been John Franklin Enders professor. There he was closely associated with Torsten Nils Wiesel. Using electro-physiological techniques, they investigated the response to light of cells in the cerebral cortex. This led to the identification of regions responsive to specific photo-stimuli, and to a detailed mapping of the whole visual cortex. Hubel and Wiesel shared a Nobel prize in 1981.

Hussein, King 1935–
King of Jordan. His childhood was marked by the family's poverty and by the experience in 1951 of seeing his grandfather assassinated; he attacked the assassin and was shot at, but the bullet bounced off a medal. His education was completed with a course at Britain's Sandhurst military academy. In 1953 his father was forced to abdicate and he came to the throne. He had British and US support in his national and personal struggle to survive; and he transformed Jordan's economy, with output doubling between 1956 and 1963. He was particularly vulnerable in the Israel–Palestine conflict, because of the many Palestinians in Jordan; he joined with Egypt in the 1967 "six-day war" against Israel, and was defeated; he then helped draft UN resolution 242 calling for the return of the Israeli-occupied west bank. His efforts to integrate the Palestinian refugees in Jordan were unsuccessful, and he then had to deal with terrorist action and personal challenge from the PLO: in 1971, after a year's fighting and under the menace of civil war, he expelled them. He denounced the Israel–Egypt Camp David peace accords as unfair to the Arab states, in particular Palestine and Jordan, resisting huge pressure from the US government to help implement them. This won him Arab support, and he became the Palestinians' spokesman. This knife-edge diplomacy was typical of a king who had survived coups, wars and assassination attempts. In the Iraq–Kuwait crisis of 1990, Hussein made massive efforts, with "shuttle diplomacy", to avert the war between the UN allies and Iraq.

Jackson, Michael 1958–
US popular singer. He began his career with the Jackson Five in 1969, and in the early 1970s recorded his first solo hits *Got To Be There* (1971) and *Rockin' Robin* (1972). His album *Off The Wall* (1979) launched him into the big time. This was followed up by *Thriller* (1982), which marked the start of his preoccupation with video packaging, and *Bad* (1987). In 1988 he released a quasi-autobiographical film *Moonwalk*. He was also a brilliant dancer. Extremely wealthy, reclusive and eccentric, he was also famous for having used plastic surgery, and other interventionist means, to alter his facial appearance completely, from cheekbones to the color of his skin.

BIOGRAPHIES
John Paul II (Karol Wojtyla)

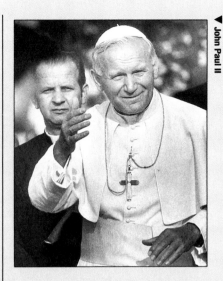

John Paul II

Juan Carlos (right)

Ruhollah Khomeini

John Paul II (Karol Wojtyla) 1920–

The first non-Italian pope in 456 years, John Paul II was a conservative who underlined the orthodox Catholic positions on such issues as abortion, divorce and contraception, addressing the public directly, avoiding the complexities of theological dogma. Becoming a priest just after World War II, Wojtyla rose quickly through the Catholic hierarchy from bishop (1958) to cardinal (1967). He became the first ever Polish pope in 1978 and immediately began a global tour involving massive rallies where he attempted to redefine the tenets of Catholicism to clarify their relation to the modern world. In 1981 an assassination attempt left him seriously wounded. His public support in troubled times for the Solidarity movement and the church in Poland may have partly provoked this attack.

Johnson, Philip 1906–

US architect. In 1932 Johnson co-wrote *The International Style: Architecture since 1922*, which defined modern architecture. He trained as an architect in the early 1940s, and achieved fame through the *Glass House* he made himself in 1949; it showed the influence of Mies van der Rohe, with whom he collaborated on the Seagram Building, New York (1958); this style climaxed in the 1980 *Crystal Cathedral* in Los Angeles, and spawned a host of imitators. Johnson produced more moderate works, with a neoclassical bent, and harmonizing with the landscape. They include the Sheldon Art Gallery (1962), and the superb New York Theater (1964). His interiors are usually impressive, with dullish exteriors.

Juan Carlos 1938–

Spanish king. The grandson of Alfonso XIII, he was groomed for the monarchy by Franco, who in 1969 nominated him as his successor. Juan Carlos came to power in 1975, and worked to obtain a democratic constitution and an amnesty for political prisoners. He adopted the role of a constitutional monarch. In 1981, Francoist soldiers occupied parliament, and held its members hostage. He denounced this action taking a courageous stand which saved the new constitution. In the same year, he visited the Americas and China. In 1982, his promise to accept any freely elected government was kept when the Socialist party came to power. Spain then joined NATO, and Juan Carlos was awarded the International Charlemagne Award, for furthering the cause of European unity.

Khomeini, Ruhollah 1900–89

Iranian Shiah Moslem leader. In 1963 Khomeini denounced the Shah's policy of land reforms, and in 1964 the Shah exiled him. He lived abroad in Turkey, Iraq and France, coordinating strikes and campaigning for the Shah's overthrow. In 1979 Khomeini returned to Iran to great popular acclaim

and launched the Islamic revolution. The Shah's caretaker government was overthrown, new ministers appointed, and a constitution establishing an Islamic state and granting Khomeini wide-ranging powers approved by referendum. Western music and alcoholic beverages became illegal, women were obliged to wear veils, and Islamic punishments were reintroduced. Khomeini's foreign policy was marked by aggression and acts of terrorism. In 1989 he declared the book *The Satanic Verses* blasphemous, and shocked the Western world by ordering the death of its British author, Salman Rushdie. He also gave support to Islamic revolutionaries in other Middle Eastern countries.

Kohl, Helmut 1930–

West German chancellor. In 1969 Kohl gained a place in the national parliament. In the same year, he became national deputy chairman of the Christian Democrat Union, and in 1973, party leader. He ran unsuccessfully for the chancellorship of West Germany in 1976, but acceded to power in 1982 in coalition with the Christian Social Union and the Free Democrats, after the fall of Schmidt's government. They won a majority in the 1983 elections, and Kohl pursued policies of moderate economic conservatism at home, and strong commitment to NATO abroad. In 1990 he masterminded German reunification, becoming Chancellor of a united Germany which was soon disenchanted with its new status in the new economic and social crisis it faced.

Lagerfeld, Karl 1938–

German couturier. Even in childhood he liked drawing clothes and would illustrate books for fun, enjoying drawing period costumes very accurately. Advised against art school because he had no interest in painting – only drawing – he won first prize against 2,000 entrants, in 1954, for a coat design entered in a competition in Paris where the family had settled. Balmain produced the coat and employed Lagerfeld, who designed for movies. He then became chief designer for Patou, but soon left, feeling restricted. Bored with fashion, he spent two years enjoying beach life; then studied art history in Italy, to discover that he was hooked on fashion. He returned to Paris with the rise of ready-to-wear, and led a group designing innovative clothes for mass-production. In 1964 he joined the house of Chloé. His international reputation for "happy clothes" was founded on his simplified construction, fluidity of line, and use of "layering"; his stitching was brilliant.

Lewis, Carl 1961–

US athlete. A runner from the age of eight, Lewis achieved a long jump of over 25 ft in his junior year, becoming the top US high-school track

athlete. He studied communications at Houston university. His coach, Tom Tellez, helped to streamline Lewis's style and eliminated a knee problem. In 1981 he came within .04 sec of the 100m world record; at the same event, he achieved a long jump of 27ft ¾in; the combination was a first; he repeated it two weeks later, this time with a jump of 28ft 3 ½in. He did not jump under 28ft thereafter. In 1983 he jumped 28ft 10 ¾in, just short of Beamon's 15-year-old record. In the 1984 Olympics he won gold in the 100m, long jump, 200m, and 400m relay, breaking records in the last two. In 1988 he won three gold medals, including the 100m and long jump; another two golds in 1992 made him the most successful track and field athlete in history.

Lloyd Webber, Andrew 1948–

The son of a musician, he began writing music aged nine, for a toy theater. After a term at Oxford University he began working with Tim Rice; in 1965 he went to the Royal College of Music; and in 1967 he composed his first full-length theater piece. *Joseph and the Amazing Technicolour Dreamcoat* (1968) brought instant acclaim to Rice and Lloyd-Webber. More brilliantly successful musicals followed, even after the partnership split. They include *Jesus Christ Superstar* (1971), which ran until 1973 on Broadway, *Evita* (1978), the record-breaking *Cats* (1981) and *Phantom of the Opera* (1986). He also produced other, mostly occasional, works, and an album. The progenitor of "rock opera", he fused different musical styles (classical, rock, folk). In 1982 he became the first composer to have three musicals running simultaneously in New York and London.

Lovelock, James 1919–

British scientist and author of the "Gaia hypothesis". After receiving his PhD and DSc from London university, Lovelock worked for the Medical Research Institute from 1941 to 1961. During this period he was Rockefeller Fellow at Harvard (1954–55) and taught at Yale (1958–59). He then took a chair in chemistry at a university in Texas, and contributed to the NASA space program. In 1964 he began to work as an independent scientist until 1967 when he became visiting professor of cybernetics at Reading, England. In 1974 he was made a fellow of the Royal Society. In 1979, in the book *Gaia*, he presented the hypothesis that the Earth is a living organism of which we are a part; it follows that we must tend the planet to ensure our own survival. This book was followed by *The Great Extinction* (1983) and *The Age of Gaia* (1988). Lovelock's radical theory has been supported by subsequent investigation and experiment, and is endorsed by many other scientists. He received several honorary degrees, and in 1986 became the president of the Marine Biology Association.

Carl Lewis

Madonna

Nelson Mandela

Lucas, George 1945–

US film director, screenwriter and producer. One of Coppola's protegés, he observed on *Finian's Rainbow* (1968) and *The Rain People* (1969), documenting the latter. *American Graffiti* (1973) won success with the critics and public but his next, *Star Wars* (1977), dwarfed everything in sight. The distinguished commentator on mythology ancient and modern, Joseph Campbell, called Lucas "the great mythologist of our age".

MacEnroe, John 1959–

American tennis player. In 1977 he reached the semi-finals of the Wimbledon Men's Singles at the age of 18. Four years later he took the title and established himself as the premier figure in men's tennis, winning Wimbledon again in 1983 and 1984. He won many tournaments, but his fits of temper on court and tendency to swagger off court won him few friends.

Madonna (Madonna Louise Ciccione) 1958–

US pop star and icon. Her mother died when she was five, and she disliked her stepmother; performing was an act of self-determination. After early appearances in school musicals, she won a dance scholarship to the University of Michigan, and in 1978 joined the Alvin Ailey Dance Theater in New York. After spending time in Paris she worked as a drummer/vocalist, and signed with a record company, releasing an album in 1983; fame followed instantly, and all her albums, such as *Like a Virgin* (1984), were hits. In 1985 she appeared in the movie *Desperately Seeking Susan*. She played to massive audiences on a series of world concert tours, and was reputed to be the world's highest-earning woman. She cultivated her own myth, projecting an aggressive and outrageous sexuality and social and religious iconoclasm which she presented with a level of irony which emphasized her toughness. However , she began to resort to plastic surgery, as well as compulsive body-building and the use in public of aggressive "minders", in a way that suggested she was taking herself very seriously. Her book *Sex* was a sensation in 1992.

Mandela, Nelson R. 1918–

Black South African leader. In 1943 Mandela, a lawyer, joined the African National Congress, and helped to found its Youth League in the Transvaal. In 1952 he organized nonviolent resistance to apartheid and in 1953, now a member of the National Executive, was barred from public speaking until 1961 when, having become a leading figure in the ANC, he was acquitted of treason after a long-running trial, and coordinated a general strike. In 1962 he was imprisoned for encouraging industrial unrest. After the Sharpeville massacre (1960) the ANC was banned, and Mandela began to advocate armed struggle.

He helped to found Umkonto We Sizwe (Spear of the Nation), the ANC's military wing, and in 1963 was charged with treason, following the discovery of an arms cache. At his trial he made a four-and-a-half-hour speech in his own defense and in 1964 was sentenced to life imprisonment. The South African authorities maintained that there would be no possibility of Mandela's release until he renounced the use of violence, which he refused to do, becoming an international figure and the symbol of black resistance. In 1990, however, F.W. De Klerk unbanned the ANC and released Mandela, who had limited success in talks with the government but maintained his goal of a nonracial democracy in South Africa. His patience, courage and persistence were rewarded when most of the legislation maintaining apartheid was dismantled at last in 1991.

Maradona, Diego 1960–

Argentinean soccer star. Born to poor parents, Maradona shone early as a footballer and was invited to join Argentinos Juniors. His international debut was as a substitute on the Argentinean team playing Hungary in 1977; his team scored a 5–1 victory. In 1978 his age barred him from the national team; but thereafter he was always included. In 1981 he transferred to Boca Juniors for a record $8 million fee; but the club defaulted on payments so he returned, and was then signed to Barcelona. In 1984 the Italian club Napoli paid $9 million for him. In 1986 an Argentinean World Cup victory was allowed even though film record clearly showed that Maradona had scored the winning goal with his hand; this, as well as a scandal associating his name with the illicit use of drugs, tarnished but did not seriously affect his reputation as a brilliant all-rounder, with masterly ball control, great stamina, speed and flexibility.

Maxwell Davies, Peter 1934–

British composer. After studying at the Manchester college of music and Manchester University Maxwell Davies won a scholarship (1957) to study in Italy with the composer Petrassi. From 1959 he taught music in a British school. This influenced his composition; it became simpler, with more awareness of the connection between composer, player and audience; he also devised a system for teaching children to perform modern music. After (1962) a period at Princeton University as a scholarship student with Roger Sessions, he set up several British ensembles to perform the music of contemporary composers. Constantly innovative in musical content and method , he traveled widely performing and lecturing. His major works include the choral *O Magnum Mysterium* (1960), the opera *Taverner* (1962–68), *Eight Songs for a Mad King* (1969), the ballet *Salome* (1978), and the *Sinfonia Concertante* (1983).

Mendini, Alessandro 1931–

Italian industrial designer. Having worked as an architect for the Milan firm Nizzoli until 1970, he became the editor of the design magazine *Casabella*, and later *Modo*, and the highly influential *Domus*. Finding his inspiration in "banality" – employing, for example, the designs and materials of everyday objects from 1950s suburban "non-culture" – he has made furniture for the avant-garde Studio Alchimia. His most famous piece is a post-Modernist coffee-set.

Menuhin, Yehudi 1916–

US/British violinist. He owned his first violin at three, after being upset at the poor sound quality of a toy one. He started lessons two years later, and gave his first public solo performance then with the San Francisco orchestra. In 1924 the philanthropist Sidney Ehrman took on financial responsibility for Menuhin's career. In 1926 came his New York debut, and a move to Europe. His 1927 Paris debut recital, of three concertos, was a great success, and he astounded critics at a performance in November 1927 with the New York symphony orchestra, because of his mature grasp of Beethoven. He appeared in a series of stunning performances with the world's top orchestras and conductors, and in 1934 made his first world tour. From 1935 to 1937 he withdrew to assess himself. Feeling he lacked technical knowledge, he set about mastering his craft. In 1959 he moved to Britain and became director of the Bath Festival, and conductor of its orchestra, renamed the Menuhin Festival Orchestra. In 1963 he opened a school for musically gifted children. Menuhin brought new and neglected composers to the public ear; he made many records, solo and with other musicians, including jazz violinist Stéphane Grappelli and Indian sitarist Ravi Shankar.

Milstein, César 1927–

Argentinean–British molecular biologist. After graduating in chemistry in Buenos Aires he spent three years as a postgraduate student in Cambridge, (1958–61). Two years later he returned there permanently to become a member of staff of the Medical Research Council, latterly at the Laboratory of Molecular Biology. His research was particularly concerned with the structure, evolution and genetics of immunoglobulins and phosphoenzymes. In particular, he is identified with the discovery of monoclonal antibodies (MCAs): that is, antibodies produced by a line of cells deriving from a single ancestral cell. Such antibodies are all uniquely identical in chemical structure and, therefore, specific for a single antigen. In 1975, with G. Köhler, he developed a technique (hybridoma technique) for producing MCAs in large quantities. They have great therapeutic and diagnostic value. In 1984 he shared a Nobel prize with Köhler and N. Jerne.

François Mitterrand

Robert Mugabe

Martina Navratilova

Mitterrand, François M. 1916–

French president. He escaped from German capture in World War II and became a resistance leader. He was elected to the National Assembly in 1946, and between 1947 and 1957, held cabinet posts in 11 different governments. He ran for the presidency in 1965. In 1971, as First Secretary of the Socialist party, he considerably increased its popularity. He ran unsuccessfully against Giscard d'Estaing in 1974, but defeated him in 1981 to become president. After a socialist majority in the general election, Mitterrand formed a government. He began a program of nationalization, increased welfare payments and the minimum wage, and gave more power to local governments. He later moderated his economic policies when worldwide recession occurred. In his foreign policy, his tough but realistic attitude to the Soviet Union encouraged détente in the later 1980s.

Miyake, Issey 1935–

Japanese fashion designer. After graduating from Tama University in 1964, he studied fashion in Paris and worked for Laroche and Givenchy before going to New York, where he held his first show in 1971, with a second in Paris two years after, by which time he had already established his own style: bold, sometimes quirky designs, using linear and geometric shapes, wrapped and layered around the body. He continued to be an innovator, combining elements of West and East in his garments.

Moro, Aldo 1916–78

Italian premier. A law professor who wrote several books on the law and related subjects, Moro entered the legislature after World War II, and held several cabinet posts, including foreign secretary (1947–48) and minister for justice (1955–57). In 1959 he became secretary of the Christian Democrats and, during a crisis, although himself a centrist, urged a coalition with the Socialists. In 1960, partly because of this, the conservative Christian Democrat prime minister, Tabouri, resigned. In 1963 Moro became prime minister and brought Socialists into government for the first time in 16 years. Defeated over a budget issue, he resigned and then formed a new cabinet. Italy's economic weakness blocked his reformist aims, and in 1966 the Socialists defeated him, but again he formed a new government. He resigned at 1968's general election, and was foreign minister (1970–72). In 1974 he was premier again, this time in a Republican coalition, which collapsed in 1976. Later that year he became president of the Christian Democrats, and helped to engineer a compromise between them and the Communists. In March 1978 Red Brigade terrorists kidnapped him; the government did not comply with their demands for the release of political prisoners, and Moro was shot dead.

Morris, Mark 1956–

US choreographer. Morris learnt folk dance and flamenco from the age of eight, then modern dance and ballet; he began choreographing around 1970. He danced with a Balkan dance ensemble, loving its community spirit and simplicity. In 1974 he studied flamenco in Madrid, returned to study ballet in New York, joined a company in 1976, but soon left, and toured Asia and Australasia. His own works were first performed in 1980 in Cunningham's studio. In 1981 he set up the Mark Morris Dance Group. His pieces reflect on the vagaries of love – New Love Song Waltzes (1982), violence – Dogtown (1983, with Yoko Ono's music), and his climactic solo O Rangasayee (1984), to an Indian raga, took audiences and critics by storm. He has also worked from literature, like Barthes' essays on semiotics, in Mythologies (1986). Morris's consummate skill and creativity has brought comparisons to Graham and Cunningham. In 1988 Morris took over the Ballet du XXme Siècle, in Brussels, from Béjart.

Mugabe, Robert G. 1924–

Zimbabwean president. In 1963, Mugabe broke away from Nkomo's Zimbabwe African People's Union (ZAPU), and helped to found the Zimbabwe African National Union (ZANU) fighting for independence and black majority rule. He was imprisoned in 1964, and in 1965 Rhodesia's white elite made a unilateral declaration of independence from Britain. Mugabe became the leader of ZANU in 1974, and was freed in 1975. In the ensuing civil war (1975–79), Mugabe and Nkomo led the Patriotic Front against the government forces. ZANU gained a majority in the 1980 elections, and Mugabe became prime minister. He successfully encouraged the European community to remain, and introduced social reform. In 1982, he clashed with Nkomo, when he announced that only policies approved by ZANU would be implemented. Mugabe later expressed an intention eventually to institute a single-party state.

Murdoch, Rupert 1931–

Australian newspaper tycoon. An Oxford MA graduate, Murdoch worked on London's Daily Express in the 1950s, and returned to Australia in 1952 to run a small paper inherited from his father; he made it into a scandal sheet. He then set up a quality national newspaper (The Australian, 1964). Back in London, in 1969 he bought the News of the World and the then leftwing Sun; he vulgarized the Sun (impossible with the News of the World) and quadrupled its circulation. In 1974 he set up a US national weekly tabloid, The Star, and in 1976–77 bought the New York Post, the New York magazine and the "hip" Village Voice, which he sold in 1985. In 1981 he bought the London Times at a low price, on condition he was proprietor only, not

contributor, and that the editor be approved by an independent panel. These strictures were prompted partly by the Sun's hysterical and bloodthirsty jingoism during the Falklands war of 1982. Murdoch now moved into TV and film company ownership, gathering power in all media; and in his native Australia moves were made to frustrate his attempts at further expansion into the TV networks.

Navratilova, Martina 1956–

Czech-born American tennis-player. After winning the Women's Singles title in Czechoslovakia from 1972 to 1974, she came to the notice of the Western public when she reached the semi-finals of the women's singles at Wimbledon in 1976, having defected to the USA the previous year. A player of extraordinary physical power as well as skill, particularly in serve-and-volley play, and iron nerves, she won the Wimbledon title eight times in the 1980s. Navratilova was probably the wealthiest sportswoman of her time, amassing no less than $2,173,556 from prize-money alone in 1984.

Nicholson, Jack 1937–

US film actor. A versatile, charismatic character who first won notice in Easy Rider (1969), he had been starring in B-movies since 1958, writing and co-producing too. Thereafter most of his films were good and his notices great. He excelled in sardonically humorous outsider roles. Credits include Five Easy Pieces (1970), The Last Detail (1973), Chinatown (1974), One Flew Over the Cuckoo's Nest (1975), Terms of Endearment (1983) and The Witches of Eastwick (1987).

Oshima, Nagisa 1932–

Japanese film director. A leader of Japan's new wave, he made films attacking traditional mores, offering radical alternatives, featuring sex and/or violence. His technique was equally innovatory, mixing fantasy and reality. He made his first feature, A Town of Love and Hope, in 1959. In the Realm of the Senses (1976) made world headlines with its realistic portrayal of sexual obsession. Other credits include Death by Hanging (1968), The Ceremony (1970) and Merry Christmas Mr Lawrence (1982).

Packer, Kerry 1937–

Australian media baron. He started his long and successful career in the press as a trainee executive in the Australian Consolidated Oven and Compress Printing in 1955, and from the mid-1970s established a dominant influence in the Australian press and in broadcasting. He caused a controversy in 1977 when he contracted 35 of the world's top cricketers to play a series of matches in Australia, televised exclusively by his own Channel Nine network.

Pol Pot

Ronald Reagan

Salman Rushdie

Pahlevi, Mohammad Reza 1919–80

Shah of Iran from 1941. In 1951, Mosaddeq, a nationalist opponent of the Shah, nationalized the British-owned petroleum industry, and became premier. In 1953, after a vain attempt to dismiss him, the Shah left the country. He returned a few days later and assumed full power, probably with US help. He denationalized the petroleum industry, and with US aid, embarked upon a process of westernization and modernization. Some Iranians criticized the pace of change as being too slow, while others opposed westernization for religious reasons. Government corruption, the secret police, and the concentration of oil revenue in a few hands were also causes of controversy. Widespread rioting occurred in 1978, and the Shah fled abroad in 1979.

Papandreou, Andreas (George) 1919–

Greek prime minister. Son of the governor of Chios, he became a Trotskyist at Athens university where he studied law. For helping to publish a radical journal, he was arrested and tortured. He left for the USA, taking a PhD in economics at Harvard (1943). He taught, and published several books on economics in the USA; in 1959 his father persuaded him to give up his career and his US citizenship to go into Greek politics. His rise was swift but the severity of his attacks on the USA, the monarchy and the military fueled the opposition. His father became prime minister in 1963; but his government fell in 1965, partly because of the meteoric rise of the younger Papandreou through the party hierarchy. Furthermore, in 1964 Andreas was charged with corruption, and although it was unproven, stripped of his ministerial posts in 1965. In 1967, after the military junta took over, father and son were jailed, and then allowed to leave the country. Andreas returned to North America where he taught and lectured. He also set up the Panhellenic Liberation Movement (PAK) and worked to bring down the Junta. When it fell in 1974, he returned to Greece, and PAK was the foundation of PASOK (Panhellenic Socialist Movement), which, under his leadership, was a very well organized party. In 1981 he led Greece's first ever Socialist government. In 1987, however, there were rumors of corruption, and the nation was further scandalized by his open adulterous affair with an ex-air hostess. In 1989 the government fell; criminal proceedings were instituted against Papandreou for fraud.

Pavarotti, Luciano 1935–

Pavarotti had a musical upbringing, and was a keen sportsman; he wanted to sing professionally, but taught(1955–57), on the advice of his family. He then sold insurance to finance his full-time study of music. He made his debut, and began to work, in 1961, after winning an international competition. In 1965 Richard Bonynge hired him for an Australian tour with Joan Sutherland. His New York début was in 1968, at the Metropolitan Opera House. He won acclaim especially in the role of Tonio in Donizetti's *La Fille du Régiment*, notably in an aria which contains nine high Cs. He became widely popular throughout Europe and North America; his recordings sold massively, and his concert performances were always sold out. Pavarotti was a superb *bel canto* singer; his voice was utterly pure and supple, even in the highest register.

Perez de Cuellar, Javier 1920–

Peruvian diplomat and UN secretary general. De Cuellar studied law in Lima and then worked in the foreign ministry. In 1944 he joined the diplomatic service and soon became first secretary of the Peruvian embassy in Paris, subsequently holding the same position in Britain, Bolivia and Brazil. He was a delegate, in 1946, to the first session of the UN general assembly. In 1961 he returned to Lima to work in the foreign ministry; the following year he became ambassador. Between 1964 and 1969 he was ambassador to Switzerland, Moscow and Poland. In 1971 he became Peru's permanent representative to the UN; and as Waldheim's special envoy to Cyprus in the 1975 ENOSIS crisis, he did avert further fighting. He was ambassador to Venezuela (1977–79) and then returned to the UN. After visiting (1981) Afghanistan and Pakistan on peacemaking missions he resigned, returned to the area later that year, then retired; but at the end of the year he was elected UN secretary general as a compromise candidate. He was an active intermediary in the 1982 Falklands war between the UK and Argentina. A key figure in the Iran–Iraq peace talks of 1988, he also made diligent but unsuccessful attempts to avert war between the UN allies and Iraq, in 1991. He was criticized for not speaking out on controversial issues such as the South African situation.

Pol Pot (Saloth Sar) 1925–

Kampuchean political leader. A member of Ho Chi Minh's resistance movement, in 1946 Pol Pot joined the Communist party, in Cambodia an underground movement. He studied radio-electronics in Paris, returned in 1953 to Phnom Penh and joined the leftwing group Pracheachon. He led the Khmer Rouge in the revolution of 1975, and became prime minister. Under his rule between one and three million people died from neglect and brutality. In 1979, Vietnam invaded Kampuchea and he was ousted. He fled to the mountains with the Khmer Rouge, to wage guerrilla warfare. The government refused to negotiate while Pol Pot was leader, and in 1985 he was officially removed from leadership of the Khmer Rouge.

Qadhafi, Muammar 1942–

Libyan revolutionary and president. A Libyan army captain and leader of the Free Officers movement, Qadhafi led a military coup and proclaimed a republic. In 1970 he closed down British and US military bases, later deported ethnic Italians and Jews, and in 1973 nationalized foreign-owned sections of the oil industry. In 1977, as president, he installed a single-party system, blending his own interpretation of Islam with revolutionary socialism. Internationally, he first allied Libya with Egypt, and sought a pan-Arab federation of Libya, Egypt and Syria. He gave unqualified support to the Palestinians and opposed the Egyptian President Sadat's peace initiatives. In 1980 Britain broke diplomatic relations with Libya after a shot fired from the Libyan embassy killed an unarmed policewoman, and the killer went free. In 1986, after reports of his involvement in several major European terrorist incidents, the US airforce bombed Libya. Qadhafi himself escaped unharmed, but his one adopted child was killed in the raid.

Reagan, Ronald 1911–

40th US president. Reagan switched from his post-World War II support of the Democrats to the Republicans in 1962, and after a long career as a screen actor, during which he aided McCarthy (q.v.), he was Republican Governor of California from 1967 to 1975. Reagan increased taxes and cut state government spending. He was elected president in 1980, standing on the ticket of traditional American values and military strength. In 1984 Reagan was re-elected for a second term by a large majority. He greatly raised military spending at the expense of nonmilitary spending, and lowered taxes, doubling the national debt in five years. He initially reverted from détente to cold war, but, after some difficulty concerning his Strategic Defense Initiative policy, his most notable achievement was the signing in 1988 of the INF Treaty with the Soviet Union, the first ever agreement to dismantle nuclear weapons. The latter years of the Reagan administration were overshadowed by the Iran–Contra scandal in which it was alleged that members of the administration had sold arms to Iran hoping to obtain the release of hostages in the Lebanon, and that some of the profits had been diverted to the rightwing Contra forces in Nicaragua. Reagan retired in 1988.

Richards, Viv 1952–

West Indian cricketer. He made his debut for the island of Antigua in 1971, and captained Somerset from 1974 to 1986, and led the West Indian team from 1985. Widely considered one of the finest batsmen of the century, he used his sporting celebrity to promote cultural solidarity in his native West Indies.

▼ Andrei Sakharov

▼ Martin Scorsese

▼ Paul Simon

Rushdie, Salman 1947–

Indian-born British novelist. Rushdie, son of a wealthy Muslim family, was educated in Britain at Rugby school and Cambridge university. After graduating in 1968 he worked in fringe theater, and as an advertising copywriter. His first novel, *Grimus* (1975), was a surrealistic account of an American Indian in the West. *Midnight's Children* (1981) won the prestigious British Booker Prize; it was a rich, picaresque work, dealing through the history of a family with the history of partition in the subcontinent. *Shame* (1983) was shortlisted for the Booker Prize. Publication of *The Satanic Verses* (1988) precipitated a nightmare, when, after riots as Muslims (most of whom had not read the book) protested at a passage in which a group of prostitutes play at being the wives of the prophet Muhammad, the Iranian Muslim leader Ayatollah Khomeini pronounced a "fatwa" or sentence of death on Rushdie. The writer went at once into hiding, protected by British police. He continued to write, and his next novel, *Haroun and the Sea of Stories*, was published in 1990.

Sa'adawi, Nawal el- 1930–

Egyptian doctor, novelist, sociologist and feminist. After first graduating in 1944 she studied in 1966 at Columbia University, New York. She returned to Egypt and worked as a doctor and a psychiatrist at Cairo University Hospital. She eventually became director of the Egyptian ministry of health, and editor of the government magazine *Health*. *Women and Sex* (1972) dealt openly and searchingly with sexual taboos and the problems of women in Muslim culture, and called for changes in the position and treatment of women both inside and outside the home. As a result of its publication she was dismissed from her posts. She continued to write, producing many novels and short stories, as well as some non-fiction works; all addressed the issues facing women in Islam. She began to publish a feminist magazine *Confrontation*. Her book on women in Islam, *The Hidden Face of Eve*, was published in the UK in 1980. In 1981 she, along with thousands of others, was denounced by President Sadat, taken by force from the home, and imprisoned without trial for "crimes against the state". Released a few months later after Sadat's assassination, she wrote an account of her prison experiences. She favors the novel form, and her writing is rather honest, intelligent, compassionate, and courageous, than polemical. She is an international campaigner for justice. Her books are very widely read in Egypt and abroad.

Sadat, Muhammad Anwar el- 1918–81

Egyptian president. During World War II, Sadat cooperated with the Germans and was imprisoned twice by the British. In 1950, he joined Nasser's Free Officers movement, and was involved in the military coup two years later. He was then general secretary of the National Union party (1957–61), and vice-president (1969–70). Although he soon resigned this post he became president by default on Nasser's death in 1970, and began a process of social and economic liberalization, expelling many Soviet advisors in 1972. In 1973, he ordered an unsuccessful attack on the Israeli-occupied Sinai Peninsula. After the ceasefire, Sadat restored relations with the United States, and worked to attract Western aid and investment. He later repudiated the 1971 friendship pact with the Soviet Union. He also began to adopt a more conciliatory attitude toward Israel, and in 1975 consented to a mutual policy of nonbelligerency, and the reopening of the Suez Canal. In 1977, he visited Israel and presented a peace plan in the Knesset (Israeli parliament). In 1978, he met with Begin at Camp David, and agreed in principle to a treaty in return for Egyptian control of the Sinai Peninsula. Later the same year, he and Begin were awarded the Nobel Peace Prize, and in 1979 they signed the peace treaty; it proved unpopular with religious fundamentalists. Sadat responded with repression, and was assassinated in 1981 by an army officer and three Islamic fundamentalists.

Saddam Hussein 1937–

Iraqi president. Orphaned early, Saddam was used to violence as a child, and is said to have shot his first victim, with his own gun, at the age of ten. He attended Baghdad and Cairo universities. In 1957 he joined the Ba'ath party; in 1962 he survived a death sentence for his attempt to kill General Qassim. He became a leader of the Cairo Ba'ath party, and as such returned to Iraq in 1963. The following year, while in jail for conspiracy, he was elected to Ba'ath national leadership. He played a major role in the revolution of 1968, and was on the Revolutionary Command Council until 1979, when he became Iraq's president and prime minister. His rule was repressive and bloodthirsty; he conducted the war with Iran (1980–88), armed largely by the western powers and the Soviet Union. The poison gas massacre he ordered in 1988 of over 5000 Kurdish Iraqis was a particularly well publicized and hideous event. In 1990, after accusing Kuwait of manipulating oil prices to Iraq's detriment and stealing Iraqi oil, he invaded it, destroying its infrastructure and maiming, torturing and killing its citizens. The United Nations passed a resolution ordering Iraq out; sanctions were applied. In early 1991 Allied forces went to war against Saddam; his forces were soon routed; he left oil wells blazing and the Gulf polluted with a massive oil slick. Revolution ensued in Iraq, and Saddam resumed his regime of murderous brutality against his own people, chiefly the Kurds, who became the object of international concern; US troops were redeployed in Iraq to protect them. Saddam wrote the book *One Trench or Two*.

Sakharov, Andrey Dimitrievich 1921–89

A Soviet nuclear physicist and political dissident, Sakharov became internationally renowned as an advocate of civil liberties and reform in the USSR. His early years were very successful – a doctorate at the age of 26 and subsequent work on the development of the Soviet Union's first hydrogen bomb, for which he was made a full member of the Soviet Academy of Sciences at the age of 32. However, in 1961 he openly stated his objection to Soviet nuclear tests in the atmosphere, fearing their harmful effects. In 1968 he called for a reduction in superpower nuclear arms holdings and an integration of capitalist and communist systems. These opinions and his active defense of human rights in the USSR led to a State campaign against him. He lost his professional position, was imprisoned and in 1980 exiled to Gorky. He was awarded the 1975 Nobel Peace Prize for his contribution to the defense of human rights. Gorbachev's reforms saw Sakharov reentering mainstream Soviet society and taking political office; he continued to campaign for social reform.

Schmidt, Helmut 1918–

West German chancellor. Awarded the Iron Cross during World War II, in 1946 Schmidt joined the Social Democratic party. Between 1949 and 1969 he served twice alternately in the Hamburg municipal government and the Bundestag. He served as defense minister (1969–72), and as finance minister (1972–74), consolidating what was known as the "economic miracle". He became chancellor in 1974, and worked to defuse tension with the Communist states. He also enjoyed good relations with the USA, and supported the EEC. Economic problems at home resulted in the collapse of the coalition with the Free Democrats, and after a vote in the Bundestag, Schmidt resigned the chancellorship in 1982.

Scorsese, Martin 1942–

US film director. A highly regarded filmmaker whose most successful films emphasize character rather than dramatic plot, his first major film was *Mean Streets* (1973). The disturbing vision of urban life and jumpy camerawork were typical of his work in *Taxi Driver* (1976) and *Raging Bull* (1979). His more "commercial" projects have included *Alice Doesn't Live Here Anymore* (1975) and *New York, New York* (1977).

Shamir (Yizernitzky), Yitzak 1915–

Israeli prime minister. Shamir studied in his native Poland and in Israel. He fought with the Israeli freedom fighters (Irgun) in World War II, and was detained by the British. In 1945 he returned to Israel, and entered politics in 1955, working in intelligence until 1965. In 1973 he entered the Knesset (Israel's parliament). Foreign minister from 1980 to 1983, he became prime minister on Begin's

▲ Manuel Soares

▲ Roger Sperry

▲ Sylvester Stallone

resignation, and tried to form a coalition with Labor; in the face of opposition, he clearly demonstrated his natural authority. After an inconclusive election in 1984, he formed a coalition government ("National Unity") with power to alternate between him and Shimon Peres as foreign minister and then prime minister. The arrangement was questioned; in 1986, when Shamir took over as prime minister, it was obvious that it did work; it also sustained internal unity in the two parties (Labor and Likud).

Shevardnadze, Eduard 1928–
Soviet politician. His father and brother were prominent in the Georgian Communist Party, and in 1946 he became an instructor in Komsomol, the Communist Youth League, joining the CPSU itself in 1948. He graduated in history by mail. By 1957 he was the first secretary of the Georgian Komsomol, and in 1959 he joined its supreme soviet. He held first secretary posts for two districts in the early 1960s; drafted in, he also rose in the ranks of the MVD (civilian police) and in 1965 took charge of the Georgian ministry of public order (so becoming police chief), which in 1968 became the ministry of internal affairs; he was also made a general in the MVD. He undertook a major drive against crime in this unruly republic. In 1972 he became first secretary of the Georgian Communist Party, where he successfully combated corruption. In 1976 he joined the Communist Party Central Committee, as a candidate member in 1978 and a full member in 1985, when he succeeded Gromyko as foreign minister; he built good relations with the USA and helped pave the way for the 1985 summit between Reagan and Gorbachev. In 1986 he established trade agreements with Japan. He also settled old disputes with the UK. Gorbachev's right-hand man, he resigned in 1990, declaring that he saw his nation reverting to military dictatorship. In 1992 he became president of his native Georgia following some months of internal unrest.

Simon, Paul 1941–
US popular singer/songwriter. He made his recording debut with Art Garfunkel, as "Tom and Jerry"; for the next five years he recorded solo; at law school, he met Garfunkel again and dropped out of school in 1963. In 1966 they released the album *Sounds of Silence*, which sold over two million copies worldwide. Their popularity increased with *Mrs. Robinson*, and 1970's *Bridge Over Troubled Water* was a multi-million seller. In 1971 the two split, and Simon continued solo. In 1978 he acted, in the movie *Annie Hall*, and then signed with Warner Brothers; he wrote, directed and acted in the 1980 film *One-Trick Pony*. He was adventurous in his musical partnerships, including Philip Glass among the guest artists on *Hearts and Bones* (1983), and controversially working in South

Africa with black African musicians to record *Graceland* (1986). For this Simon was briefly blacklisted by the African National Congress and the UN. He subsequently produced an album by the black African band Ladysmith Black Mambazo. His 1987 UK concert tour with two African singers, Miriam Makeba and Hugh Masakele, was picketed by antiapartheid protesters. Simon's next album, *Rhythm of the Saints* (1990) also used African musicians and arrangements.

Soares, Mario 1924–
Portuguese president. A Sorbonne law graduate, from 1946 to 1948 Soares was on the Central Executive of the Democratic Youth Movement. After 13 prison sentences, he was exiled to France, all for counter-dictatorship activity. Returning after a coup in 1974, he became foreign minister, and brought peace to Portuguese colonial Africa. In 1976 he became socialist leader of a coalition government until 1978 when the issue of land reform brought the government down, and was elected in 1983 for a second term. In 1986 he was elected President; he renounced Socialist Party leadership, and swore to lead the people, whatever their politics; he was now able easily to work with the rightwing prime minister Caraco. Regarded and respected internationally as an elder statesman, he was largely responsible for Portugal's entry into the EC.

Sottsass, Ettore 1917–
Austrian-born Italian industrial designer. A graduate of Turin Polytechnic, he set up office in the city in 1946. Closely associated with Olivetti from 1957, he always maintained a quirky independence. In the 1960s he dabbled in Pop, and later produced bizarre furniture designs for the Studio Alchymia. In 1981 he formed the radical "Memphis" group, where he continued his career as a designer of witty and outrageous furniture and initiated an international revolution in style and design.

Sperry, Roger Wolcott 1913–
US psychobiologist. After studying psychology and zoology he did several years of research at Harvard, Yerkes and the National Institutes of Health before being appointed professor of psychobiology at the California Institute of Technology (1954–84). Initially his research was with amphibians which, unlike mammals, can regenerate a severed optic nerve. In them, he was able to demonstrate a specific difference in function between the two halves of the brain. Turning to the brains of primates and humans he found a similar difference in function. In the left hemisphere the processing of verbal messages is generally dominant: in the right, emotional and spatial interpretations. Sperry was awarded a Nobel prize in 1981.

Spielberg, Steven 1947–
US film director and producer. He shot his first film at 12, won a contract with Universal after college. Unafraid of sentiment, he shows childhood as a constant preoccupation. The most successful American director of the seventies and eighties, his box-office smashes include *Jaws* (1975), *Close Encounters of the Third Kind* (1977), *Raiders of the Lost Ark* (1981), *E.T.: The Extra-Terrestrial* (1982) and *The Color Purple* (1985).

Springsteen, Bruce 1949–
US rock singer. He played guitar in a band at 14, and wanted stardom, despite family disapproval. In 1973 Columbia released his first album; it sold slowly, but in 1974 a Boston music journalist wrote "I saw rock and roll's future and its name was Bruce Springsteen". The glare of fame came in 1975, in response to his album *Born to Run*, which went gold that year. "The Boss" was popular for his driving rhythms, strong , full sound, poetic, meaty lyrics, social concern, and his enormous energy. Other albums followed, such as *Nebraska*, which dealt with the suffering of the socially deprived. By 1985 13 million copies of *Born to Run* had sold worldwide, and Springsteen was the most popular American singer since Presley.

Stallone, Sylvester 1946–
US film actor, screenwriter and director. He decided early that acting was for him but met with no encouragement. He landed bit parts in films and then the lead in a low-budget movie. He wrote his own star part, *Rocky* (1976), sold the rights and made a fortune at the box office. All his later roles depended upon his muscular physique and right-wing politics. With *Paradise Alley* (1978) he began directing as well as writing. Credits include the *Rocky* and *Rambo* series.

Stockhausen, Karlheinz 1928–
German composer. An accomplished pianist by his teens, Stockhausen studied with Messiaen in 1952; his *Kreuzspiel* (1951) is a response to Messiaen's seminal *Modes de Valeurs*. In 1952 he cofounded an electronic music studio in Cologne, producing his first mature work, *Kontrapunkte* (1953), before studying phonetics and acoustics at Bonn University (1954–56). He introduced physical space as a musical parameter, as in *Gesang der Jünglinge* (1956) and *Gruppen* (1957), in which sound-sources are arranged around the audience. His quest for a "music of the whole world" led him to use "found" material electronically manipulated in *Telemusik* (1966) and *Hymnen* (1967), the latter being a visionary mosaic of anthems and such "found" material. Influenced by Eastern philosophy, he made his music a tool in his quest for spiritual enlightenment. From 1977 Stockhausen worked on *Licht*, a cycle of seven transcendental operas named after the days of the week.

▲ Meryl Streep

▲ Mother Teresa

▲ Margaret Thatcher

Streep, Meryl (Mary Louise) 1949–

US actress. Not popular with other children in high school, she had voice coaching for four years after the discovery in 1961 that her singing voice was beautiful. She appeared in high school plays, and by the age of 16, after bleaching her hair, losing her spectacles and her braces, managed to conform. Her outstanding acting ability showed up during her time at Vassar, where she majored in drama. After graduating she worked in summer stock, and then won a scholarship to Yale Drama School. By 1975 she had gained a Master's degree, and a reputation as a marvellously versatile actress. She won critical acclaim in a number of stage plays, and was nominated for a Tony and other awards. For her part in the TV mini-series *Holocaust* she won an Emmy. In her first movie, *Julia* (1972) she had a supporting role; in 1979 she enhanced her reputation with three films, including *Kramer vs. Kramer*; now viewed as America's finest actress, she continued to make movies in many styles, such as *The French Lieutenant's Woman* (1980), *Sophie's Choice* (1982) and *Out of Africa* (1985). Snubbed when she was dropped as Evita in favor of Madonna, she showed audiences how well she could have done it in *Postcards from the Edge* (1991) in which she sang a storm.

Tambo, Oliver 1917–93

President of the African National Congress (ANC). He gained his BSc in 1941, and studied for an education diploma, but was expelled for taking part in a student strike. He taught science and math at his old school, as well as politicizing his pupils. In 1944 he cofounded the ANC Youth League, advocating militancy. He joined the ANC national executive in 1949. After qualifying as a lawyer he formed the first black South African legal partnership, with Nelson Mandela. In 1954 he was put under a banning order for two years; he continued to campaign, and in 1955 became ANC secretary general; 1957 saw the completion of the new ANC constitution he had been drafting. In 1956 he was arrested and charged with high treason; the charges were dropped in 1957. In 1958 he became ANC deputy president. The following year a five-year banning order was placed on Tambo. In 1960, at the request of the National Executive, who believed – correctly – the ANC would be outlawed, he reluctantly left for Bechuanaland (Botswana),and helped to unite, briefly, the ANC, the South African Indian Congress, and the Pan-African Congress (PAC). He traveled the world as the ANC's expatriate leader, visiting the United Nations and attending OAU meetings. In 1965 he helped set up an ANC guerrilla training unit in Tanzania; this became the military HQ. In 1967 he became acting president of the ANC; in 1969 he and the national executive were heavily criticized; but he reestablished his

leadership and was elected president. In 1977 he was named as president-general. He attributed the ANC's success to those who struggled in South Africa. In 1990 Nelson Mandela, at last released from prison, became deputy president of an unbanned ANC and took over from Tambo, by then hospitalized after a slight stroke.

Te Kanawa, Kiri 1944–

New Zealand soprano. She had a famous singing teacher as a school teacher, and soon won competitions at home and in Australia. She worked as a popular singer and recording artiste until 1966 when she went to the London Opera Centre. Stardom came suddenly in the 1970s; she appeared at the Royal Opera House, Covent Garden, in many Mozart roles, including the Countess in *The Marriage of Figaro*, and as Mimi in Puccini's *La Bohème*. Constantly busy, she made her New York debut at the Metropolitan Opera House as Desdemona in Verdi's *Otello*. In 1981 she sang at the wedding of the Prince of Wales and Lady Diana Spencer, broadcast to over 600 million viewers. In 1982 she was awarded a CBE.

Teresa, Mother 1910–

Yugoslav nun and founder of a charitable order. While at school she decided to be a missionary in India. She taught at a girls' convent school in Calcutta from 1929 until 1946 when on a train journey she heard God calling her to live and work among the poor. She moved to the slums of Calcutta, establishing the order of the Sisters of Charity, which spread through India and into other countries. Her work focused on caring for poor, sick and dying children. Her book, *Gift from God* appeared in 1975. She was awarded the 1979 Nobel Peace Prize and in 1985 the US Presidential Medal of Freedom.

Thatcher, Margaret Hilda 1925–

British Conservative prime minister. MP for Finchley from 1959, after holding government and shadow posts, she was elected party leader in 1975. She became the first female British prime minister in 1979. A rightwing Tory, Thatcher took a strong line on law and order and defense and advocated the end of government control of industry, tax and public expenditure costs and the limitation of trade union power. Economically, she adopted the monetarist policies. Unemployment nearly tripled during her first two terms, and in the early 1980s Britain lost 20 percent of its manufacturing industry. Homelessness increased by approximately 60 percent between 1981 and 1987, and the social security reforms of 1988 reduced payments to many poor people. Despite her unpopularity, Thatcher's conduct in the Falklands war led to her landslide victory in the 1983 general elections. Her second term was marked by a continuation of monetarist policy and a growing

emphasis on liberalizing the economy, marked by the privatization of major public concerns. In 1985 she signed the Anglo-Irish agreement. She developed a warm relationship with US president Reagan, and allowed the use of British bases for the US bombing of Libya in 1986. In 1987 she achieved a record third term in office, and privatization policies continued, unemployment decreased, but inflation and the trade deficit rose sharply. She supported the idea of a common European market, but took a lone and controversial stand against full European monetary union, and was forced to resign in 1990.

Tonegawa, Susumu 1939–

Japanese molecular biologist. He studied science at Kyoto University and did postgraduate research at the University of California (1963–69). He then spent 10 years in Switzerland at the Basle Institute for Immunology, before returning to the USA in 1981 to teach at MIT. His research addressed a puzzling aspect of the human immune system. How does it manage to produce the vast variety of antibodies and antigens, numbered in millions, required to meet every contingency? Tonegawa showed in the 1970s that the cells which produce antibodies (T-cells) each contain about a thousand pieces of relevant genetic material. Permutations make possible at least a billion antibodies. Tonegawa was awarded a Nobel prize in 1987.

Torvill, Jayne 1957– and Dean, Christopher 1958–

British ice dancing champions. Torvill, a clerk and Dean, a policeman, first skated together in 1975. In 1978 they were UK champions; they retained this title until they turned professional in 1984. Awarded OBEs in 1980, they were European champions in 1981 and 1982 (injury prevented an attempt in 1983). They won the world championship in 1981, and again in 1982, 1983 and 1984. In 1984 they also won an Olympic gold medal with their gracefully erotic interpretation of Ravel's *Bolero*; they won maximum points from all judges, an unprecedented event. They retained their brilliance, creativity and popularity as professionals. Dean continued to create dances for other amateur skaters. Their massive success was due to their utter dedication, finesse, imagination and the uncanny rapport which allowed them to execute the most complex movements in unison or perfect harmony; their choice of music also was inspired.

Tutu, Desmond 1931–

Anglican archbishop of Cape Town. Tutu taught until 1958 when he trained as a priest. He took an MA in theology in the UK in 1966, when he returned to South Africa. He taught at a seminary and then lectured in theology at Lesotho university. In 1972 he took a post in London. In

Desmond Tutu

Lech Walesa

Ahmad Zaki Yamani

1975 he was created dean of Johannesburg, and in 1976 bishop of Lesotho until 1978 when he returned to Johannesburg as the general secretary of the South African Council of Churches (SACC). In 1979 his denunciation of Danish trade with South Africa led him into conflict with the government. Tutu's passport was confiscated; he was arrested after a march protesting the detention of other churchmen. In 1981 he visited the USA where he spoke with the UN secretary general; he then visited European religious leaders. On his return his passport was again confiscated. In 1984 he received the Nobel Peace Prize, for his constant advocacy of nonviolent change. In 1985 he was created bishop of Johannesburg. He traveled the world calling for tough sanctions. In 1985 he condemned black-against-black violence. He offered to mediate between the government and black leaders; after refusing initially, President Botha met with him and other black leaders in 1986. In this year he became archbishop of Capetown. He was elected head of the All Africa Council of Churches; he called again for tough sanctions. He cofounded the Committee for the Defence of Democracy to continue the work of the restricted organizations. He called for the cessation of all diplomatic relations with South Africa.

Veil, Simone 1927–

French politician. In 1944 Weil's family was taken to Auschwitz. Her parents and brother died there, but she returned in 1945, graduated in law and received the diploma of the Paris Institute of Political Studies. From 1959 to 1965 she was assistant public prosecutor. In 1970 she became the first female secretary general of the Higher Council of judges. In 1974 Chirac appointed her minister of health; in 1978 he reappointed her, and extended her responsibilities to include the ministry for family affairs. In 1977 she had been appointed chairman of the Information Council for Electro-Nuclear Energy. In 1979 she was elected to the European Assembly, resigned her government posts, and later that year became the president of the first elected European Assembly. She held office until 1982.

Walcott, Derek 1930–

West Indian poet and playwright. Walcott studied in St Lucia, graduating in 1933, and then taught at the West Indies' University until 1958. While there, he began writing folk plays. In the 1960s he directed Trinidad Theater Workshop, and *In a Green Night: Poems 1948–60* was published. *The Dream on Monkey Mountain and Other Plays* (1970) shows his use of traditional Creole idioms and tales. *Another Life* (1973) is an autobiographical poem. Walcott uses Caribbean dialect, and traditional literary forms, in work which is humorous, compassionate, informed by history, and immediate.

Waldheim, Kurt 1918–

Austrian president and UN secretary general. After voluntary military service he studied law in Vienna until being drafted in World War II. In 1944 he received his doctorate and became a diplomat. He was first secretary at the Austrian embassy in Paris (1948–51), and then worked in the foreign ministry, as a UN observer, and as ambassador to Canada. From 1960 to 1964 he was political director of the foreign ministry. He then became his country's permanent representative to the UN. He was foreign minister in a Conservative cabinet from 1968 to 1970. In 1971 he failed in his first attempt for the presidency; he was then elected UN secretary general, and re-elected in 1976. In 1981 the Chinese blocked his re-election, and Perez de Cuellar, a compromise candidate, replaced him. Scandal erupted around him during his 1986 presidential campaign when the World Jewish Congress asserted that he had been actively involved as a Nazi in the extermination of Jews in World War II. He claimed he had been an interpreter only, with no knowledge of the "final solution", and that his failure to mention his wartime experience had not been with intent to deceive. Despite considerable pressure from foreign governments, he continued his campaign, and was elected with 54 percent of the vote.

Walesa, Lech 1943–

Polish trade unionist and politician. An electrician in the Lenin shipyard in Gdansk, in 1980 Walesa led an unofficial strike after a sharp rise in food prices. Industrial action escalated, and Walesa became head of an interfactory strike committee, which succeeded in having many of its demands met, and was then renamed Solidarity. In 1981 martial law was imposed, Solidarity outlawed, and Walesa interned for a year. In 1983, martial law was lifted, and he was awarded the Nobel Peace Prize. In 1989 following strike action and negotiation between Walesa and the government Solidarity was again legalized and its representatives were allowed to contest some parliamentary seats and won a majority; Poland thus became the first Eastern bloc country since World War II to have a non-Communist leader, Solidarity member Tadeusz Mazowiecki. In 1990, Walesa was elected president and took on the Polish economic crisis.

Yamani, Ahmad Zaki 1930–

Saudi Arabian politician and oilman. Educated at Cairo, New York and Harvard universities, he established a private law practice and became director of several companies. Finance minister (1956–58), he was legal advisor (1958–60) to and member of the Saudi Council of Ministers (1960–86) and minister of state (1960–62). In addition he became minister of Petrol and Mineral Resources (1962–86) and director of the Arabian

American Oil Company (1962–68). The king ultimately controls oil policy in Saudi Arabia but Yamani was given considerable independence as petroleum minister. He also became chairman of the General Petroleum and Mineral Organization (1963–86) and of the Saudi Arabian Fertilizer Company (1966–86). As secretary general (1968–69) and chairman (1974–75) of the Organization of Arabian Petroleum Exporting Countries (OAPEC) he held great influence in an increasingly powerful organization. During the 1970s Yamani withstood threats from the USA and fellow OAPEC members. However, he lost favor with the Royal family in 1986 after oil revenue fell and was dismissed from government office.

Yeltsin, Boris 1931–

Russian politician. A construction engineer, he joined the Communist Party in 1961, and worked for it from 1968. As first secretary (1976) of the Sverdlovsk District Central Committee, he became known as a reformer. In 1985 President Gorbachev made him secretary of the Central Committee for Construction. In 1986 he became first secretary of the Moscow City Party Committee, and took on the task of purging the system of corruption. Pro-*glasnost*, in 1986 he entered the Politburo as a candidate member, and rocked the establishment by making a speech blaming himself for inertia and hypocrisy under Brezhnev. He repeatedly condemned corruption, and was effective in eradicating it. He simplified agricultural production and eliminated middlemen, and ended pointless stockpiling. Impatient with the pace of *perestroika*, in 1987 he angrily proffered his resignation from the Moscow committee and the Politburo, then, reprimanded by Gorbachev and "dismissed" for his criticism of the leadership, he "confessed" the sin of ambition. This episode aroused public concern about the genuineness of *glasnost*, especially when he was relegated to a provincial post. In 1988 he called on the workers to strive for *perestroika*, and asked for rehabilitation. It was refused, but in 1989 he was elected by a landslide victory of 89 percent as Moscow city deputy, and entered the new legislature. As head of the committee on construction and architecture, he toured the USA in late 1989. He then told Gorbachev he had six months to make his reforms work. Yeltsin's popularity grew, and he presented a serious challenge to Gorbachev's leadership. In early 1991 he called on Gorbachev to resign, and expressed bitter hostility to the leadership in terms he afterward acknowledged were excessive. However, the two men made an uneasy alliance to tackle the Soviet Union's snowballing domestic problems; Yeltsin persuaded striking miners to return to work. On the collapse of the Soviet Union he became president of the Russian Federation, and tried to implement a changeover to a market economy.